Praise for
THE LAGASSE GIRLS' BIG FLAVOR, BOLD TASTE—AND NO GLUTEN!

"Going gluten-free does not mean going without thanks to Jilly and Jessie Lagasse. These two sisters invite us to their table to share the best recipes from their food-centric family. *Big Flavor, Bold Taste—and No Gluten!* has it all— mac 'n' cheese, oatmeal raisin cookies, chocolate pecan pie, and New England clam chowder. Pull up a chair. You are in for a treat!"

—**BETH HILLSON**, author of *The Complete Guide to Living Well Gluten Free* and *Gluten-Free Makeovers*

Praise for **THE GLUTEN-FREE TABLE**

"The Lagasse girls definitely know fun and flavorful food and with this book, they're showing us all that gluten-free doesn't have to mean flavor-free. These awesome recipes will put the fun back on your gluten-free table and even the king himself, Emeril, throws in a few for good measure!"   —**GUY FIERI**

"Now that I am also forced to cook gluten-free for my family, I am delighted to have this remarkable resource! Jilly & Jessie Lagasse's *The Gluten-Free Table* not only offers heartfelt advice but also delicious recipes that everyone can enjoy. With these ladies, the sky is truly the limit!"   —**CHEF JOHN BESH**

"The Lagasse sisters share their delicious solutions and recipes for living a gluten-free life. An easy, great cookbook to start with if gluten is a problem for you or a loved one."   —**GALE GAND**

"Jilly and Jessie Lagasse have gone and done it. They've taken the warm, soulful food that connects them to their Dad and translated it into the language of gluten-free, so that we may have the pleasure of sharing both the food and the love, safely, with our own families. Thank you, Lagasse Girls!"

—**NICOLE HUNN, AUTHOR OF *GLUTEN-FREE ON A SHOESTRING***

ALSO BY JILLY LAGASSE AND JESSIE LAGASSE SWANSON

The Gluten-Free Table: The Lagasse Girls Share Their Favorite Meals

THE Lagasse Girls'

BIG FLAVOR, BOLD TASTE— AND NO GLUTEN!

100 Gluten-Free Recipes, from E.J.'s Crunchy Fried Chicken to Momma's Strawberry Shortcake

JILLY LAGASSE *and* JESSIE LAGASSE SWANSON

Da Capo
LIFE
LONG

DA CAPO LIFELONG

A MEMBER OF THE PERSEUS BOOKS GROUP

Designed by Lisa Diercks

Set in Abril Text by Lisa Diercks

Cataloging-in-Publication data for this book is available from the Library of Congress.

First Da Capo Press edition 2014

ISBN: 978-07-382-1787-1 (Hardcover)

ISBN: 978-07-382-1788-8 (e-book)

Published by Da Capo Press

A Member of the Perseus Books Group

www.dacapopress.com

Da Capo Press books are available at special discounts for bulk purchases in the U.S. by corporations, institutions, and other organizations. For more information, please contact the Special Markets Department at the Perseus Books Group, 2300 Chestnut Street, Suite 200, Philadelphia, PA, 19103, or call (800) 810-4145, ext. 5000, or e-mail special.markets@perseusbooks.com.

10 9 8 7 6 5 4 3 2 1

THIS BOOK IS DEDICATED TO ALL OF THOSE FELLOW GF'ERS OUT THERE, WHO DESERVE TO EAT DELICIOUS FOOD EVERY DAY OF THE WEEK.

CONTENTS

INTRODUCTION

BIG FLAVORS AND BOLD TASTE, TO US, JUST SCREAMS COMFORT FOOD. What do you think of when you hear the words "comfort food"? Two deceptively simple words can mean so many things to so many people. Maybe for you, the phrase conjures up vivid memories of Thanksgiving stuffing or the secret recipe chocolate cake only served on birthdays and the things you felt when you ate that special treat as a child. Or maybe you find yourself thinking of your grandmother or your mom—a beloved person or even a place comes to mind (your honeymoon in Italy, your girls' weekend in Vegas). Every person defines "comfort food" in his or her own way. When you're diagnosed with celiac disease or gluten sensitivity, you may think you have to say good-bye to all of the comforting foods you love. It's hard enough adopting a new way of eating—but throw into the mix the idea that you can't have your favorite fried chicken, mac 'n' cheese, or oatmeal raisin cookies, and it's downright unfair and intimidating.

We know what that's like—in 2001 Jessie was diagnosed with gluten sensitivity, and, in 2004, Jilly was finally diagnosed with celiac disease. The following years saw us both on the path to good health, but that required a lot of persistence, perseverance, patience, and experimentation. We had to take charge not only of our health but also of our kitchens (and if you know our dad, you know what that means!). We both spent several years adapting and de-glutening our favorite old recipes, while simultaneously adding new dishes to our portfolios. Our first book, *The Gluten-Free Table,* is all of that hard work encapsulated in cookbook form: it really was a labor of love and an accurate representation of what the food in our homes looked like in the years after our diagnoses. Since then, though, our tastes have changed, our lives have changed, and all of these delicious gluten-free products have entered the mix. As a natural result, our menus have become more diverse, and we've been able to develop many new recipes that produce comforting, tasty food but remain gluten-free (GF). Even though Jessie's boys do not currently have to follow a GF diet, they happily and unwittingly eat most of the GF foods Jessie presents to them. Admittedly, though, they can be a bit picky at times, but Jess has still been able to find good gluten-free workarounds so that they are eating balanced GF meals that they WANT to eat. J.P. does like to add mustard to almost everything, gluten-free or not, but we say go with whatever works, right?

It was pretty easy for us to think of our favorite comforting recipes, but, to make sure we cast a wide net, we started asking other people about their favorite dishes. Before we knew it, our friends, family, and even some strangers had helped us home in on the kinds of foods that gave them joy and evoked memories of home and happiness. This wonderfully diverse and warm group of recipes is the result.

Many of these recipes everyone will be familiar with, though there are some specific to our family and the New England town where we grew up. In cooking these foods, we were sometimes transported back in time and could practically see, taste, and smell those precious and fleeting childhood treasures. As small children, we always associated our Great-Gramma Cabral's house with delicious-ness. Be it her beloved banana bread or her Portuguese kale soup, there was always something warm in winter and refreshing in summer for us to enjoy. After a long afternoon of sledding in the park across from her house, a bowl of her Por-tuguese soup with fresh Portuguese bread was the greatest comfort in the world. Or maybe it was the early smells of Thanksgiving dinner we'd wake up to while at our Grandma and Grandpa Kief's house in the Adirondacks. All of the cousins got to spend Thanksgiving together, playing and putting on a yearly Thanksgiving Day play for our family. The smells of Grandpa Kief's stuffing and a freshly baked apple pie still bring us back to those wonderful times.

The memories and stories we could share are practically endless! We can still close our eyes and smell Dad's wonderful duck and andouille gumbo (page 276) simmering away while we finished opening our Christmas gifts. And we can prac-tically taste Mom's delicious chocolate pecan pie (page 318) melting in our mouths. All these associations remind us of the people who helped make us who we are today. That's "comfort food."

But these big memories and big flavors aren't limited to childhood reminiscing. Your background, where you grew up, or where you've traveled—these all make up each person's palate. Who would have thought Jilly would choose a spicy chicken curry over chicken noodle soup when she is ill? After years spent living in London, Jilly now craves foods like a good shepherd's pie with gravy (page 262), a Sunday roast dinner, or a spicy Indian curry of any variety. For Jessie, immersed in New Orleans culture and flavor since right after high school, her favorite comfort foods involve a lot of Louisiana accents, like gumbo of any kind, or red beans and rice. She's also been known to indulge in many a blueberry muffin (page 81) or Maw-Maw's Deviled Eggs (page 29), perennial foods she's always loved but that aren't necessarily connected with any specific memory or experience. And that's how these recipes work, too—they're dishes you simply feel good cooking, eating, and sharing.

Of course, for us, there was one major hurdle: almost all the recipes we had listed were traditionally gluten filled. Think about it: pot pies with warm, flaky crusts, thick floury-sauce-laden casseroles, creamy soups, stuffings, muffins, and biscuits.

Luckily, our years of gluten-free eating and experimentation helped us out tremendously. Since these are many of our favorite foods, we'd been playing around with gluten-free versions for years. Here you'll find these favorite dishes in a gluten-free form while staying true to the original tastes and flavors. Because that, in the end, is our goal. If you have a gluten intolerance or celiac disease, we want you to be able to share in the food AND the memories, and to not have to go without the dishes you find most comforting. We want you to be at the same table—literally and figuratively!—with everyone else. So go ahead. Dig into some hot crab dip with homemade garlic Parmesan crackers (page 32), savor some beef stewpot with a biscuit crust (page 258), and slice off a chunk of our chocolate raspberry layer cake (page 292). These recipes and so many others will take the "c" out of celiac and put it back in "comfort."

Our mission has always been to demonstrate that gluten-free most certainly does not mean flavor-free; the title says it all: big flavor and bold taste. Even with a gluten issue, people can still be comforted with the foods they grew up eating, loving, sharing, and craving. We truly hope you enjoy all the wonderful dishes we have shared here. They come from our kitchen and most certainly our hearts.

After all, food is love and that love is meant to be shared!

Jilly Lagasse and Jessie Lagasse Swanson

THE JOURNEY TO GLUTEN FREEDOM

NO MATTER WHY YOU'RE HERE, BECAUSE OF NECESSITY, CURIOSITY, OR some other reason, this little compendium has got LOTS for you to love! Some of you might be new to this whole gluten-free game and are looking for ideas and direction for where to take your new diet. Perhaps you are a parent with a newly diagnosed child looking for all the help and answers you can get! (Gluten . . . what the **** IS gluten and how do I get it out?!) Fret not. If you are new to gluten freedom, don't worry. Just breathe and remember that there are still so many delicious things for you to eat! And this book will show you just how bold and flavorful your newly gluten-free life can be.

If this ain't your first GF rodeo, and you've perhaps been diagnosed for some time, you might be stuck in the same ole food routine and are craving a bit of yummy newness. Some diverse recipes to actually get excited about! Old favorites that've been off limits because they're chock-full of gluten? Yep, we've got that. Some new dishes to impress the ladies and gents? Yep, we've got that too. The most perfect chocolate layer cake with buttercream frosting to make for your daughter's ninth birthday? Yep, we absolutely have GOT that! We hope this book provides you with a bit of inspiration to get your taste buds riled up and back on track!

We also welcome all of you who might not have celiac disease or a gluten intolerance but who may just want to try out a gluten-free diet to see how you feel without gluten. Though we strongly advise you to get a proper diagnosis from a trained medical physician and not just a self-diagnosis courtesy of WebMD, we still embrace your being here and hope we can help you too! More and more people are finally starting to make the connection between what they put into their bodies and how their bodies feel and function. . . . And with all this new awareness, more and more people are looking at their own kitchens, thinking about how to feed themselves better. For some people, whenever you have digestive issues, you will be advised to follow what is called an elimination diet. For two weeks or longer, depending on your doctor's recommendation, you might cut out of your diet all dairy products or all wheat- and gluten-containing products or all poultry, and so on and so on. Then, slowly, you reintroduce the different categories of foods to see what the possible offending foods might be. Many people who do this start to realize that they feel a lot better once they cut out certain foods! Perhaps some of their ailments and former symptoms have vanished, or perhaps they have more energy or are getting better sleep. The difference is often so noticeable that they permanently adopt this new diet and lifestyle.

Whatever your reason for being with us, we applaud all of you gluten-free followers, new and old! We truly believe that a life without gluten can be very bold, flavorful, and satisfying.

We must admit, though, that we didn't always think or feel this way. Never did we think we'd see the day when people would choose to eat this way without it being a medical necessity. At the time of our diagnoses, that seemed absurd! The gluten-free product sphere consisted of cardboard-like bread with no flavor, and a few terribly textured packaged cookies. "Yuck" was an understatement. But, oh how things have changed. Gluten freedom has never tasted so good and has never been easier to achieve! We are amazed, on a daily basis, to see all the delicious gluten-free products popping up in grocery stores, and to see how many restaurants are offering a gluten-free menu or, better yet, are completely gluten-free! It warms our hearts and our tummies to see all the growth in just the past few years since publishing our last book, *The Gluten-Free Table*, in 2012. And we strongly believe the more we keep spreading the GF word, the more of this amazement is yet to come.

But, like we said before, back when we were diagnosed, "amazing" was the last word we'd have used to describe the GF foods available or our feelings about our GF prospects. For Jessie, before her diagnosis, she had spent months suffering from troubling digestive issues and had spent countless hours consulting traditional physicians who never seemed to be able to help her. Finally, she visited a naturopathic doctor. After only two visits and a few untraditional tests, Jessie was diagnosed with a gluten intolerance in 2001. At the time, the damage caused by the unrecognized culprit had taken its toll on Jessie's body and so she was required to follow a pretty comprehensive elimination diet for one year. But what an astounding difference this solution made. She felt better than she had in a long time, and so she embraced the change wholeheartedly. After one year, Jessie was able to reintroduce gluten, dairy, and many other previously banned foods into her diet to a small degree. Now, she is able to indulge in a gluten-filled sandwich or pizza slice every few days without it causing major mischief for her. But, she still has to be vigilant of her offending foods and not overindulge while at her son's class birthday parties or at her Friday night pizza party. Although neither of her boys

Green Bean Casserole with Crispy Onions, page 170

Momma's Strawberry Shortcake with Homemade Biscuits, page 283

are required to follow a gluten-free diet at this point, they do so for the most part and don't miss the gluten a bit.

Jilly, however, can never cheat. That's because she has full-on celiac disease. Jilly had years of health struggles and digestive issues and was constantly misdiagnosed with everything under the sun. She even had one doctor tell her she was just allergic to bananas and that if she cut them out of her diet, she'd be fine. Really? Bananas? She continued to struggle until she moved abroad to London in 2004.

As she sat on her new doctor's table giving him her laundry list of ailments, he instantly said, "Oh dear, sounds like you have celiac disease. We'll do the test." And sure enough, the simple yet magical blood test came back positive. After following a strict gluten-free diet, she saw an immediate recovery in just a few short weeks. She wasn't hunched over in toe-curling pain from tummy cramps anymore, she had energy again, her eczema vanished, and even her hair started to grow . . . a bit!

HELP! I THINK I'VE BEEN GLUTENED!

WE WANTED TO SHARE OUR OWN DIAGNOSIS STORIES TO ILLUSTRATE how different and drastic the effects of gluten can be on a gluten-sensitive or gluten-allergic person. There are distinct medical differences between a person with a gluten sensitivity and one with celiac disease. We will leave that complex discussion to those with the expertise, but, as far as our understanding and experience go, one significant and relevant difference has to do with eating gluten AGAIN after diagnosis. If you have a sensitivity, like Jessie does, that means your body has an intolerance to gluten and you may display the same symptoms or reactions as someone with celiac disease, BUT you may eventually, with proper medical supervision, be able to eat gluten again in limited quantities without experiencing long-term damage. This has been the case for Jessie. (We have to note here: if you've been diagnosed with an intolerance and have been following a GF diet, please don't try to get gluten back into your life without talking to your doctor first! It's truly different for everyone.)

Since Jilly has celiac disease, if she were to have a bite of real bread or wheat-thickened gravy, she'd practically die! Or at least have such a violent reaction, she'd wish someone would put her out of her misery. We know, it may seem a tad dramatic, but you haven't seen her reaction when she accidentally gets "glutened." Everyone's "Oops, I got glutened" reactions are different, just like the symptoms of this disease themselves. They vary greatly from person to person. Jilly can pretty much tell within 20 minutes of eating something she shouldn't have. And, once the realization hits, it is a mad dash to get back home for a good two-day marathon of misery! You probably have your own similar stories of accidental glutening to share, and so you understand perfectly. If you've been on the GF train for a while, you know the ins and outs of gluten and every answer to the question "What IS this disease?"; if you're newly diagnosed or cooking for someone who has celiac disease, here's a basic rundown of the gluten beast and the trouble it can cause.

Celiac disease, also known as celiac sprue, is an autoimmune disease of the small intestine that makes it impossible to digest the protein found in wheat flour called gluten. It is a hereditary illness, which means you are genetically predisposed to the disease. So, not only do you have your mother or father to thank for

Indian Chicken Salad Sandwiches on Homemade Socca Bread, page 132

those lovely blue eyes, you can also thank them for never being able to eat a real slice of pizza again.

For reasons not yet understood, the disease can develop at any age and can lie dormant in your system until later in life. Some believe it can be triggered by an extreme stress or trauma. The real danger is that, if left untreated, celiac disease can lead to several other serious health issues. Because it is an autoimmune disease, it is very likely you'll pick up a few more along the way. We know, not exactly the winning lottery ticket you were hoping for. Other illnesses and health issues one could develop include disorders like Hashimoto's thyroiditis, multiple sclerosis (MS), systemic lupus, Graves' disease, rheumatoid arthritis, osteoporosis, type 1 diabetes, eczema or dermatitis herpetiformis, anemia or iron deficiency, problems with infertility and miscarriage(s), some neurological conditions like epilepsy and migraines, and intestinal cancers.

Because the disease can have such significant and lifelong effects if not identified, we highly recommend that anyone who thinks they might be affected go get tested sooner rather than later. Wonderfully, diagnosis is pretty easy. It is simply a blood test that will screen you for certain autoantibodies, the term used to describe the particular antibodies responsible for the body's autoimmune reaction to gluten. Usually, people who have celiac disease will have a higher level of these autoantibodies in their blood. In order for the test to be accurate, however, you MUST be tested while still consuming a gluten-filled diet. So, before you cut the gluten out on your own accord, call your doctor and schedule the blood test while you're still all gluteny! Because this disease affects the small intestine, your doctor may want to do a biopsy as well, to see just how much damage you have. It's perfectly normal and it's actually pretty cool to find out!

If you are thinking about asking for the blood test or even the biopsy, you've probably already started to note certain "symptoms" you're experiencing that have caused you to consider celiac disease as the culprit. Though the symptoms people experience are varied and diverse, there do tend to be some common symptoms that appear across the board. Children and infants may experience any of the following (though it seems that digestive symptoms tend to be more common in youth):

- **abdominal bloating and pain**
- **chronic diarrhea**

- vomiting
- constipation
- pale, foul-smelling, or fatty stool
- sudden weight loss or weight gain
- fatigue or lethargy
- irritability and behavioral issues
- dental-enamel defects of the permanent teeth
- delayed growth and puberty
- short stature
- failure to thrive
- attention deficit hyperactivity disorder (ADHD)
- eczema or an itchy skin rash known as dermatitis herpetiformis

Adults may experience any of the following, along with the digestive issues mentioned above:

- unexplained iron-deficiency anemia
- fatigue or lethargy
- bone or joint pain
- arthritis
- bone loss or osteoporosis
- depression or anxiety
- tingling numbness in the hands and feet
- seizures or migraines
- missed menstrual periods
- infertility or recurrent miscarriage
- canker sores inside the mouth
- eczema or dermatitis herpetiformis
- hair loss
- sudden weight loss or weight gain

Currently there aren't any known drugs or medical treatments to treat celiac disease. The only real known solution is to adhere to a strict gluten-free diet for the remainder of your life once you are properly diagnosed. However, there are

HEY, IS THIS ON THE TEST? GF FACT AND FIGURES

Just in case you are like us and are always interested in random gluten-related facts (yes, Jessie still watches *Jeopardy* every chance she gets!), we thought we'd share some interesting factoids. For instance, celiac disease (CD) is estimated to affect every 1 in 100 people worldwide, and, unfortunately, there are roughly 2.5 million Americans who are still undiagnosed.

Here are a few more interesting nuggets, courtesy of www.celiac-disease.com:

- 1 out of every 133 Americans (about 3 million people) has CD.
- 97% of Americans estimated to have CD are not diagnosed.
- CD has over 300 known symptoms although some people experience none.
- Age of diagnosis is key: If you are diagnosed between ages 2 to 4, your chance of getting an additional autoimmune disorder is 10.5%. Over the age of 20, that rockets up to 34%.
- 30% of the U.S. population is estimated to have the genes necessary for CD.
- CD affects more people in the U.S. than Crohn's disease, cystic fibrosis, multiple sclerosis, and Parkinson's disease combined.
- People with CD dine out 80% less than they used to before diagnosis and believe that less than 10% of eating establishments have a "very good" or "good" understanding of GF diets.
- It takes an average of 11 years for patients to be properly diagnosed with CD, even though a simple blood test exists.
- GF foods are, on average, 242% more expensive than their non-GF counterparts.
- The Food Allergen Labeling and Consumer Protection Act became law in 2006, allowing for easier reading of food labels for those with CD. What took so long?
- 12% of people in the U.S. who have Down syndrome also have CD.
- 6% of people in the U.S. who have type 1 diabetes also have CD.
- Among people who have a first-degree relative diagnosed with CD, as many as 1 in 22 of them may have the disease.

exciting new medical developments being tried and tested as we speak, or type, as the case may be. We have very high hopes for some kind of treatment—be it for just the reaction or for the disease as a whole—sometime in our lifetimes.

WHAT I REALLY WANT TO KNOW IS, CAN I EAT THIS?

WHILE WE FIND ALL OF THE STATISTICS AND MEDICAL INFORMATION TO be valuable and exciting, what really gets our hearts racing is talking about all the food we can eat on a gluten-free diet. As I'm sure you know, or will soon find out in the many pages to come, we both have very different personalities, preferences, tastes, and needs. Yes, we are sisters, but we are apples and oranges, my friends. The one thing that we both agree on, the one thing that brings us back to the table over and over again . . . is the food! Well, the food gets us to the table, but then we once again differ on what we'd like to put on the table. Many of Jessie's recipes are great for larger families or crowds and are usually pretty quick and easy to throw together. Mostly, that's because cooking huge portions is something our dad has always taught us to do. But it is also because her house is like Piccadilly Circus, with people constantly coming in and out and eating all the while!

Jilly has gotten into healthy foods more than ever and prefers to eat light with the occasional indulgence. She has also had to cut dairy out of her diet almost completely (who can say no to a bit of paneer?!), so that has forced her to cook in a whole new way . . . coconut oil instead of butter and dairy-free yogurt instead of Greek yogurt, for example. She is also a single gal about town, so she cooks mostly for friends and loves to take her time in the kitchen perfecting yumminess for her next cocktail or dinner party.

The beauty of this difference, though, is that it has resulted in a fantastically diverse array of recipes for this book. There is pretty much something here for everyone. An important thing to keep in mind, too, is that the recipes are somewhat fluid and adaptable. You can double a 4-serving recipe if feeding a crowd or cut one of Jessie's 6- to 8-serving monsters down to 2 to 4 if necessary. And you can and should always adjust ingredients or seasoning to suit your preference. Just because we like cayenne in our au gratin potatoes doesn't mean you have to. Cooking should be fun, and you should always make it your own! So, look at

Baked "Fried" Shrimp Tacos with Mango Salsa and Homemade Zingy Tartar Sauce, page 160

these recipes as a tasty blueprint from which you can build whatever gluten-free creation your heart desires.

All of this talk about cooking and recipes is great, but maybe you are wondering what you can even cook WITH now that you need to banish the gluten from your life and your pantry. Here are some helpful lists of all the things you can and should have in your gluten-free pantry and also a list of things to avoid.

Meme's Eggplant and Ricotta Lasagna, page 221

First things first: you'll need to start getting your flour on. . . . We are dedicated users of a premade all-purpose flour blend by Arrowhead Mills called Gluten Free All Purpose Baking Mix. It is a blend of rice flour, sorghum flour, tapioca starch flour, baking powder, rice bran extract, and xanthan gum. We fully understand that there are certain blends of flours and certain specific flours that are better for certain types of gluten-free recipes. And we have caught a lot of slack for using a premade blend in the past. However, our reason for doing so is simple, and it is this: to make your life simpler! Most people don't have the time, the money, or the desire to research and then mix all sorts of flour blends for different recipes. It also standardizes our recipes so that you have consistency along with great taste and flavor. Of course, by all means substitute your own flour blend if you'd like. Our way is not the only way, for sure!

In addition to a solid all-purpose flour blend, there are a substantial number of flours that could earn a place in your gluten-free pantry, including:

- almond flour/meal
- chestnut flour
- coconut flour
- pecan flour
- hazelnut flour
- chickpea flour (a.k.a. garbanzo bean, gram, or besan flour)
- fava bean flour
- finely milled rice flours (white or brown)
- soy flour
- amaranth flour
- buckwheat flour
- millet flour
- sorghum flour
- tapioca flour or starch
- cornmeal
- arrowroot starch
- potato starch and potato flour

Some of these flours may be totally new to you; the good news is that you can find most of them in your local grocery store, or you can order them in bulk online (see Resources, page 333, for a list of our favorite places to shop online). In addition to flours, some helpful ingredients to have on hand for all of your gluten-free baking needs include:

- xanthan gum
- guar gum

- agave syrups (light and dark)
- gluten-free baking powder and baking soda
- cornstarch
- honey
- molasses
- sugars (light and dark brown, granulated, confectioners', and coconut)
- all-natural, unsweetened applesauce
- coconut oil
- coconut milk
- shredded coconut
- condensed milk
- high-quality fruit preserves and jams
- high-quality chocolate (milk, semisweet, and dark)
- dried fruit (such as cherries, cranberries, and apricots)
- nuts (such as pecans, almonds, peanuts, walnuts, and cashews)
- vanilla pods and vanilla extract
- loads of spices (such as whole and ground cloves, whole and ground cardamom, cinnamon sticks, nutmeg, allspice, and ginger)
- cream of tartar
- salt

As with flours, some of these ingredients might be totally unfamiliar; the good news about the GF boom is that these ingredients, too, are now more readily available locally or online.

Here are a number of gluten-free pastas, grains, cereals, and dried legumes we use often in our cooking and suggest you stock up on, too.

- quinoa and quinoa pasta (we like Ancient Harvest brand)
- gluten-free rice-based pastas (all shapes, noodles, and lasagna sheets)
- gluten-free corn-based pastas (all shapes, noodles, and lasagna sheets)
- gluten-free rice and tapioca flour noodles, vermicelli, and pad thai noodles
- certified gluten-free oats and oatmeal products
- cornmeal, grits, and polenta

- corn- and rice-based tortillas
- rices (such as brown, white, jasmine, basmati, and wild)
- rice cakes (check the label on any flavored varieties)
- dried peas (such as black eyed and green split)
- dried beans (such as red kidney, pinto, black, and great Northern white)
- dried lentils (such as green, yellow, red, and black)

Here are some canned and bottled goods, seasonings, and sauces we can't live without. Please note that, while we recommend using a few of our dad's products in our recipes, like his Emeril's Original Essence seasoning, it is simply because we were taught to cook using these ingredients and thus they are what we used when we de-glutened all of our favorite recipes. Again, any alternative of your choice will suffice.

- canned whole tomatoes, diced tomatoes with chili, tomato sauce, tomato paste, tomato purée, etc.
- canned or jarred olives and artichoke hearts
- canned beans (such as aduki, red kidney, black, black eyed peas, and great Northern)
- rice wine vinegar
- cooking sherry
- sesame oil
- gluten-free soy sauce or tamari
- olive oil, vegetable oil, coconut oil, sunflower oil, avocado oil
- high-quality truffle oil
- all-natural peanut butter
- all-natural almond butter
- jarred salsas
- hot sauces (such as Tabasco, Tapatio, Crystal, and Sriracha, a chile-garlic sauce)
- nuoc mam cham, or fish sauce
- Thai-style sweet chile dipping sauce
- gluten-free satay sauce
- high-quality mayonnaise, ketchup, and relish

- mustards (such as whole grain, Dijon, and American)
- grated horseradish or horseradish sauce
- grated ginger and pickled ginger
- gluten-free stock cubes and stocks (such as vegetable, beef, and chicken)
- all-natural spices and seasonings
- Emeril's Original Essence seasoning
- freshly ground black pepper
- crushed red pepper flakes
- Thai green and red curry pastes
- Indian curry pastes and powders (such as mild, medium, or hot curry powder, Madras paste, tandoori spice, and garam masala)

See, just when you thought your shelves were going to be super bare without gluten, here are some more options! You can have:

- Any fresh, frozen, or canned varieties of vegetables. Just be sure to buy them plain, unseasoned, and without any premade sauces.
- Any fresh fruit, fruit juices, fruit cups, and dried fruits you fancy. Just be sure to check the labels if by "fresh fruit," you mean a can of cherry pie filling!
- Any breads, cookies, cakes, noodles, pastas, crackers, cereals, and tortillas made from any of the flours mentioned above.
- Most dairy products; most milk and milk products, cheeses, and yogurts are generally safe. Be sure to check the labels, though, on any flavored ice creams, yogurts, smoothies, frozen yogurts, creamers, malted milk–flavored drinks, and even some margarine blends.
- All meats, poultry, fish, shellfish, and eggs are safe, but be sure to check the labels on all prepackaged deli meats, hot dogs, and sausages, premade meatballs, and some canned or frozen meats. Also check any pre-marinated items, as who knows what they actually marinated the meat IN.
- Agave syrups, honey, molasses and treacle, sugars, jams and preserves, chocolates, and most marshmallows and meringues are all fine. Check labels, though, when buying hard candies, cough drops, and even some

candy bars, as they can contain sneaky gluten products in the list of ingredients. So read carefully!

- Mostly all spices, if natural, are safe as well. Just check the labels of premade blends to be sure.

Phew! It may seem like a lot of info—and it is, since there are truly tons of GF possibilities (which is a good thing, right?). But what about all the sneaky places that gluten could be hiding?

New England Clam Chowder, page 203

Quick and Easy Enchilada Pie, page 272

HEY YOU, SNEAKY GLUTEN! ARE YOU IN HERE?

WHETHER YOU ARE AWARE OF IT OR NOT, GLUTEN LOVES NOTHING MORE than to hide in things that you couldn't possibly think to look for him in. Thankfully, with the FDA having passed several new guidelines for food labeling, it's easier than ever to identify products that are really gluten-free. It's mandatory for all known food allergens, such as soy, nuts, eggs, milk, wheat, and dairy, to be

CLEARLY labeled in the "this product may contain" bit of the package. Manufacturers also have to clearly label if the product has been made on any shared equipment and in any shared environment. And now, the newest FDA ruling requires all products labeled "gluten-free" to meet a standardized "less than 20 parts per million" test. This ensures that the products that SAY gluten-free actually ARE! Gone are the days of reading through each and every product's ingredient list—though we usually still do it out of habit! Still, if you forget to read the label, just remember that gluten is typically used in some unexpected ways. Gluten is usually used as a thickener or to bulk up items, so it can be in something as simple as a can of soup or a package of sausages. It is in some preservatives, food stabilizers, modified food starches, malt flavoring, and hydrolyzed vegetable protein and hydrolyzed plant protein, also known as HVP/HPP (which is actually made from wheat). It can also be used as a flavor enhancer (what the heck is that?!) and even in some of your medications, vitamins, and Communion wafers! (Personally, we love that there are gluten-free Communion wafers and matzos available now. Gluten-free accommodations for your spiritual growth, anyone? Yes, please!) . . . Here is a list of things we still give a yellow light to, as they may have gluten hiding in them. Check your labels and proceed with caution with the following:

- **creamy soups or sauces (Ask yourself, how did it get so thick? Is it from the help of a wheat flour roux or thickener containing gluten?)**
- **bouillon or stock cubes**
- **cheese sauces and dips (such as premade Alfredo pasta sauces and queso dips)**
- **pasta sauces**
- **varieties of seasoned potato and corn chips**
- **licorice (all flavors and colors)**
- **premade deli meats, packaged cold cuts, salamis, hot dogs, sausages, self-basting turkeys, frozen seasoned meats and fish, and pre-marinated meats and fish**
- **store-bought or premade, prepackaged meatballs (they will almost always contain breadcrumbs to thicken)**
- **gravy, gravy mixes, and premade gravies**
- **premade dips and dip mixes**

- French fry varieties that are seasoned, breaded, or coated (they could be coated with a wheat flour blend)
- imitation crabmeat and crab sticks
- crackers and cereals
- health bars, protein bars, and protein powders
- prepackaged dry soup mixes
- prepackaged rice mixes
- spice blends (they may use wheat flour as a binder)
- soy sauce

I'M AWFULLY THIRSTY! CAN I DRINK THAT?

ALL THIS TALK ABOUT THE CANS AND CANNOTS OF YOUR GLUTEN FREE-dom must be starting to make you a little thirsty. (No, just us?) Well, believe it or not, the yes's and no's don't just pertain to food, my friends. They also pertain to the ole beverages as well. So have a cocktail—just make sure it's a safe choice first!

Most teas, coffees, and soft drinks are fine. However, alcoholic beverages can be tricky. According to the National Institutes of Health's Celiac Disease Awareness Campaign, beer should be avoided—unless it is gluten-free. Traditional beers are made with barley and occasionally some other wheat-containing grains, so they are a big no-no, obviously. There are some super-delicious gluten-free beers on the market nowadays, so things are looking better if you are a beer-loving celiac. Wines are generally gluten-free, but if you're thinking about sampling some vino that has added flavors, you might want to sip—or skip—instead of slurp. The NIH also says that cocktails made with distilled alcohol are safe and according to about. com, most authorities say that people with celiac disease can safely drink distilled alcoholic beverages, even those that are made with gluten grains. How does that work? The distillation process supposedly removes all of the gluten protein molecules responsible for reactions to gluten, rendering the drinks gluten-free. But this is where things get interesting. There are some brands that may use barrels that contained wheat or barley to produce these tasty alcohols, or use added flavors, and you could possibly have a reaction from the cross-contamination. The Celiac Sprue Association (www.csaceliacs.info) recommends celiacs consume only potato-based vodka, rum and tequila (all made from non-gluten grain sources), along with preservative- and dye-free wines and brandies and gluten-free beer. So what's a thirsty person to do? Go with your gut, of course. Check labels and websites. Remember, what might cause one of us to react to something, might be perfectly fine for you—and vice versa! If you find yourself feeling a bit

Sugar Cookie Jam Thumbprints, page 305

rough around the edges the next day—more than that half margarita warrants—there's a good chance you got glutened from your drink. So just stay away from that brand.

SPREAD THE LOVE BUT NOT THE BREADCRUMBS, PLEASE

OKAY, SO YOUR PANTRY IS NOW READY TO GO AND YOU WON'T GO thirsty ever, ever again. So, let's cook something, shall we? We have a bunch of helpful tips to get you on your way to making your kitchen a gluten-free, safe zone. Some of you might not have the luxury of having an entirely gluten-free kitchen at home. So, if you are one of the many living with gluten partakers, you'll need to take the proper precautions to make sure you avoid cross-contamination as best as possible. Some people have such a severe reaction to gluten and wheat that the mere sharing of a toaster oven can send them into "Oops, I got glutened"-ville. Cross-contamination happens when wheat and gluten come into contact with gluten-free products and, in turn, "contaminate" them. This can happen by sharing cutting boards, colanders, butter, margarine, and jars of peanut butter and jam . . . yep, lots of things. Here is a helpful list of some kitchen culprits and some tips to keep yourself and your kitchen free from cross-contamination.

- **TOASTERS AND TOASTER OVENS:** Let's face it—crumbs get everywhere, especially in these pups, whose bread and butter is, well, toasting bread! It's best to have a dedicated GF toaster or toaster oven.
- **CUTTING BOARDS:** We find it helpful to have different color-coded or designated cutting boards in the kitchen that are dedicated for gluten-free use only. This really helps cut down on one of the most common forms of cross-contamination.
- **COLANDERS:** Just like with the cutting boards, we highly recommend having a designated gluten-free colander in your kitchen. Shared colanders are hard to keep completely gluten-free and aren't too expensive, so, to avoid cross-contamination, we think it's best to just have a separate one.
- **UTENSILS, CUTLERY, POTS & PANS:** Make sure to wash them all very well with hot, soapy water. This is cheaper than buying two sets of everything, although we won't stop you from doing so. And NEVER use the

Spicy Tomato Soup with Grilled Cheese Dippers, page 123

same pot of boiling water to boil both gluteny and gluten-free pasta! If it's unavoidable, boil the gluten-free pasta first.

■ **BBQ GRILLS AND OTHER COOK TOPS:** Make sure all are properly cleaned before cooking any gluten-free foods on them to avoid the risk of cross-contamination.

■ **BAKING EQUIPMENT:** Any measuring cups, spoons, scales, mixing bowls, food processor bowls, blenders, baking sheets, cake pans, and muffin trays should all be very carefully washed before using. As for flour sifters and electric mixers: think of all those nooks and crannies where gluteny flour can get stuck. A flour sifter can be particularly hard to scrub completely clean, and mixers can sometimes hold on to a dried bit of dough.

■ **FRYING OIL:** Either in pans or in a large deep-fat fryer, you have to be careful here depending on how sensitive you are. But to be safe, don't share your oil, or, as with pasta water, fry your GF food first (and don't reuse the oil another day).

■ **CONDIMENTS:** Yes, all those things you can dip a butter knife into and out of and spread on both gluteny and non-gluteny items are at risk of cross-contamination. While you may have a super-GF-savvy family, there's still enough chance of cross-contamination that you may want to keep separate condiments and label 'em GF.

DON'T WORRY, JUST BE HAPPY AND EAT

IF YOU'RE FEELING OVERWHELMED AND ARE REACHING FOR A GLUTEN-laden baguette . . . put it down and slowly back away. In the next 299 pages, we'll prove just how scrumptious and flavorful this bold new road can be. You will still get to have most, if not all, of the things you miss since being diagnosed. With just a turn of the page, you'll find recipes for breakfasts, lunches, starters, accompaniments, mains, and, of course, desserts. And we've included a Resources guide on page 333 to help you order or locate some of the products we use and to share some fantastic websites that can help answer your questions and assist you in gathering information and obtaining the education you might need. So high five, fist pump, and booty shake away because your new life of yumminess, happiness, and health starts now!

LOOKING FOR DAIRY-FREE OR QUICK & EASY RECIPES?

We know that a lot of GF folks need to be DF, too, so you'll find dairy-free recipes designated with this icon: DF. The dairy-free icon is a great guideline. However, be on the lookout for recipes where we give suggestions on how they can be made dairy-free with a few simple adjustments.

Strapped for time? As much as we love to be in the kitchen, busy schedules (jobs, kids, pets, carpools . . . sound familiar?) can make a homemade meal, delicious as it is, seem like a real chore. Quick & Easy to the rescue! Recipes with this icon Q+E can be made in about 30 minutes. There are a few that push the 45-minute mark, but they are so easy, we wanted to make sure you're aware of those, too!

For a quick guide to our Dairy-Free or Quick & Easy Recipes, check out the lists on pages 329–332.

For Starters

ROWING UP, WE ALWAYS HAD LOTS OF PEOPLE AROUND: friends, extended family, and their friends and family. This tendency to gather wasn't limited to holidays or special occasions either. It would and did occur regularly, after an afternoon softball game, a Wednesday night carpool drop-off, or with no precipitating occurrence at all. These pop-up social gatherings might end after some shared snacks, or they might continue straight through a whole meal. The food we'd serve at these events wasn't fancy or complex. But that never stopped everyone from partaking in whatever there was to eat AND from having a wonderful time together doing so.

As adults, we've found that those kinds of everyday events and holiday soirees conjure up warm memories for us. We now have, almost naturally, the same kind of environments in our grown-up homes. Not a night passes without Maw-Maw Patsy (Jessie's mother-in-law), Gramma Luz (Jessie and Jilly's mom), or the neighbor kids stopping by Jessie's house. And holidays and birthdays are still full of family and friends spending time together, eating, chatting, laughing, and, yes, more eating.

One difference in our present homes over our childhood one, though, is the food! Not only are the options we offer now gluten-free, but they

Crispy Sriracha and Lime Chicken Wings, page 41

also tend to be a bit more complicated than chips and jarred salsa! Jessie's house, which is admittedly more chaotic than Jilly's, tends to be full of dips and quick snacks like the Spicy Crab Dip with Homemade Garlic Parmesan Crackers (page 32) or her version of Maw-Maw's Deviled Eggs (page 29). Jilly, who is very adept at preparing a nice dish to begin her dinner parties, leans toward the more complex offerings like the Cucumber and Smoked Salmon Rolls with Chive Cream (page 52) or the Warm Apple and Brie Tartlets (page 65). Either way works and all of the options are delicious. We hope that you agree and find yourself beginning your family meals or get-togethers with some of these recipes. And that, in the end, they can become a part of the shared memories you and your family look back on fondly in years to come.

MAW-MAW'S DEVILED EGGS

 **MAKES 24 PIECES**

LIKE SO MANY OF MAW-MAW PATSY'S RECIPES, THIS ONE WAS never written down. So, Jessie had to watch her make this a bunch of times while peppering her with questions about possible quantities and measurements. We think, after some trial and error, that we have a version true to Maw-Maw's original one (including her secret ingredients: relish and Cajun spices!). You can easily make a larger quantity of eggs, if you want; just increase the other ingredients proportionally, and you should be fine! This is a quick and easy recipe and will take you 30 minutes or less to make.

12 large hard-cooked eggs, cooled and peeled
2 teaspoons sweet relish
¼ teaspoon garlic powder
½ teaspoon Emeril's Original Essence seasoning or Cajun seasoning of your choice
3 to 4 tablespoons mayonnaise, depending on your preference
1 teaspoon dried parsley
Salt and freshly ground black pepper (optional)
Paprika, for garnish

1. Slice the cooled hard-cooked eggs in half lengthwise. Empty the yolks into a small mixing bowl and set the halves on your serving dish.

2. Add to the yolks the sweet relish, garlic powder, Essence, mayonnaise, and parsley. Mix the ingredients together until the yolks are mashed up and the filling is uniform. You can taste it here to see if you want to add any salt and/or pepper. Maw-Maw doesn't, so we leave it up to you whether to add anything else!

3. Using a teaspoon, gently fill each egg white cup with the yolk filling. Once all the eggs are filled, sprinkle a small bit of paprika over the eggs for garnish. Serve immediately or refrigerate until ready to serve.

NOTE: To get perfectly hard-cooked eggs each time, place a single layer of eggs in the bottom of a pan and cover with 1 to 2 inches of cold water. Over high heat, bring the eggs to a boil for only a minute or so. Then, remove the pan from the heat, cover it, and let it sit for 10 to 12 minutes. After that time has elapsed, run the eggs under cold water for a few minutes in order to stop the cooking process and then set them aside until they are cool enough to handle and peel.

EASY ARTICHOKE DIP

Q+E   MAKES 4 TO 6 SERVINGS

THIS FIVE-INGREDIENT BEAUTY IS QUICK AND EASY TO MAKE and is super delicious. In fact, we usually keep an extra jar of marinated artichoke hearts in the pantry just in case we need to whip up some dip for unexpected guests. If you can't find artichoke hearts in olive oil, you can substitute a 14-ounce can of artichoke hearts, drained, and 2 to 4 tablespoons of olive oil. Pretty soon, you'll be keeping some artichoke hearts in your pantry, too! This is a quick and easy recipe and will take you 30 minutes or less to make.

1   (12-ounce) jar marinated artichoke hearts in olive oil
½   teaspoon minced garlic, or more to taste
⅔   cup grated Parmesan cheese
5   dashes green Tabasco (or hot sauce of your choice), or more
    to taste
    Freshly ground black pepper

1. Preheat the oven to 350°F.

2. Combine all the ingredients in a blender or food processor and blend until well combined and the artichoke hearts are broken down. Scrape down the sides using a rubber spatula, if necessary, and reblend to capture any unprocessed pieces.

3. Pour the mixture into an 8-inch square baking dish and bake for 10 to 15 minutes, or until the dip is warmed through and starting to bubble around the edges.

4. Remove it from the oven and serve warm with your favorite crudités or tortilla chips.

SPICY CRAB DIP WITH HOMEMADE GARLIC PARMESAN CRACKERS

 MAKES 6 TO 8 SERVINGS

CRAB-BOIL FLAVOR IN A DIP, ANYONE? THIS TASTY AND SPICY crab dip can be served warm or cold, and it can be paired with homemade crackers or any store-bought variety. So many options! The crackers alone are somewhat bland, but that is to complement the spiciness of the dip. Feel free to doctor the recipe by adding additional types of cheese or herbs like crushed rosemary or thyme if you'd prefer. This is a quick and easy recipe but will take you about 45 minutes to make as opposed to the usual Q&E time of 30 minutes or less.

CRACKERS

- 2 cups gluten-free flour blend (we like Arrowhead Mills Gluten Free All Purpose Baking Mix), plus extra for rolling
- ¼ teaspoon salt
- 1 tablespoon xanthan gum
- 1 teaspoon garlic powder
- ½ teaspoon freshly ground black pepper
- ¾ cup water
- ¼ cup extra-virgin olive oil
- ½ cup grated Parmesan cheese

DIP

- 8 ounces cream cheese, room temperature
- ¼ cup sour cream
- 1 teaspoon hot sauce of your choice

¼	teaspoon crab-boil liquid (we like Zatarain's)
2	teaspoons minced garlic
½	cup grated Parmesan cheese
¼	teaspoon cayenne pepper
¼	cup thinly sliced green onions (green parts only)
2	tablespoons freshly squeezed lemon juice
	Salt and freshly ground black pepper
16	ounces crab meat, picked over for shells

1. Preheat the oven to 350°F.

2. First, make the crackers. Sift together the flour blend, salt, xanthan gum, garlic powder, and pepper in a large mixing bowl.

3. Once the dry ingredients are evenly mixed, add the water and olive oil and mix by hand until a dough forms.

4. Incorporate the cheese into the dough and divide it into two equal-size balls or chunks.

5. Lightly flour a sheet of waxed paper and place one ball in the center. Flour the top of the ball lightly and cover with another piece of waxed paper.

6. Gently roll out the dough as thinly as possible. You can either cut out precise squares or rectangles, or you can go the more artistic route and cut the dough into whatever shapes you'd like. Just try to keep the sizes approximately the same so they cook evenly. We like to use a pizza cutter to cut the dough, as it produces a nice, clean cut, but a sharp knife will also work.

7. Gently transfer the pieces of dough to a greased baking sheet and bake for 15 to 20 minutes, or until the edges are golden brown. Remove from the oven and let cool.

8. Repeat the process until you have baked all of your dough. (Leave the oven at 350°F for the dip.) Set the crackers aside until the dip is ready.

9. Combine all of the dip ingredients except the crab in a large mixing bowl. Stir until everything is mixed together evenly. Gently fold in the crab.

10. Transfer the mixture into an 8-inch square baking dish and bake for 25 to 30 minutes.

11. Remove the dip from the oven and transfer to a serving dish. Serve warm with the prepared crackers or refrigerate the dip until thoroughly cooled and serve that way. Both ways are delicious.

ROASTED VEGGIE DIP À LA BABA GHANOUSH

Q&E DF MAKES 2 CUPS

BABA GHANOUSH IS LIKE HUMMUS'S COOLER, YUMMIER EGG-plant sister, and it is absolutely the inspiration for this scrumptious roasted veggie dip. This dip features the fabulous eggplant of course, but we've also added some zucchini and grape tomatoes into the roasting pan mix for a deliciously healthy dip that will make a great addition to any get-together. Roasting the vegetables takes some time, but the end product is well worth it. We like to serve this with crudités, our favorite lentil chips, or gluten-free crackers. This is a quick and easy recipe but will take about 45 minutes to make instead of the usual Q&E time of 30 minutes or less.

1½ to 2   pounds eggplant, ends discarded, peeled, sliced in half lengthwise, and coarsely chopped into equal pieces

½   pound zucchini, ends discarded and coarsely chopped into equal pieces

1   cup grape tomatoes

1   tablespoon minced garlic

⅛   teaspoon cayenne pepper (optional)

⅛   teaspoon smoked paprika
Salt and freshly ground black pepper

¼   cup olive oil

3   tablespoons plus 2 teaspoons freshly squeezed lemon juice, divided

2   tablespoons coarsely chopped fresh parsley

3   tablespoons tahini (paste made from ground sesame seeds)

1. Preheat the oven to 400°F. Grease a large roasting pan or baking sheet with nonstick cooking spray and set aside.

2. In a large bowl, combine the eggplant, zucchini, grape tomatoes, garlic, cayenne, paprika, and some salt and pepper and stir well to combine all the ingredients.

3. Transfer the seasoned vegetables into the prepared pan.

4. In a small bowl or measuring cup, combine the olive oil and 3 tablespoons of the lemon juice with a bit more salt and pepper. Stir well and then pour all over the vegetables in the pan, distributing it as evenly as possible. Give a quick stir to coat all the vegetables and roast for 40 to 45 minutes, or until the eggplant is soft and tender. Depending on your oven, this may take an extra 5 minutes.

5. Remove and let the vegetables cool in the pan for a few minutes.

6. Add the vegetables to a blender or food processor. Pulse for a few moments to blend down all of the vegetables. Scrape down the sides.

7. Add in the remaining 2 teaspoons lemon juice, parsley, and tahini and blend well until the dip is nice and creamy and few chunks remain. It will still be a bit chunky, but you want to blend it as smooth as possible.

8. Serve either slightly warm or cold with your favorite gluten-free crackers, lentil chips, pita bread, or crudités.

SHRIMP-STUFFED MUSHROOMS

MAKES 26 TO 32 MUSHROOMS (with size variations)

THESE MINI MOUTHFULS OF WONDERFULNESS ARE SO FAST TO make and yet they are so decadently delicious. Although they are simple to make, it can sometimes be difficult to get the filling into the mushrooms efficiently. We use a teaspoon to fill the mushroom cavity and stuff the filling in. It works well and helps you get that nice, heaped-filling result. You can also use your fingers to stuff the mushroom caps and mold the stuffing on top of the mushrooms, if preferred. Be sure to not overcook them, or else they can collapse in on themselves. You want the mushrooms tender but firm enough to maintain their shape. This is a quick and easy recipe and will take 30 minutes or less to make.

2	tablespoons plus 1 tablespoon extra-virgin olive oil, divided
½	pound small (51/60) shrimp, peeled and deveined, tails removed (see note)
2	teaspoons minced garlic
½	cup gluten-free breadcrumbs
1	teaspoon Emeril's Original Essence seasoning or Cajun seasoning of your choice
¾	cup grated Pecorino Romano cheese
2	tablespoons minced fresh parsley
	Salt and freshly ground black pepper
2	tablespoons chicken stock or water
26 to 32	large white stuffing mushrooms (2- to 2½-inch diameter), stems removed

1. Preheat the oven to 400°F. Lightly grease a large baking sheet with nonstick cooking spray.

2. In a medium skillet, heat 1 tablespoon of the olive oil over medium-high heat. Sauté the shrimp and garlic until pink and opaque, about 3 to 5 minutes. Transfer to a cutting board and set aside while you make the filling.

3. Stir the breadcrumbs, Essence, cheese, parsley, and salt and pepper to taste together in a small mixing bowl.

4. Add the remaining 2 tablespoons olive oil and the chicken stock and mix thoroughly.

5. Once the shrimp are cool enough to handle, chop them into small pieces. Add the chopped shrimp to the breadcrumb mixture and stir it up until all the ingredients are mixed together evenly.

6. Using a teaspoon, fill each mushroom cavity with stuffing, using the teaspoon to shape a nice heaping mound of stuffing. You can also use your fingers to push the stuffing down into the mushroom. Place the stuffed mushrooms on the prepared baking sheet.

7. Bake for 15 to 20 minutes, or until the mushrooms are tender and the filling is browned on top.

8. Remove from the oven, let cool for 5 minutes, and then serve.

NOTE: 51/60 shrimp will cook down to 71/90 size. If you want to buy shrimp that are already peeled, deveined, and have the tails removed, look for 61/70 shrimp. They get cut up for this recipe, so the only real difference the size will make is texture and cook time. However, even large shrimp cut up very small would taste fine.

CRISPY SRIRACHA AND LIME CHICKEN WINGS

MAKES 4 TO 6 SERVINGS (ABOUT 22 WINGS)

THESE CHICKEN WINGS ARE ABSOLUTELY WORTH THE TIME and effort to make, and that is a fact, Jack. The spicy, garlicky Sriracha combined with the zesty, tart citrus is the best tag team for a sauce we could have dreamt up. We also can't think of anything better for these perfectly crispy, crunchy lil' wings to take a dunk in! And, like our recipe for E.J.'s Crunchy Fried Chicken (page 213), we use a blend of superfine white rice flour and cornstarch to get a really nice, crispy coating on the chicken. We guarantee you that these will please anyone who may turn his or her nose up at the whole "gluten-free thing." So dunk on, my friend. May the Sriracha be with you!

SRIRACHA AND LIME SAUCE

1	stalk fresh lemongrass, outer brown leaves peeled and discarded
½	cup freshly squeezed lime juice
2	tablespoons white vinegar
2 to 4	tablespoons Sriracha sauce (4 if you want it very spicy!)
3	tablespoons granulated sugar
3	tablespoons nuoc mam cham (fish sauce)
2	teaspoons freshly grated ginger or ginger purée (from a jar)
2	teaspoons minced garlic
1	tablespoon roughly chopped fresh mint
1	tablespoon roughly chopped fresh cilantro

2½   pounds high-quality chicken wings, separated at joints, no wing tips

¾   cup freshly squeezed lime juice

½   cup cool water

2   teaspoons granulated sugar

2   teaspoons garlic salt

1½   cups superfine white rice flour

¼   cup cornstarch

1½   teaspoons onion powder

1   tablespoon Emeril's Original Essence seasoning

    Vegetable oil, for frying

1. First, make the sauce. Place the stalk of lemongrass on a cutting board and, using either a heavy wooden spoon or a meat mallet, beat the stalk a few times to release the flavors. You don't need to take out all your day's frustration on it . . . just a few whacks will do it!

2. In a small, nonstick saucepan, combine the lemongrass stalk with all the ingredients except for the mint and cilantro. Over medium-low heat, bring it to a gentle bubble.

3. Once bubbling, turn the heat down to low and simmer for 3 to 4 minutes, or until the sugar dissolves, stirring occasionally. Turn off the heat.

4. Using a fine-mesh strainer, strain this liquid into a heatproof glass jar or bowl. Stir in the fresh mint and cilantro and allow to cool to room temperature before refrigerating until needed.

5. Now make the chicken wings. Rinse the chicken wings well and pat them dry with paper towels. Place all the wings into a gallon-size resealable plastic bag.

6. In a measuring jug or medium bowl, combine the lime juice, water, sugar, and garlic salt. Mix well and pour into the bag with the chicken wings. Seal the bag and refrigerate for at least 2 hours but no more than 8 hours, turning the bag occasionally to make sure the wings are marinating evenly.

7. After the marinating time, take the chicken out of the fridge and allow it to come to room temperature.

8. In another gallon-size resealable plastic bag, combine the rice flour, cornstarch, onion powder, and Essence and shake well.

9. Line a large baking sheet with aluminum foil.

10. Transfer the wings about six at a time from the bag of marinade into the bag of flour mixture and shake to coat the wings evenly. Lay them on the prepared baking sheet. Continue this process, working in batches, until all the wings have been floured.

11. Now let's fry the chicken wings. You'll need a large baking sheet lined with paper towels here. If you have a deep fryer, fry the wings until golden brown and cooked through following the manufacturer's instructions for chicken. If you don't have a deep fryer, use an 8- to 10-inch cast-iron skillet or Dutch oven. Fill the pan with vegetable oil until the pan is halfway full. DO NOT fill the pan up fully with oil!

12. Over medium-high heat, heat the oil until it reaches 350°F, being sure to check it with a candy/deep-fry thermometer. You want the oil not to dip below 350°F or rise any higher than 375°F, so try to keep the oil in this window.

13. Once it reaches 350°F to 375°F, carefully fry the chicken wings in batches, about six to seven wings per batch. You don't want to overcrowd the pan. Cook for about 5 minutes on the first side, until golden brown and crispy. After 5 minutes, carefully flip the wings using metal tongs and cook for another 5 to 6 minutes on the other side, until crispy and brown. We suggest you use a meat thermometer to check the internal temperature of the chicken to make sure the wings are properly cooked through. The internal temperature should be at least 165°F. If you are worried about the wings being fully cooked, you can always cook them in a 375°F oven for another 10 minutes on a baking sheet.

14. Once fried, transfer the wings to the paper towel–lined baking sheet to cool. Continue frying in batches until all the chicken wings are cooked.

15. Once all the wings are cooked, take the Sriracha sauce out of the fridge. You'll need a clean pair of tongs and a cooling rack placed over a large baking sheet or roasting pan to catch any drips.

16. Using the tongs, dunk one of the cooked wings into the sauce. Submerge it quickly but make sure it's well coated. Place it onto the rack and continue this process until all the wings have been dunked in the sauce. Serve immediately while hot. Discard any remaining sauce.

EASY CHICKEN SATAY SKEWERS

  MAKES 10 SKEWERS

WHO DOESN'T LOVE THAT YUMMY PEANUT SATAY DIPPING sauce you get in Thai or Vietnamese restaurants? Well, we clearly do because we wrote a whole recipe based on that sauce! The satay sauce does double duty here by being a delicious marinade for the chicken and also serving as a dipping sauce bonus! This is a great dish to have the kiddies help you out with as well. They love to help stir and mix the sauce and thread the chicken onto the skewers. These skewers are perfect in the oven as directed below, but they are delish on the grill, too, especially when you get some charred bits. Just remember: if you're using wooden or bamboo skewers as opposed to the metal variety, you'll need to soak them in water for 20 to 25 minutes before using. This will ensure they don't burn when cooking, either on the grill or in the oven. This is a quick and easy recipe but will take about 45 minutes instead of the usual Q&E time of 30 minutes or less.

½   teaspoon minced fresh ginger or ginger purée (from a jar)
½   teaspoon minced garlic
1   teaspoon lime zest
2   tablespoons freshly squeezed lime juice
1   tablespoon honey
2   tablespoons gluten-free soy sauce or gluten-free tamari
1   tablespoon sesame oil
2   teaspoons curry powder or garam masala
¼   cup smooth peanut butter
1   tablespoon chopped cilantro, plus more for garnish if desired
1   cup coconut milk, divided

1   pound boneless, skinless chicken tenders

1   teaspoon vegetable or sunflower oil, for the pan
      As many skewers (bamboo, wood, or metal) as chicken tenders
      (we had 10)

1. In a medium bowl, combine all the ingredients except for the coconut milk, chicken tenders, and vegetable oil and mix well until it forms a thick paste.

2. Take half of this marinade and place it in a small saucepan with ½ cup of the coconut milk. Stir well to incorporate and set aside.

3. Add the remaining ½ cup of the coconut milk to the bowl with the remaining half of the marinade and stir well to incorporate. Add the chicken tenders to this, cover, and marinate in the fridge for 20 minutes.

4. While the chicken is marinating, brush a large baking sheet with the vegetable oil using either a pastry brush or a paper towel, or coat well with nonstick cooking spray.

5. Preheat the oven to 400°F.

6. Over low heat, gently warm the marinade and coconut milk mixture in the saucepan for 3 to 4 minutes, or until it's warmed through. Transfer this to a small bowl for dipping.

7. Take the chicken out of the fridge and thread one tender onto one skewer, going back and forth on the skewer in an "S" shape, almost like you're sewing it on. Place each skewer on the prepared tray.

8. Bake for 25 minutes, or until fully cooked through. Turn once during cooking. Alternatively, you can grill the skewers on the BBQ for 10 minutes, also turning halfway through cooking.

9. Serve the skewers on a large plate or serving platter with the satay sauce for dipping. Sprinkle a bit more chopped cilantro on top of the skewers, if desired.

CRISPY COD FISH CAKES WITH HORSERADISH SAUCE

(DF) MAKES 6 TO 8 (½-CUP-SIZE) CAKES

FISH CAKES ARE ANOTHER ENGLISH STAPLE THAT JILLY adopted from her years of living in London. But really, who doesn't like a hot and crispy fish and potato cake fried to golden-brown perfection, this side of the pond or the other?! It doesn't matter where you're from or where you live, this is a delicious starter to any meal. This can easily be made into a main meal as well—just serve two fish cakes per person. Feel free to substitute the cod with any white-fleshed, flaky fish you might prefer. Also, if you don't have tapioca flour for the coating, superfine white rice flour works just as well. Just be sure your pan is piping hot before placing the cakes in it so you get a nice crispy coating. Happy fishing!

FISH CAKES

¾	pound cod fillets, or any other white fish you like (tilapia, haddock, etc.)
1	tablespoon olive oil
1	teaspoon Emeril's Original Essence seasoning or Cajun seasoning of your choice
1	pound potatoes, peeled, diced, and placed in a saucepan of cold water
2	tablespoons Dijon mustard
2	tablespoons finely chopped chives
1	tablespoon finely chopped parsley
6 to 8	dashes Tabasco

Salt and freshly ground black pepper

2 tablespoons Horseradish Sauce (recipe follows)

Tapioca flour, for coating (a few tablespoons)

Vegetable oil, for frying

Arugula, for serving (optional)

HORSERADISH SAUCE

½ cup high-quality mayonnaise

1 tablespoon prepared horseradish (as close to pure, grated horseradish as you can find)

1 tablespoon Dijon mustard

1 teaspoon finely chopped parsley

2 teaspoons freshly squeezed lemon juice

Salt and freshly ground black pepper

1. First, make the fish cakes. Place the cod fillets on a plate and drizzle the olive oil and the Essence on both sides of the fish.

2. Heat a sauté pan or skillet over medium-high heat and add the fish. Cook the fish for a few minutes on each side until cooked through. Depending on the thickness of your fish, this could be for about 3 to 4 minutes on each side.

3. Once cooked, take the fish out of the pan and let it rest on a cutting board or plate until cooled.

4. Over high heat, bring the saucepan of potatoes and cold water to a boil and cook the potatoes until fork-tender, about 10 to 15 minutes, depending on size. Drain and allow to cool.

5. While the potatoes are cooking, in a medium bowl, combine all the ingredients for the horseradish sauce and mix well. Set aside.

6. In a large bowl, add the cooled potatoes, and using a fork, a masher, or your hands, mash the potatoes a bit so they aren't so chunky. You want some chunks, but not too much.

7. Add the cooled fish fillets to the bowl. Using a fork or your hands, flake the fish and mix it well with the mashed potatoes.

8. Add the mustard, chives, parsley, Tabasco, salt and pepper, and 2 tablespoons Horseradish Sauce to the bowl. Using a spoon, mix all the ingredients together well to form the fish cake batter.

9. Dust a few tablespoons of tapioca flour on a cutting board. You'll need a baking sheet here as well. Dust your hands with a bit of tapioca flour and, using a ½-cup measuring cup, scoop an even amount of the cake mixture, dump it into your floured hands, and coat all sides of the mixture with the flour, flattening it out slightly to make a patty. Place on the baking sheet and continue until all the fish cakes are formed.

10. Place the baking sheet in the fridge for 20 minutes to allow the cakes to set.

11. After 20 minutes, in a large sauté pan or skillet, heat a few tablespoons of vegetable oil over medium-high heat. Fry the fish cakes for 4 to 5 minutes on the first side until golden brown before flipping and cooking the other side for another 3 to 4 minutes until brown and golden.

12. Transfer the cakes to a paper towel–lined plate or baking sheet to allow to de-grease slightly. Serve warm with a bit of the remaining horseradish sauce dolloped on top and some arugula underneath each cake, if desired.

CUCUMBER AND SMOKED SALMON ROLLS WITH CHIVE CREAM

SERVES 8 TO 10 (TWO ½-INCH-THICK SLICES EACH)

WE JUST LOVE THE FLAVOR COMBINATION OF SMOKY SALMON with an herby dill and caper-filled cream cheese spread all rolled up in a crisp cucumber package. It is the perfect nibble to get any gathering off to a yummy start. We like to serve this in slices on top of a really crunchy cracker, like Glutino Original Bagel Chips. But feel free to use any gluten-free cracker you prefer. Or, perhaps try serving this on some toasted pieces of your favorite gluten-free baguette. No matter how you slice it and no matter how you serve it, this works!

6	ounces cream cheese (preferably low-fat), at room temperature
1	tablespoon finely minced chives
1	tablespoon finely minced fresh dill
1	teaspoon drained and finely minced capers
2	teaspoons freshly squeezed lemon juice
1	teaspoon Dijon mustard
	Pinch of Emeril's Original Essence seasoning or Cajun seasoning of your choice
	Freshly ground black pepper
1	cucumber (preferably English seedless), peeled, ends trimmed, and halved crosswise (not lengthwise)
8	ounces high-quality smoked salmon slices, as low in sodium as you can find
20	of your favorite gluten-free crackers, for serving (we like Glutino Original Bagel Chips)

1. In a small bowl, combine the softened cream cheese, chives, dill, capers, lemon juice, mustard, Essence, and a bit of pepper. Stir well and set aside.

2. Take the peeled cucumber and, either with a mandoline or a ribbon peeler, slice the cucumber lengthwise to create thin ribbons. Do this until you reach the seeds, then flip the cucumber to another side and repeat again until you reach the seeds. Repeat this process on all four sides of the cucumber and dispose of the seedy center bit.

3. On a large paper towel–lined plate, lay out all the ribbon slices and cover with another piece of paper towel. Press down gently to absorb some of the moisture.

4. On a large cutting board, lay out a large piece of plastic wrap.

5. Working across the plastic wrap, layer the slices of cucumber vertically, slightly overlapping each piece until all the cucumber ribbons are laid out almost to make one large, long piece.

6. Making sure the cream cheese mixture is at room temperature and softened, spoon half the mixture on top of the cucumber slices. Using a spatula or spoon, gently spread this mixture over the top of the cucumber slices as evenly as you can to make a complete layer. Please refer to the process pictures for an idea of what this should look like.

7. Next, layer the slices of smoked salmon on top of the cream cheese layer, overlapping the pieces slightly, again to make one complete layer.

8. Spoon the remaining half of the cream cheese mixture on top of the

salmon and again, very carefully spread this out as evenly as possible, making a complete layer.

9. Now for the fun, slightly difficult part: the rolling! Taking the edge of the plastic wrap closest to you, gently fold and roll all this over to create a solid log shape, if you will, keeping it as tight as possible. You want to use the plastic wrap to help you maneuver and roll, but you do not want it to get wrapped up in the middle of the filling.

10. The plastic wrap should now be wrapped tightly around the log. Twist the ends and place the entire roll on a baking sheet. Refrigerate for 20 minutes to allow the roll to set slightly.

11. After 20 minutes, gently peel back the plastic wrap to expose the cucumber salmon roll. Using a paper towel, blot the roll to absorb any moisture that may have formed.

12. With a sharp knife, slice the roll as evenly as possible into 16 to 20 slices. This may require a little patience, as the roll is a bit delicate. Take your time here.

13. Serve each slice of the roll on top of a bagel chip or any gluten-free cracker you prefer. Serve and enjoy immediately.

PORK AND MUSHROOM SPRING ROLLS WITH GINGER AND CITRUS PONZU DIPPING SAUCE

DF   MAKES 14 TO 16 SPRING ROLLS

WE LOVE SPRING ROLLS AND THUS REFUSE TO GO WITHOUT just because we can't have gluten! We use those fabulous store-bought spring roll wrappers you find in the Asian or international section of your local grocery store . . . you know the ones. You've seen these wrappers a million times but never knew what to do with them! They're made with rice and tapioca flour and are surprisingly easy to work with once you get the hang of it. The sky is the limit with the potential tasty filling options once you conquer your spring-roll-rolling fear. However, this pork and mushroom combo is definitely our favorite. We've given you two options for serving: a healthy version and, of course, a naughty version (fried spring rolls anyone?). Either way, try these as an appetizer for your next get-together and be prepared for everyone to ask when you had time to take an "art of spring roll making" class! Serve them with our Ginger and Citrus Ponzu Dipping Sauce to complete your tasty journey.

1½ tablespoons vegetable oil

2 teaspoons minced garlic

1½ teaspoons freshly grated ginger or ginger purée (from a jar)

1 pound ground pork

1½ cups finely diced mushrooms (shiitake, oyster, or baby bellas)

½ cup drained and finely diced water chestnuts

½ cup finely sliced green onions (green and white parts)

2 tablespoons rice wine vinegar

1	tablespoon plus 1 teaspoon gluten-free tamari or gluten-free soy sauce (preferably low-sodium)
1	tablespoon sesame oil
½	teaspoon crushed red pepper flakes
14 to 16	spring roll wrappers (also called rice pancakes by some brands)
	Vegetable oil (if frying)

YOU'LL ALSO NEED

Large shallow bowl or pan filled with cold water (large enough for a whole spring roll sheet to lie flat in)

Clean cutting board for rolling

2   large plates

2   dampened cloths or paper towels to cover the rolled spring rolls and keep them from drying out

1. First, make the filling. In a large sauté pan over medium-high heat, place the oil, garlic, ginger, and ground pork. Cook until the pork is cooked through, for about 5 minutes, stirring frequently and using a wooden spoon to crumble the meat as it cooks.

2. Add the mushrooms and water chestnuts to the pan and cook until softened, about 3 to 4 minutes, stirring frequently.

3. Add the green onions, rice wine vinegar, tamari, sesame oil, and pepper flakes to the pan and stir. Turn the heat down to low and cook for 2 minutes to allow the vinegar to evaporate and the flavors to marry.

4. Turn the heat off and set the pan aside to cool. Once cool, place the mixture in a large bowl.

5. Now for the assembly. Place one wrapper sheet in a shallow pan or bowl of cold water and, with your hands, gently move the sheet back and forth until it becomes soft and tacky, about 30 seconds. It will go from a solid sheet to a translucent, malleable sheet.

6. Immediately take it out of the water and gently lay it flat on a clean cutting board. Let it dry for a few seconds before placing 2 tablespoons of the filling mixture onto the middle of the wrapper as compactly as you can.

7. With clean hands, gently fold the bottom of the wrapper over so it covers the filling completely. Then fold in the sides tightly over the filling, as if you were wrapping a little present. (You want the spring rolls to be as compact and even in size as possible.)

8. Roll the wrapper upward as neatly as possible to form the completed spring roll.

9. Once rolled, place on a large plate and cover with either a dampened cloth or paper towel to keep from drying out.

10. Repeat steps 5 to 9 until all of the rolls are assembled. If you aren't frying them, serve the spring rolls immediately with our Ginger and Citrus Ponzu Dipping Sauce. If you are frying, proceed to steps 11 to 15.

11. If frying, fill a small heavy pan with high sides (such as a cast-iron skillet or a wok) halfway with vegetable oil and turn the heat to medium high. These rolls are too fragile for a deep fryer, so please trust us when we say: pan fry only. The oil temperature should be around 180°F so as not to damage the delicate wrappers.

12. Once the oil has reached 180°F, place one of the spring rolls onto a large, metal slotted spoon or pick up with tongs and carefully drop the roll into the hot oil. It should bubble up immediately. If not, the oil isn't hot enough to fry yet. Fry a few rolls at a time, making sure not to overcrowd the pan so you have room to maneuver and flip them.

13. Fry until golden brown on all sides, for about 1 minute, turning with the slotted spoon or tongs so they cook evenly.

14. Once golden brown, remove the cooked rolls with your slotted spoon or tongs and place on a large paper towel–lined plate to de-grease and cool.

15. Repeat steps 12 through 14 until all the spring rolls are fried. Once cool enough to handle, serve immediately with our Ginger and Citrus Ponzu Dipping Sauce.

GINGER AND CITRUS PONZU DIPPING SAUCE
MAKES ABOUT 1 CUP

THE COMBINATION OF PUNCHY GINGER AND TART CITRUS really works well to balance all the divine saltiness of the Pork and Mushroom Spring Rolls. This sauce is a perfect accompaniment, though it works deliciously well as a marinade, too. Try it either on its own as a dipping sauce or marinate your favorite fish, steak, or chicken in it for a tasty stir-fry in a snap. It makes a good amount, so you should have plenty of leftovers—just store in an airtight container in the fridge.

½ cup gluten-free tamari or gluten-free soy sauce (preferably low-sodium)

¼ cup pulp-free orange juice
Juice of 1 lemon (about 2 tablespoons; we use a Meyer lemon)

1 tablespoon water

1 tablespoon rice wine vinegar

½ heaped teaspoon freshly grated ginger or ginger purée (from a jar)
Pinch of light brown sugar

1. Place all the ingredients in a bowl and whisk until well combined and the sugar has dissolved.

2. Store in an airtight container and keep refrigerated until needed. Sauce may need a quick stir before use.

Pork and Mushroom Spring Rolls, page 56

SAVORY CHEDDAR SCONES WITH RED ONION MARMALADE

 MAKES 8 (¼-CUP-SIZE) SCONES

WHAT'S NOT TO LIKE ABOUT A PIPING HOT, CHEESY SCONE? These little bites of heaven are made that much more delicious with the red onion marmalade. You could, of course, just skip the marmalade and serve these with your favorite soup or even a bowl of our Home-Style Chili with Gluten-Free Beer (page 211) to sop up all the scrumptiousness. We've used coconut oil instead of the usual shortening or butter, but feel free to use whichever you prefer. We found that these work best when mixed by hand instead of using a food processor. For a dairy-free alternative, simply omit the cheese in the recipe and substitute the milk with your favorite dairy-free version. We know you'll be baking lots of these! This is a quick and easy recipe and will take 30 minutes or less to make.

SCONES

1½ cups gluten-free flour blend (we like Arrowhead Mills Gluten Free All Purpose Baking Mix)

1 teaspoon baking powder

½ teaspoon xanthan gum

½ teaspoon salt

¼ cup coconut oil, shortening, or unsalted butter

½ cup cold milk (we used whole milk but any % will work)

1 medium-size egg, lightly beaten

½ cup high-quality finely shredded sharp Cheddar cheese
Kosher sea salt, for sprinkling (optional)

1   tablespoon olive oil
2   cups thinly sliced red onion (halve the onion before slicing)
1   teaspoon minced garlic
    Pinch of salt
    Freshly ground black pepper
2   tablespoons cooking sherry
2   tablespoons loosely packed light brown sugar

1. Preheat the oven to 425°F. Position an oven rack in the middle and lightly coat a baking sheet with nonstick cooking spray.

2. First, make the scones. Sift the flour, baking powder, xanthan gum, and salt into a medium bowl.

3. Add the coconut oil and, USING YOUR HANDS, blend the oil into the flour mix as finely as you can until it looks and feels like small breadcrumbs. You want to work out the lumps as much as you can.

4. Add the milk and the lightly beaten egg to the bowl and mix well using a fork. It will be thick and a bit lumpy, almost resembling thick oatmeal.

5. Add the shredded cheese to the mixture. Use a wooden spoon to gently fold it in until all is well combined and it forms one big ball of dough.

6. Using a ¼-cup measuring cup, scoop out ¼ cup of the mixture and work each scoop in your hands by gently rolling and patting, as if you were making a hamburger patty. Place on the prepared baking sheet. Repeat this process until all eight scones have been formed.

7. Sprinkle a bit of kosher salt on each scone, if desired, before baking on the middle rack. Bake for 14 to 16 minutes, or until the tops of the scones are golden brown and a bit crispy.

8. While the scones bake, make the marmalade. Warm the olive oil in a small sauté pan or saucepan over medium-low heat for 1 minute.

9. Add the onions, garlic, and a pinch of salt and pepper and cook until soft, about 8 to 9 minutes, stirring frequently.

10. Once softened, turn the heat down to low. Add the sherry and brown sugar and cook for 4 minutes, or until it starts to reduce and thicken into a syrupy consistency, stirring often.

11. Remove from the heat and let cool slightly. Serve on top of your warm scones. Any remaining marmalade can be kept in an airtight container and stored in the fridge for up to 1 week. It's delicious served with your favorite cheeses.

WARM APPLE AND BRIE TARTLETS

THE DELICIOUS COMBINATION OF APPLE AND BRIE IS WIDELY known, and it frequently shows up in salads, appetizers, and even desserts. For this twist, we paired the two with some caramelized sweet onions and put them in a little GF version of a tartlet. Instead of using an actual tartlet pan, we chose to use a muffin tin since most people have the latter but not the former. It is important to get your dough as thin as possible or else the crust flavor can overwhelm the delicate apple. Just work with your dough in small batches, and it should maintain its shape long enough to successfully roll it out and transfer it into the muffin tin.

2	recipes Basic Pie Crust dough (page 70) (see note)
	Gluten-free all-purpose flour or baking mix, for dusting
2	tablespoons extra-virgin olive oil
4	cups julienned sweet yellow or white onions (such as Vidalia)
1	tablespoon Dijon mustard
2	tablespoons light brown sugar
1⅓	cups peeled and diced Granny Smith apple, mixed with 2 teaspoons freshly squeezed lemon juice
1	tablespoon chopped fresh thyme
¼	teaspoon garlic powder
	Salt and freshly ground black pepper
6	ounces Brie cheese
	Fresh chives, chopped, for garnish (optional)

1. Grease two standard twelve-cup muffin tins with nonstick cooking spray.

2. Prepare two recipes of the Basic Pie Crust dough (page 70), being sure to divide and refrigerate it in four disks instead of two.

3. Preheat the oven to 350°F.

4. Working with one disk of dough at a time, flour a piece of waxed paper and place the dough disk in the center of the waxed paper. Lightly flour the top of the disk and cover with another piece of waxed paper. Using the waxed paper keeps the dough from sticking to the rolling pin and makes it much easier to work with. Roll out the dough as thinly as possible (shoot for ⅛-inch thickness). Using a 2½-inch-diameter cookie cutter, cut out disks of dough and gently transfer them to the bottom of the muffin cups. Gently press the dough down so that it fits snugly in the bottom of the tin and comes up the side enough to make a slight lip.

5. Repeat this process until you have dough in twenty-four muffin cups. Discard any extra dough.

6. Next, you need to blind bake the tartlets. Place small pieces of parchment paper in the bottom of each cup so that it covers the crust. Fill each cup with a few dried beans, which will act as pie weights for each tartlet. Bake at 350°F for 15 minutes.

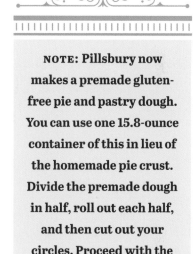

NOTE: Pillsbury now makes a premade gluten-free pie and pastry dough. You can use one 15.8-ounce container of this in lieu of the homemade pie crust. Divide the premade dough in half, roll out each half, and then cut out your circles. Proceed with the recipe as directed.

7. Remove from the oven, let cool completely, and then carefully remove the beans, the parchment, and the tartlet shells from the tin. Alternatively, you can leave the shells in the muffin tin. Set the tartlet shells aside until you are ready to fill them.

8. While the tartlet shells are baking, make your caramelized onion concoction. Heat the olive oil in a large skillet over medium heat. Add the onions, mustard, and

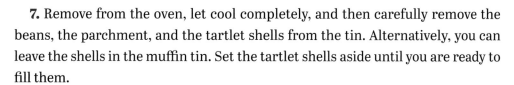

brown sugar and begin to sauté. You'll need to stir them often to prevent burning and to help the caramelizing process. (Be aware that the whole caramelizing process can take anywhere from 20 to 30 minutes total, depending on the size of your onions.)

9. Once the onions have been sautéing for about 15 minutes and are on the way to browning, add the apples, thyme, garlic powder, and salt and black pepper to taste. Stir to incorporate and continue cooking until the onions are completely caramelized, deep golden brown but not burned, roughly for another 5 to 10 minutes longer. If your onions finish cooking before the tartlet shells are cool, remove them from the heat and set them aside. Once you are ready to assemble, take your

Brie out of the fridge to let it come to room temperature. This makes it a bit more malleable to work with when pressing down into the tartlet shells.

10. Once the tartlet shells have cooled and the onion mixture is cooked, slice your Brie into twenty-four equal-size pieces.

11. Preheat the oven to 350°F.

12. If you have removed your tartlet shells from the muffin tin, lay them out on a large, ungreased and unlined baking sheet. Alternatively, you can assemble the tartlets inside the tin and remove the finished product carefully with a fork or small spatula. We differ here in our preferred methods: Jilly prefers to assemble in the tin and then remove and Jessie prefers to assemble on the baking sheet. Either way will work.

13. Using your fingers, gently press one Brie slice into each tartlet crust so that it fills the bottom as evenly and thinly as possible. Use your fingers to gently press down and smooth out the Brie slice as much as you can.

14. Then fill each tartlet with approximately 1 teaspoonful of the onion mixture.

15. Once all the tartlets have been filled, bake them on the ungreased, unlined baking sheet or in the tins for 3 to 5 minutes so the cheese can melt and the tartlets and filling can warm through.

16. Remove the tartlets from the oven and let cool briefly, about 2 to 3 minutes. Garnish with some freshly chopped chives, if desired, and serve warm.

$\mathscr{B}$ASIC PIE CRUST RECIPE AND PREPARATION INSTRUCTIONS

HERE IS OUR TRIED AND TRUE RECIPE FOR A CRISPY, GOLDEN-
brown gluten-free pie crust using a premixed, gluten-free flour blend. Because working with gluten-free flour is somewhat different than working with traditional gluten-filled flours, we thought it would be helpful to provide you with some specific instructions and helpful hints for preparing the ideal gluten-free pie crust. The biggest point to remember: COLD, COLD, COLD. Keep your butter cold, use ice to make ice water (don't just get cold water out of the tap), and chill your dough as directed. It really does make a difference!

1	cup gluten-free flour blend (we like Arrowhead Mills Gluten Free All Purpose Baking Mix), plus more for dusting
¼	teaspoon salt
½	teaspoon xanthan gum
½	cup (1 stick) COLD unsalted butter, diced into small cubes
1	large COLD egg
2 to 4	tablespoons ice water

1. In a food processor, mix the flour, salt, and xanthan gum to combine.

2. Add in the cold butter cubes and pulse until the mixture resembles fine crumbs, with no large pieces of butter remaining unincorporated.

3. Add the egg and 2 tablespoons of ice water and then pulse again until a dough forms. Depending on the flour blend you use, you may need to add additional ice water. You want the dough to be somewhat sticky, and it should hold together easily when squeezed.

4. Remove the dough from the food processor and transfer it to a large resealable plastic bag. Squish the dough down into a large disk of even thickness (as thin as your plastic bag can accommodate). Alternatively, you can wrap the dough in plastic wrap and flatten it into a disk that way. Refrigerate for at least 30 minutes or up to 3 days.

5. Once the dough is thoroughly chilled, transfer it from its wrapping to a floured sheet of waxed paper. Sprinkle the top of the dough with a bit more flour and top with another similarly sized sheet of waxed paper.

6. Using a rolling pin, roll out the dough while it is between the sheets of waxed paper. This eliminates the sticking issue and helps keep the dough together better.

7. Once the dough is of the desired size (about a 12-inch-diameter circle for a 9-inch pie tin) and has as even a thickness as possible, gently peel off the top layer of waxed paper.

8. Transfer the dough sheet into the pie tin by either inverting the crust from the waxed paper into the tin or gently removing the dough from the bottom sheet of waxed paper and placing it in the tin.

9. Once the dough is safely in the pie tin, gently press the dough down so it fits snuggly along the bottom and up the sides of the tin. If any part of the crust breaks, gently piece it back together. It will cook together just fine, don't worry!

10. Carefully trim the edges of the crust so that you have a ½- to 1-inch overhang. Fold the edges over and crimp them as desired.

11. Now it is time to blind bake your crust. Preheat the oven to 350°F.

12. Gently place a piece of parchment paper or foil along the bottom of the crust. Fill the bottom with pie weights or dried beans. Bake the crust for 15 minutes.

13. Remove the crust from the oven and carefully remove the parchment/foil and weights/beans. Using a fork, poke some holes in the bottom of the crust and return it to the oven for another 5 minutes.

14. Let cool completely before using.

SMOKY PEA AND TRUFFLE CROSTINI WITH GOAT CHEESE, GRAPE TOMATOES, AND PEA SHOOTS

 MAKES 32 CROSTINI

THESE SWEET LITTLE CROSTINI ARE NOT ONLY DELICIOUS TO the eye, they are just as delicious to eat! Who knew you could turn a humble bag of frozen peas into such an hors d'oeuvres masterpiece? These are surprisingly simple to whip up, and you will impress all your guests when passing a tray of them around. If you want your pea purée a bit more smoky, just add a pinch more smoked paprika. If you prefer it a bit more salty, feel free to salt or pepper this to your preferred taste and, as always, if you wish to omit the cheese in this, feel free. Have fun with this tasty lil' starter and make it your own. This is a quick and easy recipe and will take 30 minutes or less to make.

 1 (1-pound) bag frozen peas, thawed
 1 tablespoon plus 1 teaspoon high-quality white truffle oil
 ½ teaspoon minced garlic
 ½ teaspoon smoked paprika
 ⅛ teaspoon salt, or more to taste
   Freshly ground black pepper
 32 (½-inch) slices of your favorite gluten-free baguette (we like Udi's for this recipe)
 6 ounces goat cheese, crumbled
 16 grape tomatoes, sliced in half lengthwise
   Pea shoots (or any sprout you like: radish, alfalfa, sunflower)

1. Place the peas in a medium saucepan over medium heat, cover, and warm them gently for 3 to 4 minutes, stirring once or twice.

2. Transfer the warm peas to a blender or food processor and blend until smooth.

3. Add the truffle oil, garlic, smoked paprika, and salt and pepper to taste and blend until well incorporated and smooth. Alternatively, you can transfer the blended peas to a large bowl and mix all the remaining ingredients in with a spoon.

4. Transfer the mixture to a large bowl. You should have roughly 2 cups of the puréed pea mixture.

5. Preheat the oven to 350°F.

6. Divide the slices of baguette, also known as your crostini, between two ungreased baking sheets.

7. Spoon a tablespoon or so of the pea mixture onto each crostini. If you have any remaining pea mixture, you can either store or discard.

8. Top the pea mixture with a bit of crumbled goat cheese and gently press it down to flatten slightly.

9. Bake for 4 to 5 minutes to warm everything through.

10. To garnish, place one grape tomato half onto the goat cheese, pressing it down so it stays in place, followed by one or two pea shoots on top of the goat cheese, almost like it is shooting out of the crostini.

11. Continue until all the crostini are garnished with a grape tomato half and pea shoots.

12. Transfer to a serving dish or platter. Crack some fresh black pepper and sprinkle a bit of salt on top of the crostini and serve still slightly warm. If you need to warm these up again, simply place them back on the baking sheet and flash them again at 350°F for a few minutes.

Breakfast

WHEN WE WERE CHILDREN, MORNINGS TENDED TO BE HECTIC and fast-paced (sound familiar?). Rarely did we have a weekday morning to sit down and enjoy a traditional breakfast. It didn't happen too often on the weekends either, since those mornings were generally filled with sports practices or errands. The large family-style, all-sit-down-together breakfast meals tended to occur at holidays when the family and extended family were all together and everyone had the time to prepare the classic breakfast-style feast. We usually had some version of bacon, eggs, chorizo, muffins, cinnamon rolls, biscuits, and fruit. In later years, the breakfast casserole or quiche supplanted the previous buffet-style options. Though the presentation changed, there were always the key foods represented. You will see, for us, what those were and still are by glancing at the chapter contents here.

Many, as you'll also see, were very gluten-centric. Cinnamon rolls with icing, breakfast biscuits, and quiche crust all demand a solid, effective dough component, and it was difficult for us to develop a gluten-free version for a while. We think that we've cracked it now and have created very scrumptious gluten-free versions of our most favorite and treasured breakfast items. We hope that you and your family agree!

Ooey Gooey Cinnamon Rolls, page 86

FRUIT AND YOGURT PARFAITS WITH HOMEMADE GRANOLA

 MAKES 4 SERVINGS

ONE OF THE FIRST SNACK REPLACEMENTS JESSIE STARTED making for herself after she was diagnosed with her gluten sensitivity was granola. The version we settled on here is Jessie's bare-naked version: it has no nuts, seeds, or fruits added. We've offered our preferred proportions for additions as optional items below, in case you prefer to add some favorites. Just keep in mind that you may have to increase the amount of coconut oil and maple syrup to compensate for the additional fruits and nuts. As for the parfait itself, please feel free to use any seasonal fresh fruit and any flavor of yogurt you like. If dairy is an issue, feel free to substitute your favorite dairy-free yogurt here. So enjoy some freedom here! This is a quick and easy recipe and will take 30 minutes or less to make.

GRANOLA

2	cups quick-cooking gluten-free rolled oats
¼	cup high-quality maple syrup
2	tablespoons coconut oil
1	tablespoon honey
1	teaspoon vanilla extract
	Pinch of salt
½	teaspoon ground cinnamon
¼	teaspoon ground nutmeg
½ to ¾	cup nuts of your choice (optional)
½ to ¾	cup dried fruit of your choice (optional)
¼ to ½	cup seeds of your choice (optional)

2 cups regular vanilla yogurt (or dairy-free vanilla yogurt)
2 cups sliced strawberries or fruit of your choice
   Honey, for garnish (optional)

1. Preheat the oven to 325°F.

2. Combine all the granola ingredients in a medium bowl. Be sure to mix well and break up the coconut oil with your hands. The warmth of your hands while mixing should help it soften and distribute into the other ingredients evenly.

3. Once the mixture seems to be evenly mixed and the oats evenly coated, spread it out in an even layer on a large greased baking sheet.

4. Bake for 10 to 15 minutes, or until the granola just starts to turn golden brown. It will remain slightly damp and won't crisp up until you remove it from the oven. So, please be sure not to leave it in the oven too long, waiting for it to crisp, or it will most likely burn.

5. Remove from the oven and allow the granola to cool on the baking sheet for 10 minutes or so.

6. Once the granola has cooled, it is time to assemble the parfaits. Begin by scooping ¼ cup of granola into the bottom of each of four serving glasses.

7. Top this layer with ¼ cup yogurt followed by ¼ cup of fruit in each glass.

8. Repeat the process with the remaining granola, yogurt, and fruit.

9. Top with a drizzle of honey, if desired, and serve.

TRADITIONAL BREAKFAST BISCUITS

Q+E **DF** MAKES 6 (¼-CUP) BISCUITS

THIS IS A FANTASTIC, BASIC GLUTEN-FREE BISCUIT RECIPE that is a great go-to and a base in so many of our other dishes. If dairy isn't an issue, add a bit of shredded cheese and you have our Savory Cheddar Scones (page 62). Pop them on top of our tasty Beef Stewpot (page 258) to make the biscuit crust. Or, for that sweet tooth among us, use the biscuit as a tasty sponge to soak up all that deliciousness in our Momma's Strawberry Shortcake (page 283). We also love them plain and hot out of the oven with homemade jam or local honey drizzled all over the top. We do find, though, that this recipe works best when you use your hands to blend the dough as opposed to a food processor. Also, if you do not have a dairy issue, these will work deliciously well using unsalted butter and regular whole milk. Let us know what you cook up with this recipe. This is a quick and easy recipe and will take 30 minutes or less to make.

1½ cups gluten-free flour blend (we like Arrowhead Mills Gluten Free All Purpose Baking Mix)

1 teaspoon baking powder

1 teaspoon xanthan gum

½ teaspoon salt

¼ cup coconut oil (or COLD unsalted butter diced into small chunks)

½ cup COLD dairy-free whole milk such as Lactaid (or regular whole milk)

1 medium egg, lightly beaten

1. Preheat the oven to 425°F and position an oven rack in the middle.

2. Sift the flour, baking powder, xanthan gum, and salt into a medium bowl.

3. Add the coconut oil to the bowl and, with your hands, blend it into the flour mix until it resembles fine breadcrumbs. Again, we find hands work best as opposed to a food processor here.

4. Add the milk and egg to the bowl and mix well. It will be thick and a bit lumpy, almost resembling oatmeal.

5. Using a ¼-cup measuring cup, scoop out a ¼ cup of the dough and place on an ungreased baking sheet. Using your hands, gently pat down each biscuit a bit. Repeat until all six are on the pan.

6. Bake on the middle rack for 12 to 15 minutes, or until they are cooked through and the tops are golden brown. Serve warm with butter or jam, if desired.

PERFECT BLUEBERRY MUFFINS

 MAKES 12 MUFFINS

WHEN JESSIE'S OLDEST SON, JUDE, WAS A TODDLER, HE LOVED walking up the street to the local bakery to get a blueberry muffin and milk. This was wonderful together time for Jess and Jude, but it was really hard for her not to cheat and eat his gluteny-muffin remnants! So, to combat her cravings, she created this delicious gluten-free version. We tested this recipe using both fresh and frozen blueberries. Both versions came out fantastic, but we think the fresh berries result in a slightly fluffier muffin. Experiment for yourself and see what you prefer. This is a quick and easy recipe and will take 30 minutes or less to make. Note that because of the differences in traditional and gluten-free flours, you may want to fill the muffin cups higher than you normally would, to increase the height of the muffins.

2	large eggs
2	teaspoons vanilla extract
½	cup dairy-free whole milk (or regular whole milk)
½	cup vegetable oil
1	cup firmly packed light brown sugar
2	cups gluten-free flour blend (we like Arrowhead Mills Gluten Free All Purpose Baking Mix)
2	teaspoons baking powder
1	teaspoon baking soda
½	teaspoon salt
¾	teaspoon ground cinnamon
1½	cups fresh blueberries, washed and dried

1. Preheat the oven to 350°F. Line a twelve-cup muffin tin with paper liners or generously grease the tin with nonstick cooking spray.

2. In a medium mixing bowl, whisk the eggs, vanilla extract, milk, oil, and sugar together until there are no lumps of sugar remaining.

3. In a large mixing bowl, sift together the flour, baking powder, baking soda, salt, and cinnamon until all the ingredients are evenly distributed.

4. Fold the wet ingredients into the dry ingredients until all the dry ingredients are incorporated and the batter has formed a thick cake-like mixture.

5. Gently fold in the blueberries so as to distribute them throughout the batter but not break them in the process. The batter should remain light brown and untainted by leaking blueberry juice. (It's okay if it gets a bit juicy, just try not to mix it that hard!)

6. Divide the batter evenly among the twelve muffin cups. It is okay to fill the cups ¾ of the way up.

7. Bake for 20 to 25 minutes, or until the muffins are golden brown and a toothpick inserted in the center comes out clean.

8. Remove from the oven and let cool slightly before serving.

YOU-WON'T-TASTE-THE-VEGGIES ZUCCHINI MUFFINS

 MAKES 12 MUFFINS

JESSIE'S FATHER-IN-LAW, ARTHUR, LIVES ON A SMALL HORSE farm about an hour outside New Orleans. In addition to his horses, he also has a considerable garden, which every year produces innumerable zucchini. This recipe was developed as a direct result of that zucchini abundance. Jessie also took the opportunity to throw in another less-than-popular vegetable, carrots, in an effort to get her kids to consume them one way or another. Well, this recipe worked on both fronts—it used up the zucchini AND both her boys scarfed these little babies right down. The muffins are moist and flavorful, and they DON'T taste like they are full of veggies. This is a quick and easy recipe and will take 30 minutes or less to make.

1½	cups gluten-free flour blend (we like Arrowhead Mills Gluten Free All Purpose Baking Mix)
1	teaspoon baking powder
½	teaspoon baking soda
1	teaspoon ground cinnamon
½	teaspoon ground nutmeg
¼	teaspoon salt
2	large eggs, at room temperature
⅔	cup firmly packed dark brown sugar
⅓	cup granulated sugar
¼	cup vegetable oil
¼	cup sour cream
¼	cup whole milk

1	teaspoon vanilla extract
1	medium zucchini (4 ounces), ends trimmed and shredded
¼	cup finely shredded carrots

1. Preheat the oven to 350°F. Line a twelve-cup muffin tin with paper liners or generously grease the tin with nonstick cooking spray.

2. Sift the flour, baking powder, baking soda, cinnamon, nutmeg, and salt together in a mixing bowl. Set aside.

3. In a large mixing bowl, stir together the eggs, brown sugar, granulated sugar, vegetable oil, sour cream, milk, and vanilla extract. You can use a whisk to beat everything together and the backside of a spoon to break up any brown sugar lumps.

4. Fold the dry ingredients into the wet ones until all ingredients are evenly mixed. Add in the zucchini and carrots and stir again until just combined.

5. Fill the muffin cups three quarters of the way up. Remember that gluten-free muffins won't rise like traditional muffins, so you can fill the tins higher than you would otherwise. Bake for 25 to 30 minutes, or until a toothpick inserted into the center of the muffins comes out clean.

6. Remove from the oven and let cool for about 5 to 10 minutes before serving warm. Alternatively, you can transfer the muffins to a cooling rack to cool completely and then serve.

OOEY GOOEY CINNAMON ROLLS

JESSIE'S BOYS JUST LOVE CINNAMON ROLLS! SHE TRIES TO limit their sugar intake, of course, so the cinnamon rolls are not a weekly indulgence. However, they are always voraciously eaten when they are on the menu, and we are sure it will be the same in your house. This version produces fluffyish rolls as long as you allow the dough to rise completely. We also like to bake them in a muffin tin because it helps them maintain their shape better. The leftovers get a bit dense and don't keep well, so try to eat them straightaway (if there are a few left, be sure to refrigerate them because of the cream cheese icing). These are truly a perfect substitute for their gluteny counterpart.

DOUGH

- 2½ cups gluten-free flour blend (we like Arrowhead Mills Gluten Free All Purpose Baking Mix)
- 2 tablespoons granulated sugar
- ½ teaspoon salt
- 1 tablespoon xanthan gum
- ¼ cup (½ stick) unsalted butter, at room temperature
- 1 tablespoon active dry yeast (not INSTANT)
- ¾ cup warm whole milk, plus 1 tablespoon for brushing
- 2 tablespoons vegetable or canola oil
- ¼ cup sour cream
- 1 large egg
- 2 teaspoons vanilla extract

1 cup firmly packed dark brown sugar

2 tablespoons ground cinnamon

¼ cup (½ stick) unsalted butter, at room temperature

½ cup cream cheese, at room temperature

1 cup confectioners' sugar

¼ cup (½ stick) unsalted butter, at room temperature

½ teaspoon vanilla extract

1. First, make the dough. We prefer to use a stand mixer, but a hand-held mixer, along with some arm work, works too. If you choose to go the hand-held route, follow the same directions as below, making adjustments as necessary. Combine the flour, granulated sugar, salt, and xanthan gum in your stand mixer bowl. Mix on low, using the paddle attachment, to evenly distribute the dry ingredients.

2. Add in the softened butter and blend on low until course crumbs form. Check to make sure the butter pieces have been distributed throughout all of the flour by hand stirring it a bit.

3. In a small bowl, stir the yeast into ¾ cup of warmed milk.

4. Add the yeast mixture, oil, sour cream, egg, and vanilla extract and beat on medium high until incorporated. Be sure to scrape down the sides so all the ingredients are incorporated into the dough. Beat on medium high for 2 to 3 minutes, until a thick dough ball forms. Scrape all of the dough into the center, cover, and let it rise for about an hour, or until it has increased in size and is getting a bit puffy. It won't get super puffy like traditional gluten dough, but it will look and feel inflated.

5. Meanwhile, make the cinnamon filling by combining the brown sugar, cinnamon, and softened butter in a small bowl. It should make a thick paste.

6. When the dough has risen, it is time to assemble the rolls. Spray a sheet of waxed paper with nonstick cooking spray and transfer your dough from the bowl to the waxed paper. Press it gently into an approximate 8 x 16-inch rectangle. Try not to roll it out because it will lose a lot of its "fluff" and get dense!

7. Gently spread the filling over the dough, leaving a ½- to 1-inch border along the edges free of filling. The filling won't spread smoothly, so just try to cover as much of the rectangle as possible in an equally thick layer.

8. Using the waxed paper as a helper, position the dough with the 16-inch side closest to you on the work surface. Use the waxed paper to roll the dough forward until you reach the border without the filling. Brush your reserved 1 tablespoon of milk onto the edge and gently press the edge into the roll so that they stick together.

9. Grease a twelve-cup muffin tin with nonstick cooking spray. Using a sharp knife or pizza cutter, cut the roll into eight equal-size slices. Place each slice into a muffin cup to help the rolls maintain their shape while cooking. Set aside to rise again in a warm, draft-free location for 45 minutes to 1 hour, or until puffy-ish.

10. Before the rolls are done rising, preheat the oven to 350°F. When they are ready for baking, bake them for 20 to 25 minutes, or until golden brown on the top.

11. About 10 minutes before you anticipate the rolls being cooked, make the cream cheese icing. Use an electric mixer to mix the cream cheese, sugar, butter, and vanilla extract until smooth and creamy.

12. Remove the rolls from the oven once cooked. Let sit for 4 to 5 minutes. Ice as desired and discard any remaining icing. Serve.

SCRUMPTIOUS LEMON POPPY SEED CAKE

OH, HOW JESSIE LOVES LEMON CAKE OF ANY KIND: LEMON pound cake, lemon bars, you name it. If it has a lemon flavor, Jessie is all over it! This lemon poppy seed cake is so moist and delicious that all of her gluten-sensitive and non-gluten-sensitive friends and family beg her to make it. You can always omit the poppy seeds if you'd prefer, and the icing is a wonderful addition but is also unnecessary. Try it all sorts of ways. Trust us, you won't need an excuse to make this recipe over and over and over.

CAKE

2	cups gluten-free flour blend (we like Arrowhead Mills Gluten Free All Purpose Baking Mix)
1	teaspoon baking powder
¼	teaspoon salt
1	teaspoon xanthan gum
½	cup (1 stick) unsalted butter, at room temperature, plus more for the pan
1½	cups granulated sugar
3	large eggs, at room temperature
½	cup sour cream
½	cup whole milk, at room temperature
1	heaping tablespoon lemon zest
2	teaspoons lemon extract
1	teaspoon vanilla extract
1½	teaspoons poppy seeds

   ¾   cup confectioners' sugar
   1   teaspoon freshly squeezed lemon juice
   1   tablespoon whole milk

1. Preheat the oven to 350°F. Grease a loaf pan with butter or nonstick cooking spray. We used a pan measuring 9 x 5 x 2¾-inches.

2. In a medium mixing bowl, sift together the flour, baking powder, salt, and xanthan gum.

3. In a large mixing bowl, beat the butter and sugar together using an electric mixer until well combined, about 3 to 4 minutes. It won't get fluffy and should stay rather granulated looking. Add the eggs, one at a time, beating to incorporate after each addition. Beat in the sour cream, milk, lemon zest, lemon extract, and vanilla extract.

4. Reduce the mixer speed to low and slowly add the flour mixture into the wet ingredients. Mix until just incorporated. Stir in the poppy seeds.

5. Pour or spoon the batter (it will be thick) into the prepared loaf pan and bake for 50 to 60 minutes, or until the top is golden brown and a toothpick inserted into the center of the loaf comes out clean.

6. Remove the cake from the oven and let it cool for 10 to 15 minutes.

7. Meanwhile, make the icing. Combine the icing ingredients in a small bowl and mix until a thick, creamy icing forms. Taste it for flavoring and add more lemon juice if preferred. The cake has a significant lemon flavor already, so be sure to factor that in before adjusting.

8. Once the cake has cooled, remove it from the pan and place it on a serving dish. Drizzle the icing evenly over the top of the loaf, cut, and serve.

FRENCH TOAST BAKE

JESSIE'S MOTHER-IN-LAW, MAW-MAW PATSY, ALWAYS MAKES this for groups! It can be made a day ahead of time or prepped and cooked right away. Personally, we like to let it sit overnight, which gives the bread a chance to soak up all the yummy egg mixture. Both ways work very well and taste fantastic, so do whatever works best for you!

FRENCH TOAST

16 ounces gluten-free French-style bread (we like Against the Grain baguettes), sliced into ½-inch-thick slices (see note)

8 large eggs

2 cups whole milk

1 cup heavy whipping cream

1 cup firmly packed light brown sugar

2 tablespoons vanilla extract

2 teaspoons ground cinnamon

TOPPING

1 cup gluten-free flour blend (we like Arrowhead Mills Gluten Free All Purpose Baking Mix)

½ cup firmly packed light brown sugar

1 teaspoon ground cinnamon

¼ teaspoon ground nutmeg

½ cup (1 stick) unsalted butter, at room temperature
Maple syrup (optional)
Confectioners' sugar (optional)

1. Preheat the oven to 350°F if you are planning to make and bake the French toast immediately.

2. Grease a 13 x 9-inch baking dish with butter or nonstick cooking spray. Layer the sliced bread evenly in the pan. We needed two rows when we tested this recipe.

3. In a large mixing bowl, whisk the eggs, milk, cream, sugar, vanilla extract, and cinnamon together. Once homogeneous, pour the mixture evenly over the top of the bread slices in the baking dish.

4. If you are making the French toast to be baked later, cover the dish tightly with plastic wrap and let it sit in the refrigerator overnight. If baking immediately, proceed to step 6.

5. If you premade the French toast and are now ready to bake it, remove it from the refrigerator and preheat the oven to 350°F.

6. Now it is time to make your crumble topping. In a small mixing bowl, mix together the flour, brown sugar, cinnamon, and nutmeg until evenly distributed.

7. Using a fork, mash in the softened butter until small crumbles form. Depending on the type of flour blend you use, you may have to add a bit more flour to get even crumbles and that is okay!

8. Sprinkle the crumb topping evenly over the top of the French toast.

9. Bake for 45 minutes to 1 hour, depending on your preferred texture; 45 minutes will result in a softer texture, while a 1-hour cook time will yield a firmer texture. Remove from oven.

10. Cover with syrup or confectioners' sugar (or both), if desired, and enjoy!

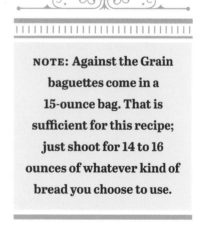

NOTE: Against the Grain baguettes come in a 15-ounce bag. That is sufficient for this recipe; just shoot for 14 to 16 ounces of whatever kind of bread you choose to use.

OATMEAL BANANA PANCAKES WITH CARAMELIZED APPLE SYRUP

THIS ALTERNATIVE TO TRADITIONAL PANCAKES AND SYRUP IS quick to mix up and is a really nice combination of flavors. It doesn't use any flour and instead relies on oats and other ingredients to make up the batter. You really need a blender or food processor to help get the right consistency for these pancakes, as the oats are tough to soften or break up on their own. Despite the unique texture, these little guys hold together well and cook quickly. The caramelized apples in the warm syrup add just the right amount of sweetness to the dish. Just remember to make the pancakes right away or else the oats in the batter will start to soak up all of the liquid, making it too thick to pour easily.

PANCAKES

- 2 cups quick-cooking gluten-free oats
- 1 large, ripe banana, peeled and broken into chunks
- 1 cup unsweetened applesauce
- 2 large eggs
- ½ cup milk of your choice
- 1 tablespoon dark brown sugar

APPLES

- 3 tablespoons unsalted butter
- 2 large, firm apples (such as Gala or Granny Smith), peeled, cored, quartered, and sliced as thin as possible
- ¼ cup firmly packed dark brown sugar

1. Preheat the oven to the "warm" setting or 200°F. Place a baking sheet in the oven. This is where you'll hold the cooked pancakes while the rest of the dish is being prepared.

2. Place all of your pancake ingredients into a food processor or blender. Purée until smooth-ish. It won't get completely smooth, but the oats should break up and it should have a thick, cake-batter-like consistency.

3. Transfer the batter into a mixing bowl to make it easier to scoop out for cooking.

4. Next, heat a medium, nonstick frying pan over medium heat. Make sure the pan has time to get hot before cooking your first pancake. Using a ¼-cup measuring cup, pour ¼ cup of batter into the hot pan. You can help spread it with the measuring cup bottom or a spoon if you think the pancake is too thick. Let the pancake cook for 2 to 3 minutes and then flip it over and cook for another 1 to 2 minutes. You want it to brown on each side but not burn!

5. Using a spatula, carefully transfer the cooked pancake onto the warmed baking sheet in the oven. Repeat the pancake-making process until all the batter is gone. We made twelve ¼-cup pancakes when we tested this, but there might be some variation.

6. Meanwhile, once you have made about half of the pancakes, it is time to caramelize the apples. In a large, nonstick sauté or frying pan, melt the butter over medium heat.

7. Add the apples and brown sugar and stir to coat. Reduce the heat to low and let the apples, sugar, and butter caramelize and the apples soften. This should only take 3 to 5 minutes, depending on the thickness of your apple slices. Once the apples are tender, remove the pan from the heat and set it aside.

8. Once you have finished cooking all your pancakes, remove the warmed ones from the oven. Divide the pancakes among four plates. Scoop approximately a quarter of the warm syrup and apple mixture atop each stack of pancakes and serve immediately.

CRÊPES À LA BANANAS FOSTER

WHEN OUR DAD FIRST OPENED EMERIL'S DELMONICO RESTAU-
rant in New Orleans, we couldn't get enough of the wonderful tableside service.
That's what they call it when the staff comes and prepares certain dishes next
to your table. One of our favorite dishes prepared for our viewing and tasting
pleasure was a classic Bananas Foster. The bananas and their syrupy decadence
are flambéed tableside, releasing a blast of colorful but controlled flames. We
figured since we enjoyed it so much, we'd share a version of it with you all. Only
this time, it's served in a tidy crêpe instead of over ice cream. Be sure to swirl
your crêpe batter around the pan to thin it out enough. And please, please, be
careful with your flambéing!

CRÊPES

- ½ cup buttermilk
- 1 cup whole milk
- 2 large eggs
- ½ cup gluten-free flour blend (we like Arrowhead Mills Gluten Free All Purpose Baking Mix)
- 2 tablespoons unsalted butter, melted, plus more for frying

FILLING

- ¼ cup (½ stick) unsalted butter
- ¾ cup firmly packed dark brown sugar
- ½ teaspoon ground cinnamon
- 6 large bananas, peeled and sliced into ¼-inch-thick rounds

¼ cup dark rum
¼ cup banana liquor (optional)
Confectioners' sugar, for garnish (optional)

1. First, prepare the crêpes. In a medium mixing bowl, whisk together the buttermilk, whole milk, and eggs until combined, about 1 minute or so.

2. In a large mixing bowl, add the flour. Pour in the egg mixture and stir so that a thin batter forms. Stir in the melted butter while whisking constantly until the butter is evenly mixed into the batter.

3. In a large, nonstick 10- or 12-inch skillet, melt a small bit of butter over medium heat. This is just to ensure that the crêpes don't stick, so you don't need much butter here.

4. Once the pan is hot, pour ¼ cup of batter into the pan. Lifting it up slightly, turn the pan in a circular motion to allow the batter to spread out and form a thin layer over much of the pan bottom. You'll see when to stop because the batter will start to cook and it won't move when you turn the pan anymore. Return the pan to the heat and cook for 2 to 3 minutes, or until the top of the crêpe has set. The edges should be slightly brown, and they should start to lift up or come away from the pan a bit.

5. Using a wide spatula, gently flip the crêpe over and cook for another 2 to 3 minutes, or until the second side is cooked through and slightly browned.

6. Remove the crêpe from the skillet and transfer to a plate.

7. Repeat steps 3 through 6 until you have made all eight crêpes. There shouldn't be much batter left, but if there is, make extra crêpes to enjoy or discard the batter since it doesn't keep very well.

8. Now, it's time to make the filling. Gently and carefully wipe out any crêpe bits from the hot skillet and return it to the stove. Over medium-high heat, melt the butter.

9. Add the brown sugar and cinnamon and stir to form a syrup-like mixture. Cook this briefly, about 2 to 3 minutes, stirring constantly to ensure it doesn't burn.

10. Add the bananas and cook for 2 to 3 more minutes, or until the bananas start to reduce a bit and the sauce begins to caramelize.

11. Carefully add the dark rum and the banana liquor, if using. Stir to incorporate. Now, here's where you perform the flambé trick. Either by tilting the pan to catch the flame on your gas range or by using one of those safety grill lighters (you know, the long plastic ones), ignite the alcohol in the pan. Be prepared: the flame will initially shoot up, but then it will die down and go out on its own. Once the flame has gone out, it is time to fill your crêpes.

12. On a flat work surface, lay out one of your premade crêpes. If they have cooled, gently warm them in the microwave or a low-temperature oven, if desired. Using a slotted spoon, scoop out a spoonful of the banana mixture and place it in the center of the crêpe. We like to tri-fold our crêpes, so we spread the mixture out from top to bottom in the center of the crêpe.

13. Next, use a teaspoon to spoon a small amount of the syrup over the bananas.

14. Then, carefully fold in each side, leaving the top and bottom ends unsealed. Either serve the crêpes individually as they are constructed or carefully transfer the filled crêpes to a serving tray to be served all together.

15. Repeat the filling process for the remaining seven crêpes. You should be left with some syrup but hardly any banana pieces once the crêpes have all been filled. Garnish the crêpes with a drizzle of the remaining syrup or a sprinkling of confectioners' sugar, if desired. And, by the way, we like to save the extra syrup and pour it over vanilla ice cream for a decadent treat! Serve and enjoy.

Mediterranean Quiche

THIS FRESH, DELICIOUS QUICHE IS SO TASTY THAT IT'S HARD not to eat WAY more than one serving. If you want a faster version of this recipe, you can always substitute a premade GF crust for the homemade version. That saves a bunch of time and still results in a fantastic quiche. And, as a helpful word of advice, please be sure to sample your feta before adding any additional salt because a lot of feta is already very salty.

1 recipe Basic Pie Crust (page 70), prepared and blind baked per recipe instructions, or 1 (9-inch) premade pie crust, blind baked per package instructions

¼ cup finely diced red onions

2 heaping tablespoons chopped fresh basil

2 teaspoons chopped garlic

4 ounces frozen spinach, thawed and drained

½ cup diced tomato

8 ounces feta cheese, crumbled

6 large eggs

½ cup half-and-half

½ teaspoon freshly ground black pepper

Salt

1. Preheat the oven to 350°F.

2. Place your blind-baked and cooled crust on a baking sheet to ensure any spillover doesn't drip onto your oven. Sprinkle an even layer of onions, basil, garlic, spinach, tomatoes, and feta in the empty crust.

3. In a small mixing bowl, combine the eggs, half-and-half, and pepper and salt to taste. Whisk until combined.

4. Pour the egg mixture into the crust and bake for 50 to 60 minutes, or until the center of the quiche is set and not jiggly.

5. Allow the quiche to cool for a few minutes before serving. This is delicious served both warm or cold.

TOAD IN THE HOLE WITH BACON-WRAPPED ASPARAGUS SPEARS

Q+E DF MAKES 4 SERVINGS

THIS RECIPE IS EVERYTHING WE LOVE ABOUT BREAKFAST: THE crisp and toasty bread, the perfectly fried egg with an ooey gooey runny yolk, and the crispy bacon, too. Jilly could eat this every day, literally, and be one happy woman. But this isn't just a regular ole everyday type of breakfast—this is the deliciously special Sunday morning brunch type of dish that goes perfectly with your newspaper and a cup of tea . . . or, let's be honest, a bloody mary or mimosa! This dish can easily be halved to serve two or multiplied to serve however many party people you have waking up on Sunday morning. Use the spears to dunk into the center of the yolk to catch all the yumminess, and you will soon be looking forward to your Sunday mornings more than ever! This is a quick and easy recipe and will take 30 minutes or less to make.

16	large asparagus spears
8	strips bacon, sliced in half (we used a lower-sodium, center-cut variety)
4	pieces of your favorite gluten-free sandwich bread (we like Glutino Genius Multigrain)
1 to 1½	tablespoons olive oil or unsalted butter, for frying
4	large high-quality eggs
	Salt and freshly ground black pepper

1. Preheat the oven to 400°F. Lightly grease a baking sheet.

2. Rinse your asparagus and pat dry. Snap each spear so it breaks naturally on its own. Wherever it breaks is where the fresh part ends and the not-so-fresh part starts. Dispose of the ends.

3. Starting at the base of each asparagus spear, wrap a piece of the bacon upward and around in a spiraling fashion to just below the tip of the spear.

4. Place the spears on the prepared pan and bake for 18 to 20 minutes, or until the bacon is nice and crispy. Please note that ovens vary and the type and brand of bacon you use and the size and thickness of your asparagus all play into the timing of this. So, keep an eye on your spears, and as soon as the bacon is crispy (not burnt!), they are done. Transfer to a paper towel–lined plate to degrease slightly.

5. About 10 minutes into your baking time, prepare the toads in the holes. Cut a 1½- to 2-inch-diameter round hole in the center of each piece of bread and discard the cut-out bit. This is where the egg will get placed. Feel free to butter both sides of the bread, if desired.

6. In a medium skillet over medium-high heat, warm about 1 tablespoon oil, though a bit more might be needed depending on your pan.

7. Once the pan is piping hot, add two slices of the bread. Gently crack an egg into each hole in the bread, being careful not to break the yolks.

8. Turn the heat down slightly to medium and cook for 3 minutes. Then carefully flip over each toad in the hole and cook for another 1 to 2 minutes before taking out of the pan and plating immediately. You want a runny-ish yolk here, so don't overcook it.

9. Repeat steps 7 through 8 for the remaining two toads in the hole, adding a bit more oil to the pan before frying. Alternatively, you can fry all four at once if you have a very large skillet.

10. Serve each toad in the hole with four asparagus spears. Season with a bit of salt and pepper over top of everything. Enjoy straightaway.

# HEALTHY HUEVOS RANCHEROS

  MAKES 4 SERVINGS

THIS IS ONE HECK OF A WAY TO START YOUR DAY, LADIES AND gents. It will certainly put you in a happy place for your long commute or even longer workday. It's surprisingly quick and easy to put together, and, if you're a member of the "I heart runny fried eggs club," this is definitely the one for you! Quick, easy, and heart healthy, too? Yep, we think we've ticked a few boxes with this one. If you only need two servings of this, fret not. You can simply keep any leftovers of the bean mixture in your fridge. Also, feel free to garnish this any way you please. Jessie likes hers with a big ole dollop of sour cream. Jilly likes hers with a big ole dousing of hot sauce. However you garnish this killer breakfast dish, we know you will enjoy it. This is a quick and easy recipe and will take 30 minutes or less to make.

1	tablespoon olive oil, plus more for frying
1/3	cup finely diced red onion
1	jalapeño, seeded and roughly diced
1/2	teaspoon minced garlic
1	cup diced tomatoes
1	(15-ounce) can black beans (preferably low-sodium), drained and rinsed
2	tablespoons roughly chopped fresh cilantro, plus more for garnish (optional)
1/2	teaspoon ground cumin
	Pinch of salt
4	(5- to 6-inch) small corn tortillas, yellow or white
4	medium eggs

1 avocado, halved and sliced

Salsa, for serving (optional; we love El Pato Salsa de Tomate con Jalapeño)

1. Preheat the oven to 425°F.

2. In a medium saucepan, heat the 1 tablespoon of olive oil over medium heat.

3. Once warm, add in the onions, jalapeño, and garlic. Stir well, turn the heat down to medium low, and cook for 3 minutes, stirring often.

4. Add in the diced tomatoes and cook for another 2 minutes, stirring often.

5. Add in the black beans, cilantro, cumin, and a pinch of salt and stir well. Cook for 2 more minutes and then turn off the heat and set the pan aside.

6. Place the four corn tortillas on an ungreased baking sheet. Bake for about 3 to 5 minutes, or until they are warm and crispy, but not burnt! Remove from the oven and set aside.

7. Next, add just enough oil to coat a medium skillet.

8. Over medium heat, get the pan nice and hot. Crack two eggs into the pan, being careful not to break the yolks and keeping them from running into each other (we use a spatula edge for this). Fry for 3 minutes undisturbed. We find it helpful to put a lid over the top of the eggs to help them cook a bit quicker.

9. After the 3 minutes, carefully flip the eggs and cook for another 1 minute on the other side before quickly, but gently, removing the eggs to a large plate.

10. Repeat steps 7 through 9 for the remaining two eggs.

11. Now for plating. Place one tortilla on each of four plates. Place one of the fried eggs on top of each tortilla, followed by a generous spoonful of the black bean mixture. We find it helpful to use a slotted spoon for this.

12. Add a few slices of the avocado to each plate.

13. Garnish with a bit of your favorite salsa or cilantro, if desired. Eat straightaway.

KIEF FAMILY BREAKFAST CASSEROLE

IN 2013, OUR MOM'S WHOLE FAMILY, A.K.A. THE KIEFS, SPENT A wonderful week together in Lake Placid, New York, to honor and remember our beloved Grandpa Kief. We did what our family usually does—ate, laughed, lazed around, and ate some more. Feeding a clan of 20-plus was a fun but challenging task! This delicious and easy breakfast casserole fit the bill perfectly . . . although we had to triple the recipe. The bottom potato layer uses store-bought shredded potatoes, found either in the freezer section or in the refrigerated section by the eggs. Just make sure you buy the unseasoned kind or else the flavor of the dish might be adversely affected. If you'd like to make this dish dairy-free, just substitute the half-and-half with a dairy-free milk and omit the cheese.

1	pound unseasoned frozen or refrigerated shredded potatoes or hash browns
½	cup diced yellow bell pepper
½	cup diced red bell pepper
½	cup diced green bell pepper
½	cup diced red onion
¾	cup roughly chopped mushroom of your choice
½	pound chorizo or andouille sausage, diced
12	extra-large eggs
1	cup half-and-half (or dairy-free whole milk)
¼	teaspoon salt, or more to taste
½	teaspoon freshly ground black pepper, or more to taste
1	cup shredded mild Cheddar cheese (optional)

1. Preheat the oven to 375°F. Grease a 13 x 9-inch baking dish (we used a Pyrex) or coat with nonstick cooking spray.

2. Layer your potatoes evenly on the bottom of the prepared dish. Pat them down.

3. Sprinkle the peppers, onion, mushrooms, and chorizo evenly on top of the potatoes.

4. In a large mixing bowl, whisk the eggs, half-and-half, salt, and pepper together until homogeneous; 30 seconds to 1 minute should do it!

5. Pour the egg mixture into the baking dish. Sprinkle the Cheddar cheese evenly over the top of the mixture, if using.

6. Bake for 40 to 50 minutes, or until the eggs are cooked and not jiggly in the center.

7. Remove from the oven, let sit for 5 minutes or so to cool slightly, and then serve.

EMERIL'S RÖSTI POTATO CAKES WITH CHICKEN CONFIT AND FRIED EGGS

WE LOVE THIS RECIPE SO MUCH, OUR DAD WANTED TO CON-tribute it. It is truly a treat of a meal that would be perfect for a special breakfast, brunch gathering, or even lunch. It does take a lot of prior planning, since you have to cook and cool the potatoes at least a few hours ahead of time and make the chicken confit at least twelve hours in advance, or more realistically, overnight. Be sure you're aware of this before proceeding. It is, however, totally worth the effort!

2	baking potatoes (about 1½ pounds), peeled
3	teaspoons salt, divided
4	tablespoons olive oil, divided
1	cup yellow onion (halved lengthwise and thinly sliced)
½	teaspoon freshly ground black pepper, divided
1	recipe Chicken Confit (recipe follows)
2	tablespoons unsalted butter, divided
6 to 8	large eggs
	Sour cream, for garnish
	Fresh dill or thyme, for garnish

1. Place the whole potatoes in a Dutch oven, cover with water, add 1 teaspoon salt, and bring to a boil over medium-high heat. Reduce to a simmer and cook for 20 minutes, or until the potatoes are just cooked through.

2. Drain the potatoes and cool completely in the refrigerator for at least 4 hours and up to overnight. The potatoes must be cool before shredding them, or they will crumble.

3. Once the potatoes have been cooked and cooled, heat 2 tablespoons of the olive oil in a large sauté pan over medium-high heat. When hot, add the onion, 1 teaspoon salt, and ¼ teaspoon black pepper and cook, stirring, until the onions are well caramelized, for about 25 minutes.

4. Coarsely grate the potatoes and place in a medium bowl. Season with the remaining 1 teaspoon salt and ¼ teaspoon black pepper. Gently fold in the caramelized onions.

5. Heat the remaining 2 tablespoons olive oil in a nonstick sauté pan over medium-high heat.

6. Divide the potato mixture into six to eight portions, forming them into 3½-inch-diameter cakes. (Do this by making them into a patty as you would a hamburger.)

7. Add the potato cakes to the pan, in batches, and cook them on one side for 5 minutes undisturbed, or until they have formed a golden-brown crust on the bottom.

8. Carefully flip them over and continue to cook until they are golden brown and crisp on both sides, cooking for a total of about 12 minutes.

9. Transfer the cooked potato cakes to a paper towel–lined plate or baking sheet.

10. Transfer the chicken confit to the pan and sauté until the chicken is hot, about 2 to 3 minutes.

11. When the chicken confit is ready, plate the potato cakes. Remove the confit from the pan and divide the chicken evenly between the potato cakes.

12. In the same pan, melt 1 tablespoon butter over medium heat.

13. When hot, fry half of the eggs (three or four, depending on how many potato cakes you have) and place one fried egg on top of each potato cake.

14. Repeat with the remaining butter and eggs.

15. Serve the rösti potato cakes with a dollop of sour cream and a few sprigs of dill.

CHICKEN CONFIT

"CONFIT" JUST MEANS A MEAT THAT'S COOKED AND PRESERVED in its own fat. As we've said, it takes some time, but the flavor is totally worth it! You will need to make this recipe one day in advance, so keep that in mind. Also, once the confit is used, the excess oil can be stored in an airtight container in the refrigerator and used like butter for cooking. The flavor is wonderful and may be used to roast potatoes, sauté vegetables such as green beans, and pan-fry veal.

2	chicken leg quarters with thighs attached, excess fat trimmed and reserved
1½	teaspoons kosher salt, plus more as needed
¼	teaspoon freshly ground black pepper
5	garlic cloves
2	bay leaves
2	fresh thyme sprigs
¾	teaspoon black peppercorns
¼	teaspoon table salt
4	cups vegetable oil

1. Arrange the leg portions on a platter, skin-side down. Sprinkle with 1½ teaspoons of the kosher salt and the ground black pepper.

2. Place the garlic cloves, bay leaves, and thyme sprigs on top of one of the leg portions.

3. Place the other leg quarter, flesh to flesh, on top.

4. Put the reserved fat from the chicken in the bottom of a glass or plastic container. Top with the sandwiched leg quarters.

5. Season with two pinches of kosher salt. Cover and refrigerate for up to 12 hours.

6. Preheat the oven to 300°F.

7. Take the chicken out of the refrigerator. Remove the garlic, bay leaves, thyme, and chicken fat and reserve.

8. Rinse the chicken under cool, running water, rubbing off some of the salt and pepper. Pat dry with paper towels.

9. Place the reserved garlic, bay leaves, thyme, and chicken fat in the bottom of a 3½-quart enameled cast-iron Dutch oven. Sprinkle evenly with the peppercorns and table salt.

10. Lay the chicken on top, skin-side down. Add the vegetable oil. (It should completely cover the chicken.)

11. Place the Dutch oven over medium-high heat and cook until small bubbles appear on the surface of the oil. Transfer to the oven and bake (uncovered) for about 2 hours, or until the meat easily pulls away from the bone.

12. Remove the chicken from the oven and set it aside, allowing the chicken to cool in the fat for at least 1 hour before proceeding. The chicken can be stored (remaining covered in the oil) in the refrigerator for up to 1 month.

Lunchtime Favorites

WE CAN'T BEGIN TO COUNT THE NUMBER OF AWKWARD moments we've experienced when lunching with friends or coworkers. Like clockwork, that bread basket will be passed or a gluten-laden appetizer will be offered, and we'll have to try to politely decline without making a scene or offending the host or chef. Fortunately, as more people have discovered their gluten issues and the term "gluten-free" has entered the general vocabulary, these awkward moments are getting fewer and farther between. However, lunch still can be difficult—especially if you're sharing a kitchen with coworkers or don't have many gluten-free options close by. We wanted to offer some easy lunch recipes that can be made and brought to work, served to a friend with celiac disease, or prepared, frozen, and thawed when needed. Some items, like the Poached Egg, Arugula, and Bacon Salad (page 142), are best made fresh and served right away. But others, like the Cuban Black Bean Soup (page 126), taste delicious warmed up straight out of the freezer. All are simple and straightforward to prepare and have a wonderful combination of flavors that will be enjoyed by both celiacs and non-celiacs alike. Say good-bye to those awkward lunches!

Spicy Tomato Soup with Grilled Cheese Dippers, page 123

MINESTRONE SOUP À LA VENUS DE MILO

Q&E DF **MAKES 6 TO 8 SERVINGS**

GROWING UP IN SOMERSET, MASSACHUSETTS, MOST OF OUR "big" events throughout childhood were celebrated at the Venus de Milo restaurant in Swansea. Proms, sport award ceremonies, and even some family events were all held at the "Venus." One of the staple menu items was their signature minestrone soup. This version is similar, but we have put our own spin on it. Depending on how brothy you like your minestrone soup, you may want to add more (we recommend 10 cups for brothy) or less (8 cups) beef stock. The orzo will soak up some of the stock, even though it is precooked, so it is probably best to err on the side of extra broth until you've made this a few times and gotten it just to your liking! This is a quick and easy recipe and will take 30 minutes or less to make.

- ½ cup gluten-free orzo
- 2 tablespoons extra-virgin olive oil
- 2 cups diced yellow onion
- 1 cup diced celery
- 2 teaspoons minced garlic
- 1 pound lean ground beef
- 1 pound frozen mixed vegetables
- 1 (14.5 to 15.5-ounce) can diced tomatoes (preferably petite diced)
- 2 bay leaves
- 1 teaspoon freshly ground black pepper
  Salt
- 8 to 10 cups beef stock (depending on how brothy you prefer your soup)

1. In a small saucepan, cook the orzo to al dente as per the package instructions. Drain and set aside.

2. In a large stockpot over medium heat, heat the olive oil. Sauté the onions and celery until they start to soften, about 5 to 7 minutes.

3. Add the garlic and sauté briefly until fragrant.

4. Add the ground beef and cook until browned, stirring frequently and breaking it up into crumbles.

5. Once the beef is browned, add the mixed vegetables, tomatoes, bay leaves, pepper, salt to taste, and the cooked orzo. Stir well. Bring the soup to a boil and then reduce the heat to low. Simmer, uncovered, for 30 to 40 minutes. Adjust the seasoning if necessary and serve.

BROCCOLI AND CHEESE SOUP

 MAKES 4 TO 6 SERVINGS

FOR A LONG TIME, JESSIE HAD TO AVOID CHEESE AS PART OF her elimination diet. But after years of diligently excluding this wonderful dietary addition, she was able to reintroduce it in small quantities. Well, this soup doesn't have "small" quantities of cheese, but it is totally worth the splurge! We use a combination of two cheeses, Havarti and Cheddar, because we think the two together add a nice flavor that is missing in a straightforward Cheddar version. Try it yourself and see what you think! This is a quick and easy recipe and will take 30 minutes or less to make.

3 tablespoons unsalted butter

1 cup diced yellow onion

1 teaspoon minced garlic

¼ cup gluten-free flour blend (we like Arrowhead Mills Gluten Free All Purpose Baking Mix)

3 cups chicken stock

¼ teaspoon ground nutmeg

1 pound frozen broccoli florets, thawed

1 cup half-and-half

1 cup shredded mild Cheddar cheese

8 ounces Havarti cheese, sliced and crumbled into small pieces (about 1 cup)

Salt and freshly ground black pepper

1. In a medium stockpot, melt the butter over medium-high heat. Add the onions and sauté in the butter until they begin to soften, about 3 to 5 minutes.

2. Add the garlic and sauté very briefly, for about 1 minute. Next, stir in the flour and cook, stirring often, for 3 to 4 minutes.

3. Once the flour has melded with the onions, garlic, and butter, add the chicken stock and nutmeg and whisk constantly until the mixture starts to boil and thicken. It WILL start to thicken and should develop a consistency that coats a spoon but isn't overly thick. If your mixture gets too thick, you can always add additional chicken stock until the soup has the consistency you prefer.

4. Reduce the heat to medium, add the broccoli, and let it simmer away until tender. This can take anywhere from 10 to 15 minutes, depending on the size of the broccoli you use. Just keep testing its tenderness until it is soft and cooked through but not too mushy.

5. Once the broccoli is tender, remove the pot from the heat. Using an immersion blender, purée the mixture right in the pot. If you don't have an immersion blender, you can use a regular blender to accomplish the same consistency. Just be careful when blending the hot mixture and transferring it from the pan to the blender and back to the pan. Be sure to hold the lid on tightly when blending as it has a tendency to want to shoot off!

6. Return the pot to the stove and set the heat on low. Stir in the half-and-half. Once the mixture is hot again, stir in the Cheddar and Havarti cheeses. Stir until the cheeses are melted and the soup is a uniform, thick consistency. Season with salt and black pepper to taste.

7. Ladle the soup into bowls and serve immediately. Fair warning: this soup is very, very rich, so a little goes a LONG way. It is delicious though!

SPICY TOMATO SOUP WITH GRILLED CHEESE DIPPERS

 MAKES 6 TO 8 SERVINGS

AS KIDS, ONE OF OUR ALL-TIME FAVORITE WINTER LUNCHES was Aunty Phyllis's tomato soup with grilled cheese sandwiches. Back then, we all liked our soup hot but bland and our grilled cheese gooey and buttery. We still like our grilled cheese ooey and gooey, but these days we prefer some bite to our soup (and Jessie's boys now love their soup hot and spicy, too!). We haven't found a better baguette for this recipe than Against the Grain's version, but feel free to use whatever French-style gluten-free loaf you like best. This can easily be made dairy-free by substituting your favorite dairy-free cheese and baguettes for the dippers. This is a quick and easy recipe that will take 30 minutes or less to make.

SOUP

2	tablespoons extra-virgin olive oil
2	cups chopped yellow onion
1	cup chopped green bell pepper
1	tablespoon minced garlic
4	cups chicken stock
2	(14.5-ounce) cans crushed tomatoes
1	(6-ounce) can tomato paste
¼	teaspoon cayenne pepper
	Salt and freshly ground black pepper
1 to 2	teaspoons granulated sugar (optional)

> 2 loaves (approximately 16 ounces) gluten-free baguettes or French-style bread (we like Against the Grain), at room temperature
>
> 1 to 2 tablespoons unsalted butter, at room temperature, plus more for the pan
>
> 8 to 12 ounces Cheddar cheese, shredded (use more or less depending on preference)

1. First, prepare the soup. In a large stockpot, heat the olive oil over medium heat. Add the onions and peppers and cook for 10 to 12 minutes, stirring occasionally, until the vegetables are soft and starting to brown slightly.

2. Add the garlic and sauté briefly, for 30 seconds to a minute. Stir in all of the remaining soup ingredients except the sugar, being sure to taste the soup before adding additional salt, as some brands of canned tomatoes are already salted.

3. Let simmer for 20 to 25 minutes, giving the flavors time to meld. If the soup is too tart or tangy for your palate, add 1 to 2 teaspoons granulated sugar to take some of the tang away.

4. While the soup simmers, prepare the dippers. Preheat the oven to 425°F and grease a large baking sheet.

5. Cut each baguette in half lengthwise. Then cut each half into quarters so you have eight pieces total per baguette.

6. Using a butter knife, spread butter onto each piece and then arrange on the baking sheet.

7. Top each with a generous amount of shredded Cheddar. Bake for 4 to 6 minutes, or until the cheese is melted and the bread is crispy but not burned.

8. Ladle soup into bowls and serve with two to three grilled cheese dippers each. Dip generously and often!

CUBAN BLACK BEAN SOUP

Q&E DF   MAKES 4 TO 6 SERVINGS

THIS SIMPLE-TO-MAKE SOUP IS BRIMMING WITH FLAVOR AND fiber. We use canned black beans as a time-saver, but you can certainly cook your beans from scratch if you prefer. While our version is cooking, we like to gently break up the beans with the back of a wooden spoon so that the soup takes on a more creamy texture. Also, there are all sorts of garnish options that pair well with this soup, but we only include the most common three. Feel free to personalize your accouterments! This soup is a terrific freeze-and-eat-later candidate. It keeps well and tastes great warmed up straight out of the freezer. So, make extra and save some for next week or even the week after! This is a quick and easy recipe but will take about 45 minutes to make instead of the usual Q&E time of 30 minutes or less.

2	teaspoons extra-virgin olive oil
1	cup chopped yellow onion
1½	cups chopped green bell pepper
4	garlic cloves, chopped
1	jalapeño pepper, seeded and minced
3 to 4	cups chicken stock (depending on how brothy you prefer your soup)
2	(15.5-ounce) cans black beans, drained and rinsed
1	teaspoon ground cumin
2	teaspoons dried oregano
2	tablespoons apple cider vinegar
	Salt and freshly ground black pepper
	Sour cream, for garnish (optional)

Diced red onions, for garnish (optional)

Chopped fresh cilantro, for garnish (optional)

1. In a large stockpot, heat the olive oil over medium heat. Add the onions and sauté until they start to soften, about 3 to 5 minutes.

2. Add the green bell pepper, garlic, and jalapeño and sauté until softened, about 10 to 15 minutes.

3. Add the stock, black beans, cumin, oregano, cider vinegar, and salt and pepper to taste. The soup won't cook down too much, so if you prefer a thicker consistency, add 3 cups of stock instead of 4 cups. You can always add more stock later if it ends up thicker than you'd like.

4. Reduce the heat to medium low and simmer uncovered for 30 minutes. Be sure to stir it every so often so that nothing sticks to the pan bottom and burns.

5. Re-season as necessary and serve either as is or with the suggested garnishes.

GRAMMA CABRAL'S PORTUGUESE KALE SOUP · DF · MAKES 6 TO 8 SERVINGS

AS WITH MANY OF OUR SOUP RECIPES, THIS IS A PURE FOOD memory for us. We have so many deliciously wonderful memories of going to Great-Gramma Cabral's house in Somerset, the little town south of Boston where we grew up. As soon as we'd reach her door, we could almost always smell one of two things: the warm smell of her banana nut bread baking away or the waft of this Portuguese kale soup. Either way, we knew something delicious was in our near future. She would serve this soup with lots of Portuguese rolls and a tub of margarine, not butter! Some people like this soup more brothy, which is why we suggest using 12 to 14 cups of stock. It is completely a matter of taste as to how brothy you prepare it. We know this soup will give your family some food memories as well.

2	tablespoons olive oil
1	pound chorizo sausage, halved lengthwise, then halved crosswise, and diced into chunks (we like Gaspar's Portuguese chouriço)
1	cup chopped yellow onion
1	tablespoon minced garlic
	Generous pinch of crushed red pepper flakes
1	pound well-rinsed, stemmed kale, chopped into 1-inch strips
2	bay leaves
	Salt and freshly ground black pepper
1	pound baking potatoes, peeled and diced (2 cups)
12 to 14	cups chicken or vegetable stock (preferably low-sodium)

1. In an 8-quart stockpot, warm the olive oil over medium heat.

2. Add the chorizo, onions, garlic, and a pinch of crushed red pepper flakes. Stir and cook until the onions soften, about 4 to 6 minutes.

3. Add half of the kale and cook down until it's a third of its size, stirring constantly, about 3 to 4 minutes. Then add the other half and cook down as well.

4. Once the kale has cooked down, add the bay leaves, a bit of salt and pepper, the potatoes, and the stock. Stir well.

5. Turn the heat up to high and bring to a gentle boil. Then turn the heat down to low. Cook uncovered for 30 to 40 minutes, or until the potatoes are cooked through but not mushy.

6. Once the potatoes are cooked through, re-season with more salt and pepper or crushed red pepper flakes to your desired taste. Turn off the heat and serve immediately with your favorite gluten-free roll or baguette. We love Gillian's French rolls or Udi's French baguettes. You can use margarine—or butter. We won't tell Great-Gramma!

NOTE: Short on time or need a break from all that chopping? One pound bags of pre-cut, pre-washed kale are widely available in grocery stores and health food stores.

DADDY'S SPLIT PEA SOUP

 MAKES 8 SERVINGS

THEY SAY CHICKEN SOUP SOOTHES THE SOUL, BUT WE DIS-agree entirely! There is something so utterly comforting about a steaming hot bowl of this split pea soup. It is also a recipe very near and dear to Jilly's heart since this is one of the first dishes our dad taught her how to make and master. It is a soup that warmed Jilly's soul on many occasions, comforted her after break-ups, and cheered her up when she didn't get that A+ on the exam she studied so hard for! We have such wonderful memories of all sitting in the kitchen, catching up, and chatting away while watching our dad make a big pot of this soup—cooked, of course, with loads of his magic ingredient: love. We hope you make this soup a part of your family's kitchen traditions like we have. It really is a beautiful thing.

1	pound dried green split peas
2	tablespoons olive oil
1	cup finely chopped yellow onion
½	cup finely chopped celery
½	cup finely chopped carrot
2	teaspoons minced garlic
¾	pound ham steak, diced
½	teaspoon salt
¾	teaspoon freshly ground black pepper
⅛	teaspoon cayenne pepper
8	cups vegetable or chicken stock (preferably low-sodium)
2	bay leaves

1. Place the dried split peas in a large bowl or pot and add enough water to completely cover the peas with about 2 extra inches over the top. Soak the peas overnight. This is to soften the peas and cut down on the cook time.

2. Drain the peas and set them aside.

3. In a 6- to 8-quart stockpot, warm the olive oil over medium-high heat. Add the onions, celery, carrots, and garlic to the pot and sweat out the vegetables until slightly softened, about 4 to 5 minutes, stirring occasionally.

4. Add in the diced ham, stir, and cook for another 5 to 6 minutes to slightly brown the ham, stirring occasionally.

5. Add in the drained split peas, salt, pepper, cayenne, stock, and bay leaves. Stir well, turn the heat up to high, and bring to a boil.

6. Allow the soup to boil on high for 5 minutes and then turn the heat down to medium low. Cook uncovered for 1 hour to 1 hour and 15 minutes, or until the peas are tender and the soup is thick and mushy. Be sure to skim off any fat that may rise to the surface. If your soup becomes too thick for your liking, add a bit more stock or water and stir well to incorporate.

7. Pick the bay leaves out of the soup and discard. Taste and re-season if desired. Serve straightaway with your favorite gluten-free roll or baguette. We love Gillian's gluten-free French rolls with this.

INDIAN CHICKEN SALAD SANDWICHES ON HOMEMADE SOCCA BREAD

MAKES 4 SANDWICHES

DID YOU JUST PASS THIS RECIPE BY WITHOUT AS MUCH AS A second glance? Yes, we see you . . . the mere thought of a chicken salad sandwich brings back painful memories of a dreaded, sad, soggy lunchbox meal from your youth. Well, don't you worry: this is a majorly pumped-up chicken salad that adults and children will be begging for in their lunchbox! It's tangy, fresh, and crisp and is delicious served on our divine socca bread. But why stop there? It's also delicious on top of your favorite gluten-free cracker or wrapped up in a tasty gluten-free tortilla. The sky is the tasty limit with this one. And if you don't like it, you don't have to sit with us in the cafeteria. To make this dish dairy-free, simply substitute your favorite dairy-free plain yogurt for the Greek yogurt in the recipe. It will taste just as delicious.

CHICKEN

- ¾ cup (6 ounces) plain Greek-style or regular yogurt (or dairy-free plain yogurt)
- 2 teaspoons tandoori masala Indian spice mix
- 1 tablespoon freshly squeezed lime juice
- ¾ pound boneless, skinless chicken breast tenders

SALAD

- ½ cup (4 ounces) plain Greek-style or regular yogurt (or dairy-free plain yogurt)
- ¼ teaspoon garam masala or mild curry powder

1 tablespoon freshly squeezed lime juice
½ cup peeled and chopped cucumber (preferably English seedless)
½ cup chopped radishes
¼ cup finely diced red onion
2 tablespoons roughly chopped fresh cilantro
2 tablespoons roughly chopped fresh mint
   Salt and freshly ground black pepper

8 pieces Socca Bread (recipe follows)

1. First, prepare the chicken. In a medium bowl, combine the yogurt, tandoori masala spice, and lime juice. Stir well.

2. Add the chicken tenders to the marinade. Stir well to ensure all the chicken pieces are well coated. Cover with plastic wrap and place in the fridge to marinate for at least 30 minutes but no longer than 24 hours.

3. After the marinating time, preheat the oven to 400°F.

4. Take the chicken out of the fridge and place the tenders onto a baking sheet or into a dish in an even layer, disposing of any remaining marinade. Bake for 20 to 25 minutes, or until cooked through, depending on the size of your tenders. Let cool completely.

5. While the chicken is cooking, make the rest of the salad. In a medium bowl, combine the yogurt, garam masala, and lime juice and mix well.

6. Add all the vegetables, herbs, and a bit of salt and pepper to the bowl and gently stir together. Set aside.

7. Once the chicken has cooled, place it on a cutting board and roughly chop into small pieces. You want them smaller than bite-size chunks. Add the chicken pieces to the bowl with the salad ingredients and mix well. Taste and season with a bit of salt and pepper, if desired.

8. To serve, evenly distribute the chicken salad mixture onto four slices of the socca bread. Top with the other four matching slices and serve immediately. Alternatively, you can serve a bit of chicken salad on each quarter piece of socca bread and wrap to eat.

SOCCA BREAD

THE CHEF DE CUISINE AT EMERIL'S DELMONICO RESTAURANT in New Orleans is an absolute talent. Chef Anthony Scanio knows great food, and it is always a treat for us to have dinner there to see what creation he'll cook up next. He is also very patient when it comes to Jilly's celiac disease needs. Whenever Jilly goes into the restaurant, he magically whips up a batch of this hot, crispy socca bread so she doesn't feel left out as her fellow diners tuck into all the hot, delicious, gluten-filled bread and rolls. Socca bread, or farinata as it is also known, is a traditional chickpea bread originating in Genoa but seen anywhere along the coast of the Ligurian Sea from France to Italy. Chef Scanio learned to make this and many other delights during his time living and studying in Italy. We are certainly glad he introduced this to us! It has proven versatile, and Jilly uses it for all kinds of great things—as a chicken salad wrapper, to dunk in Indian curries, you name it. Jilly likes to make a batch of these to serve with a nice charcuterie board when guests pop over for a glass of wine. You'll love the possibilities that this bread, which is more like a crispy pancake, will open up for you.

1	cup chickpea flour (a.k.a. besan, gram, or garbanzo flour)
¼	teaspoon salt
½	teaspoon ground cumin
1	cup plus 2 tablespoons cold water
3½	tablespoons olive oil, divided

Indian Chicken Salad Sandwiches on Homemade Socca Bread, page 132

1. Sift the chickpea flour, salt, and cumin together into a medium bowl. Add the water and 1½ tablespoons of the olive oil to the flour and mix well.

2. Pour this batter into a measuring jug or something with a spout so you can easily pour it. Let the batter rest at room temperature for at least 30 minutes but no more than 2 hours.

3. After the resting time, heat 1 tablespoon of the olive oil in a large, nonstick 12-inch skillet over medium heat. You want the pan to be piping hot before pouring in the batter (we can't stress this enough!).

4. Slowly pour half of the batter into the hot pan while moving the pan in a circular motion. Swirl the batter so that it evenly coats the pan, almost as if you were making crêpes or an omelet.

5. Cook until golden brown and firm on the first side, about 3 to 4 minutes, and then flip and cook the other side until golden brown and crispy, for another 2 to 3 minutes. You want it to be fully cooked, brown, and crispy, and not wet at all.

6. Gently turn the bread out onto a plate or cutting board and cut it as if it were a pizza into four equal slices.

7. Heat the remaining 1 tablespoon olive oil in the pan and repeat steps 4 through 6.

8. Serve warm, immediately, with the Indian chicken salad.

WARM MOROCCAN SPICED QUINOA SALAD WITH APRICOTS

 **MAKES 4 TO 6 SERVINGS**

IF YOU LIKE MOROCCAN SPICES AND CUISINE, WE THINK YOU will fall in love with this heart-healthy salad. We know it will leave you feeling satisfied and happy. We suggest serving it warm, but it is also delicious cold. You should be able to find the Moroccan spice mix ras el hanout in the spice aisle at most local grocery stores. If for some reason you can't, try your local Whole Foods Market, specialty supermarkets, or Asian markets. You could also order it online; just have a look at our Resources section to see where. It really is a key component to the dish. This quinoa is a deliciously filling vegetarian option, but if you're not a vegetarian, feel free to add any other form of protein you'd like— or try serving it with our delicious Moroccan Lamb Tagine (page 244). This is a quick and easy recipe and will take 30 minutes or less to make.

1½	cups cooked quinoa, prepared per package instructions
¾	cup vegetable stock
2	tablespoons freshly squeezed lemon juice
1½	teaspoons ras el hanout Moroccan seasoning
1	(14-ounce) can chickpeas, drained and rinsed
½	cup julienned dried plump apricots (about 12 dried apricots)
⅓	cup sliced almonds
½	cup finely chopped fresh mint
¼	cup finely chopped fresh parsley
	Pinch of salt and freshly ground black pepper

1. In a medium saucepan, mix the cooked quinoa, stock, lemon juice, and ras el hanout seasoning and stir well. Heat the mixture over low heat for 4 to 6 minutes, or until the liquid is mostly absorbed.

2. Add all the remaining ingredients to the pan. Stir well and serve immediately.

Kale and Apple Salad with Pine Nuts,
Cranberries, and Goat Cheese, page 140

KALE AND APPLE SALAD WITH PINE NUTS, CRANBERRIES, AND GOAT CHEESE

Q+E MAKES 4 SERVINGS

THIS IS A DELICIOUS AND EASY SALAD TO THROW TOGETHER, not to mention it is quite healthy, too (bonus!). We know that kale may be so last season, but we are still firm lovers and users of this super food. We recommend you buy a bag variety of the kale, most of which are already cleaned several times, to make life a bit easier. To make more of a meal out of this scrumptious salad, add some grilled chicken breasts or serve with a piece of steamed fish. This is a quick and easy recipe and will take 30 minutes or less to make. Omit the goat cheese and voilà—a dairy-free salad!

DRESSING

¼ cup apple cider vinegar

2 tablespoons extra-virgin olive oil

1 tablespoon spicy brown mustard

1 tablespoon honey

Salt and freshly ground black pepper

SALAD

1 pound well-rinsed, stemmed kale, chopped into 1-inch strips

1 cup peeled and roughly diced red apple (we used Gala)

2 tablespoons pine nuts

3 tablespoons dried cranberries (preferably no sugar added)

2 to 3 ounces goat cheese, crumbled (omit for dairy-free)

Salt and freshly ground black pepper

1. Whisk all the dressing ingredients together in a large measuring jug. Set aside.

2. In a large bowl, add the kale and pour half of the dressing on top. Stir and mix well. The acid in the vinegar will help to soften the raw kale.

3. Add the remaining salad ingredients to the bowl and toss well to combine.

4. Pour the remaining half of the dressing over top, season with a bit more salt and pepper, if desired, toss well, and serve immediately.

POACHED EGG, ARUGULA, AND BACON SALAD   (QE) (DF)   MAKES 4 SERVINGS

EVERYTHING ABOUT THIS SALAD MAKES SENSE. WHO DOESN'T like a peppery arugula salad with warm mushrooms and crispy bacon topped with a perfectly poached egg and a tangy Dijon mustardy dressing to finish? It's just delicious. (Though, you could put a poached egg on an old tire and we'd be happy.) Now, we are aware that many of you perhaps have other ways of poaching your eggs than the way we've instructed below. We say, go for it! If you have one of those fancy egg-poacher machines (jealous!), use it. If you know some clever way to poach a nice egg using your microwave (Jessie), by all means do it. However you get that egg poached is up to you, as long as the poaching journey ends with the arrival on top of this salad! If you just want to make this lovely lunch dish for two, simply halve the recipe. This is a quick and easy recipe and will take 30 minutes or less to make.

SALAD

8 strips high-quality, thick-sliced bacon, diced

1½ cups sliced lengthwise cremini or chanterelle mushrooms (stemmed and cleaned first)

Freshly ground black pepper

2 tablespoons white vinegar

4 medium high-quality eggs

3 cups arugula or lamb's lettuce

1   tablespoon plus 1 teaspoon Dijon mustard
2   tablespoons dry sherry or apple cider vinegar
     Salt and freshly ground black pepper
½   cup extra-virgin olive oil

1. In a large skillet or sauté pan over medium-high heat, fry the bacon pieces until nice and crispy, about 6 to 7 minutes.

2. Once crispy, drain the grease from the pan until you have about a tablespoon or so remaining. Add the mushrooms to the pan along with a bit of pepper. Fry until the mushrooms are nice and soft and have reduced in size, about 4 to 5 minutes. Set the pan aside.

3. Bring a medium saucepan of water to a boil over high heat. Once the water is boiling, add the vinegar and turn the heat down to medium low and simmer. You want a gentle boil here, not a rolling boil.

4. Crack each egg into a separate ramekin or small bowl.

5. Using a spoon or a whisk, briskly stir the water in one direction, almost like you are creating a whirlpool effect.

6. Slide one egg into the whirlpool and with a spoon or spatula gently nudge the egg white toward the egg yolk, almost like you are trying to cover it and keep it all together. Once this egg solidifies slightly, repeat the same process with the brisk stirring in one direction and add another egg. Again, nudge the egg white over the top of the yolk.

7. Once two eggs are in the pan, set the timer for exactly 3 minutes. After the 3 minutes, use a slotted spoon to gently transfer the eggs onto a paper towel–lined plate. Cover with a bit of foil to keep the eggs warm while you plate the salad.

8. Repeat steps 6 through 7 for the remaining two eggs.

9. Now it's time to make the dressing. In either a small bowl or a measuring jug, whisk the Dijon and sherry together with a bit of salt and pepper. While whisking continuously, pour in the oil in a slow and steady stream. Keep whisking continuously until the dressing has emulsified.

10. Place the arugula into a large bowl and pour on enough of the dressing to coat the leaves but not drown them.

11. Using a slotted spoon, transfer the bacon and mushroom mixture out of the pan and into the bowl of greens, trying to drain as much fat as possible before adding it in. Season with a bit of salt and pepper and toss together well.

12. Evenly divvy up the salad mixture onto four plates.

13. Place one of the poached eggs on top of each salad and serve immediately with a bit more dressing drizzled on top, if desired. Any remaining dressing can either be discarded or kept in the fridge in an airtight container for future use.

OM'S PASTA SALAD

 MAKES 4 TO 6 SERVINGS

IF WE WERE ASKED TO NAME A DISH THAT REMINDED US OF childhood summers, this would be it. Both of us loved when our mom made this light and refreshing dinner. We always hoped she'd make extra so it could be lunch the next day, too. She used the regular bottled Italian dressing, which is awesome on this dish, but we thought we should include a homemade dressing, too! For the Italian dressing here, you can certainly adjust the amount of herbs based on your preference. Also, try to time the cooking of your pasta so that it is done close to the time you mix it all together, so it doesn't sit in the colander for too long. This is a quick and easy recipe and will take you 30 minutes or less to make.

PASTA SALAD

8   ounces gluten-free pasta, shape of your choice (we like rotini or farfalle)
6   ounces ham steak, diced
½   cup finely diced yellow onion
8   ounces grape tomatoes, rinsed and halved
8   ounces high-quality mozzarella, diced or torn into bite-size pieces

DRESSING

1   teaspoon garlic salt
½   teaspoon granulated sugar
½   teaspoon dried oregano
1   teaspoon dried basil
1   teaspoon freshly ground black pepper

Pinch of dried thyme

½   **teaspoon dried parsley**

1   **tablespoon freshly squeezed lemon juice**

2   **tablespoons white vinegar**

⅓   **cup extra-virgin olive oil**

1. In a large pot of salted boiling water, cook your pasta until al dente. You don't want it crunchy, but you don't want it mushy either. Drain.

2. In a large mixing bowl, combine the cooked pasta with the remaining pasta salad ingredients and toss to combine.

3. Now make the dressing. In a medium mixing bowl, combine the garlic salt, sugar, oregano, basil, pepper, thyme, and parsley.

4. Stir in the lemon juice and white vinegar.

5. While whisking constantly, slowly add in the olive oil. Once the dressing is completely mixed, taste and adjust your seasoning if necessary.

6. Pour the dressing over the pasta salad mixture and stir until the pasta salad components are evenly coated with the dressing and the ingredients are evenly distributed throughout. Serve slightly warm (as your noodles will probably still be warm-ish) or refrigerate, covered, for at least 30 minutes and then serve chilled.

SUN-DRIED TOMATO PESTO PASTA SALAD

Q•E MAKES 4 TO 6 SERVINGS

THIS REFRESHING AND EASY-TO-MAKE PASTA SALAD MAKES A fantastic accompaniment, but it is hearty enough to serve as its own lunch salad. Feel free to add some additional protein in the form of cooked shrimp or chicken if you'd like to make it even more substantial. Be sure to have all your ingredients ready so that the pasta doesn't have to sit for too long. This is a quick and easy recipe and will take 30 minutes or less to make.

- 12 ounces gluten-free penne pasta, cooked al dente per package instructions
- 2 tablespoons pine nuts
- 4 garlic cloves, minced
- 1 (8.5-ounce) or 2 (4.4-ounce) jars sun-dried tomatoes in olive oil
- 1 cup packed fresh basil leaves
  Salt and freshly ground black pepper
- 4 ounces high-quality goat cheese

1. Heat a small frying pan over medium-low heat. Shaking occasionally, toast the pine nuts until golden, about 3 to 5 minutes. Transfer the toasted pine nuts into a food processor and process until finely chopped.

2. Add the garlic, sun-dried tomatoes, basil, and salt and pepper to taste. Blend until the tomatoes are finely chopped and a nice, thick sauce consistency has been achieved. Transfer the mixture into a large mixing bowl.

3. Add the cooked pasta to the pesto mixture and toss to coat. Crumble the cheese over the top of the pasta salad and gently fold it in. Re-season if necessary and serve.

JILLY'S GINGER SESAME PORK STIR-FRY

● ● MAKES 4 SERVINGS

JILLY CREATED THIS QUICK AND EASY, CHEAP AND CHEERFUL meal one night with ingredients she had left in her fridge and the dream to turn them into a healthy yet satisfying dish. (Well, that and she already had her comfy's on and really didn't want to get dressed to go out to the store!) It's surprisingly light and is jam-packed with veggies, so you won't feel too heavy after a big ole bowl of it. The mint and cilantro are fresh and lively. The ginger and citrus are bright and clean and balance the gentle heat of the crushed red pepper flakes and the crisp crunch from the cabbage, snow peas, and peanuts. If you just aren't a pork lover, you of course can substitute ground chicken or even shrimp for this. If you prefer, you can also use the larger, thicker pad thai–style rice noodles as opposed to the thin vermicelli noodles we use here. Feel free to use any vegetable combination you prefer, too. Freestyle away. We hope this inspires a lil' midweek stir-fry fest in your kitchen soon. This is a quick and easy recipe and will take 30 minutes or less to make.

1	tablespoon vegetable oil
1	tablespoon sesame oil
1	pound lean or extra-lean ground pork
½	teaspoon minced garlic
1½	teaspoons minced fresh ginger or ginger purée (from a jar)
¼ to ½	teaspoon crushed red pepper flakes (depending on how much heat you prefer)
1½	cups shredded red cabbage
1	cup halved snow peas (sliced on the diagonal)
3	tablespoons roughly chopped unsalted peanuts

¼ cup sliced green onion (green and white parts, sliced on the diagonal)

2 tablespoons roughly chopped fresh mint

1 tablespoon roughly chopped fresh cilantro

1 tablespoon nuoc mam cham (fish sauce)

1 tablespoon plus 2 teaspoons gluten-free tamari or gluten-free soy sauce (preferably low-sodium), plus more for serving

2 tablespoons rice wine vinegar

1 (6-ounce) pack of rice noodles/vermicelli noodles, prepared per package instructions and set aside in a very large bowl

1 lime, quartered, plus more wedges for serving

1. In a wok or large sauté pan with high sides, heat the vegetable oil over medium-high heat.

2. Add the sesame oil, pork, garlic, ginger, and crushed red pepper flakes. Cook until the pork is fully cooked through, about 5 to 7 minutes, stirring constantly and making sure to crumble the meat as it cooks.

3. Turn the heat down to medium and add in the red cabbage, snow peas, and peanuts. Cook for 2 minutes, stirring frequently.

4. Quickly add in the green onion, mint, cilantro, fish sauce, tamari, and rice wine vinegar. Stir well and cook for 1 minute before turning off the heat.

5. With a clean pair of kitchen shears, cut the drained rice noodles a few times to make them more manageable to work with.

6. If your pan is large enough to hold the noodles as well, add them into the pan. If not, transfer the pork mixture to the large bowl containing the drained and cut rice noodles.

7. Squeeze the juice of the four lime wedges all over the pork mixture and rice noodles and gently toss everything with a pair of tongs to combine.

8. Serve immediately in deep bowls with extra tamari and lime wedges, if desired.

RED PEPPER AND PARSLEY SPANISH TORTILLA

DF MAKES 8 SERVINGS

THIS SPANISH TORTILLA, OR TORTILLA ESPAÑOLA, IS LIKE A big, tasty Spanish omelet. There are many variations on this dish, but they almost always contain potatoes, onions, and eggs cooked in a generous amount of olive oil. Some variations use chorizo or different vegetables. You really could put anything in this and it would be delicious. The other great thing about this dish is that it can be enjoyed hot or cold pretty much anytime of day. It is usually served as a lunch, a snack, or a late-night tapas treat along with a bit of salad. If you are too nervous to try all the magic plate tricks the recipe requires, you could bake it in a 375°F oven for 10 minutes to finish it off instead of trying all of the flipping. But, we have faith in you. Go on and have a glass of sangria for some liquid courage, and you'll be flipping this tortilla like a pro in no time. Olé!

PEPPERS AND ONIONS

1	cup seeded and julienned red bell pepper
1½	cups julienned onion (halve the onion before slicing)
1½	teaspoons minced garlic
¼	teaspoon smoked paprika
	Freshly ground black pepper
	Pinch of salt
2	tablespoons olive oil

TORTILLA

3	tablespoons olive oil
1	pound potatoes (any kind you prefer), peeled and very thinly sliced using a mandoline

Salt and freshly ground black pepper

8   large eggs

½   teaspoon smoked paprika

1½ teaspoons dried oregano

3   tablespoons chopped fresh parsley

Arugula, for serving (optional)

1. Preheat the oven to 375°F.

2. In a medium bowl, toss all the peppers and onions ingredients together.

3. Place all onto a baking sheet in one even layer. Roast for 30 minutes and set aside. This can be done in advance, if desired.

4. For the tortilla, in a 12-inch, heavy nonstick skillet with high sides, heat the oil over medium heat. Lay the potatoes in a large circular pattern, slightly overlapping the pieces as you go. Continue layering in this fashion until all the potato slices are used. Season with a bit of salt and pepper and fry for 10 minutes undisturbed.

5. While the potatoes are frying, in a medium bowl or measuring jug, beat the eggs, paprika, oregano, parsley, and a bit of salt and pepper together well.

6. After 10 minutes of frying, gently flip the potatoes over in sections using a metal spatula. Re-season with a bit more salt and pepper and fry for another 6 minutes. You want all sides of the potatoes to be golden and crispy.

7. Spoon the roasted pepper and onions evenly over the top of the potatoes.

8. Pour the egg mixture all over the vegetables in the pan and gently run a spatula around the edges while turning the pan in a circular motion to help create a crust on the edge of the egg and to help it set up.

9. Turn the heat down to low and cook undisturbed for 15 minutes. Avoid fiddling with it too much—just let it cook and set.

10. Place either a plate or cutting board large enough to cover the top of the pan over the pan. CAREFULLY and in one quick motion, flip the tortilla out of the pan so the top is now the bottom. This will require a bit of maneuvering,

and we suggest wearing oven mitts to do this just to be safe. You have to be slightly aggressive with this!

11. CAREFULLY slide the tortilla back into the pan so the undercooked side is down and the potato layer is on top. Cook for another 5 minutes and then turn off the heat.

12. Now for the double-plate magic trick! Place a large plate over the top of the pan and CAREFULLY but swiftly flip the pan so the tortilla pops out, almost as you would when flipping a cake pan to remove the cake. Again, we suggest wearing oven mitts for this.

13. Prepare whatever plate, board, or platter you want to serve the tortilla on. Place it over the top of the tortilla and, once again, CAREFULLY but swiftly flip the plates so the bottom is now the top, which should be the crispy potato layer.

14. Let cool for a few minutes before slicing. Serve and enjoy either warm or cold with a bit of arugula on the side, if desired.

EMERIL'S CHICKEN, SAUSAGE, AND WHITE BEAN CASSOULET WITH BASIL PESTO AND PARMESAN TUILES

MAKES 4 TO 6 SERVINGS

WE HAVE TO THANK OUR DAD FOR THIS PERFECT COLD winter's day lunch dish! It is light but healthy, comfortingly tasty, and easy to prepare. Even the tuiles and pesto, which may sound intimidating, can be whipped up very quickly and easily. Although our dad calls for bone-in chicken thighs here, we tried it with both bone-in and boneless thighs, and both ways are just as tasty. We like to use a large pair of tongs to remove the chicken and sausage from the pan after they have been browned. This helps reduce the chances of being accidentally hit by a bit of grease splatter! So, cozy on up to a nice big bowl of this cassoulet and enjoy the whole experience.

3	pounds bone-in chicken thighs
3	teaspoons sea salt, divided
1	teaspoon freshly ground black pepper, divided
4	tablespoons olive oil, divided
3 to 4	links sweet Italian sausage (about 1 pound), casings pricked with a fork
2	yellow onions, diced
1	large carrot, diced
1	stalk celery, diced
3	garlic cloves
1	sprig fresh thyme
1	sprig fresh rosemary

<table>
<tr><td>1</td><td>sprig fresh oregano</td></tr>
<tr><td>1</td><td>bay leaf</td></tr>
<tr><td>4</td><td>(15.5-ounce) cans cannellini beans or other white beans, drained and rinsed</td></tr>
<tr><td>1</td><td>(14.5-ounce) can diced tomatoes</td></tr>
<tr><td>1</td><td>quart chicken stock</td></tr>
<tr><td>⅛</td><td>teaspoon crushed red pepper flakes</td></tr>
<tr><td></td><td>Basil Pesto (recipe follows), for garnish</td></tr>
<tr><td></td><td>Parmesan Tuiles (recipe follows), for garnish</td></tr>
</table>

1. Season the chicken thighs with 2 teaspoons of the salt and ½ teaspoon of the pepper.

2. In a large Dutch oven over medium-high heat, add 3 tablespoons of the olive oil and, when hot, brown the chicken, working in batches, on all sides, about 6 to 8 minutes per batch. Transfer the chicken to a platter.

3. Add the sausages to the pan and brown on all sides. Transfer the sausages to the same platter as the chicken. Cut each link in half, cover, and set aside.

4. Add the remaining tablespoon of olive oil to the pan and decrease the heat to medium. Add the onions, carrot, celery, and garlic and cook for 8 to 10 minutes, or until the vegetables are tender.

5. Tie the herbs and the bay leaf together using kitchen string. Add the herbs, cannellini beans, tomatoes, stock, remaining teaspoon of salt, remaining ½ teaspoon of pepper, and crushed red pepper flakes to the pot and bring to a simmer over medium-high heat.

6. As soon as it comes to a simmer, transfer the chicken back to the pot. Bring to a boil and simmer, partially covered, until the chicken is very tender, about 45 minutes to 1 hour.

7. Add the sausages back to the pot and cook for 10 minutes longer.

8. Serve the cassoulet in shallow bowls, garnished with Basil Pesto and Parmesan Tuiles.

BASIL PESTO

2   bunches fresh basil (1 cup packed leaves)
2   garlic cloves, smashed
3   tablespoons shelled pistachios, toasted
¾   cup olive oil
¼   cup grated Parmesan cheese
¼   teaspoon kosher salt
     Pinch of freshly ground black pepper

1. Combine all the ingredients in the bowl of a food processor and purée until smooth.

PARMESAN TUILES

1   tablespoon olive oil
¾   cup coarsely grated Parmesan cheese

1. Preheat the oven to 350°F. Grease a baking sheet with the olive oil.

2. Spoon the Parmesan onto the baking sheet in mounds (about 2 tablespoon-fuls each), spacing the mounds about 2 inches apart.

3. Bake until the cheese is crisp and lightly browned, for about 5 minutes.

4. Remove from the oven and allow to cool briefly, then remove the tuiles from the baking sheet using a metal spatula.

BAKED "FRIED" SHRIMP TACOS WITH MANGO SALSA AND HOMEMADE ZINGY TARTAR SAUCE

MAKES 4 SERVINGS (2 TORTILLAS PER PERSON)

THIS IS THE PERFECT SUMMERTIME MEAL, WITH THE FRESH and crisp mango salsa served on top of crunchy baked, not fried, shrimp (the secret? cornmeal). The peppery arugula is perfect with the zingy tartar sauce, which offers a nice bit of cooldown from that helloooo jalapeño. Now, we admit we are very spoiled here in New Orleans with our fresh Gulf seafood, so naturally, we recommend using the freshest shrimp you can get your hands on. If you have to use—dare we say—a frozen bag variety, it will work just fine. Simply follow the directions for thawing on the package and be sure to pat dry. Feel free to add as much jalapeño as you can stand. We hope this dish inspires you to shake up your midweek lunch routine and helps to make a little fiesta in your mouth!

MANGO SALSA

1 cup diced fresh mango (we used yellow-golden mangos)

½ jalapeño, seeded and finely diced (more or less depending on heat preference)

¼ cup finely diced red onion

2 tablespoons freshly squeezed lime juice

2 tablespoons roughly chopped fresh cilantro

TARTAR SAUCE

½ cup high-quality mayonnaise

1 tablespoon Dijon mustard

2   tablespoons capers, finely chopped

2   teaspoons freshly squeezed lemon juice

6 to 8   drops Tabasco

Freshly ground black pepper

SHRIMP

1   pound high-quality, medium-size fresh shrimp (we used 31/40 count shrimp, but use the size you prefer)

½   cup Greek-style yogurt (or mayonnaise if dairy is an issue)

2   teaspoons Emeril's Original Essence seasoning or Cajun seasoning of your choice, divided

1   cup plus 2 tablespoons finely milled cornmeal, yellow or white

8   (5-inch) high-quality, small corn tortillas (we like Food For Life's Sprouted Corn Tortillas), for serving

Few handfuls arugula, for serving

1. First, make the mango salsa by combining all the ingredients in a small bowl. Stir well, cover, and refrigerate until ready to serve.

2. Do the same for the tartar sauce, combining all the ingredients in another small bowl. Season with enough Tabasco and freshly ground black pepper to your liking. Cover and refrigerate until ready to serve.

3. Now make the shrimp. Peel and devein the shrimp and remove the heads and tails. Rinse well and pat dry with paper towels.

4. In a medium mixing bowl, whisk together the yogurt and 1 teaspoon of the Essence.

5. Add the shrimp to this and, using a wooden spoon, stir well to ensure all the shrimp are evenly coated. Place in the fridge for 10 minutes, uncovered.

6. In another medium bowl, combine the cornmeal and the remaining 1 teaspoon of Essence and stir with a fork.

7. Preheat the oven to 425°F. Lightly grease two large baking sheets with non-stick cooking spray.

8. After the 10 minutes, take the shrimp out of the fridge. Working in batches, toss the shrimp in the cornmeal mixture. Make sure each shrimp is evenly coated before placing it onto the greased baking sheets.

9. Bake for 12 minutes. Pull the baking sheets out and flip each shrimp so that they'll get golden brown and crispy on both sides. Turn the oven temperature down to 350°F and cook for another 8 to 10 minutes.

10. When the shrimp are almost done cooking, go ahead and warm your corn tortillas, one at a time, in a medium dry skillet over medium heat, flipping once. They should only need about 30 to 40 seconds per side.

11. Pull the mango salsa, tartar sauce, and arugula out of the fridge and get ready to assemble.

12. To serve, evenly divide the shrimp among the warmed tortillas, roughly 3 shrimp per tortilla, depending on how many shrimp you have. Spoon a bit of the mango salsa on top, followed by a few arugula leaves. Finish with a dollop of the tartar sauce and serve.

Accompaniments

"WE GO TOGETHER LIKE RED BEANS AND RICE" OR "LIKE PEANUT butter and jelly" or "like cookies and milk." There's really nothing like the satisfaction of chasing a whopping bite of fried chicken with a forkful of mac and cheese. Or piling a bite of Thanksgiving turkey on top of a mounded spoonful of your favorite stuffing. Some foods just go together—that's why we worked hard to come up with a well-rounded group of accompaniments you can proudly serve up next to your favorite meats, fish, or tofu. Not only are they all tasty and delicious AND gluten-free, but they are easy to make and are able to be personalized to whatever tastes and preferences you have. If you like a special kind of cheese, try substituting it into Mookie's Three-Cheese Mac recipe (page 191). If you don't like chorizo but do like Polish sausage, try using that in your version of Gramma Hilda's Traditional Portuguese Stuffing (page 188). And, as always, add or take out the spice and the salt at will. The goal in all of our recipes is that YOU end up with a dish you love and want to make again and again. So don't be afraid to play around a bit and find which accompaniment you like best with your fried chicken or meatloaf!

Roasted Brussels Sprouts in Spicy Mustard Sauce, page 166, and Duck Fat Roasted Potatoes (a.k.a. Roasties), page 176

ROASTED BRUSSELS SPROUTS IN SPICY MUSTARD SAUCE

DF MAKES 4 TO 6 SERVINGS

JILLY'S FABULOUS MUM-IN-LAW, MS. JACKIE, TAUGHT HER ALL about these tasty little sprouts and a million other things while Jilly lived in London. Ms. Jackie always said to trim the outer rough or brown leaves off, and then to mark an "X" on the bottom of each sprout with a paring knife. She claimed this was to help them cook faster, and it was the way her mum had taught her. Jilly took her word for it, and for most things when it came to the kitchen, because Ms. Jackie knew her stuff. We recommend trying to use the smaller, baby Brussels sprouts for this, as the bigger the sprouts get, the more bitter they can taste and the longer they need to cook. Try these zingy sprouts and our scrumptious Duck Fat Roasted Potatoes (a.k.a. Roasties) on page 176 for the ultimate accompaniments to your next Sunday roast dinner.

SPROUTS

1½   pounds Brussels sprouts, ends trimmed, any brown outer leaves discarded, and an "X" marked on each sprout bottom using a paring knife

Pinch of baking soda (tip of a knife's worth, about ⅛ teaspoon)

1½ to 2   tablespoons olive oil (depending on size of sprouts)

Salt and freshly ground black pepper

SAUCE

1   tablespoon freshly squeezed lemon juice

1   tablespoon cooking sherry or dry sherry

1 tablespoon apple cider vinegar

1 tablespoon whole grain mustard (with seeds)

1 tablespoon Dijon mustard

1 tablespoon grated horseradish (or horseradish sauce if you can't find grated)

1 tablespoon fresh thyme leaves

½ teaspoon minced garlic

1. Preheat the oven to 400°F.

2. Place your prepared sprouts in a colander and rinse well with cool water. Drain and place them in a 6- to 8-quart stockpot and fill halfway with cold water. Add the pinch of baking soda to the pan.

3. On medium-high heat, bring the sprouts to a boil and boil them just until fork-tender, about 6 to 8 minutes, depending on size. You don't want to overcook them. Drain and place a handful of ice cubes on top to shock the sprouts and stop them from cooking further.

4. Drain any remaining liquid from the sprouts and place them in a large roasting pan. Drizzle the olive oil on top and add a generous amount of salt and pepper.

5. Roast for about 35 to 45 minutes, flipping a few times while cooking to ensure all sides get browned and roasted.

6. While the sprouts are roasting, make the sauce. In a small bowl or measuring jug, mix all the sauce ingredients together, stir well, and set aside.

7. When the sprouts are nice and roasty, remove the pan from the oven and pour all of the sauce over the sprouts straightaway. Gently give them a stir to ensure they are all well coated in the sauce.

8. Leave in the warm pan for 4 to 5 minutes to release the flavors of the sauce before serving warm.

ERBED SUGAR SNAP PEAS

 MAKES 6 TO 8 SERVINGS

ADMITTEDLY, JESSIE HAS NEVER BEEN A BIG SUGAR SNAP pea fan . . . she really just likes broccoli, broccoli, and more broccoli! However, this recipe produces some really tasty snap peas that even Jessie will eat with her meal. They're super easy and fast to make, and the combination of the herbs with the slightly sweet snap pea is really quite complementary. We prefer to use the dried herbs for this, but you can always substitute fresh ones if you'd rather—just remember to use 1 tablespoon of fresh herbs for every 1 teaspoon of dried called for in the recipe. Try these peas with our Crispy Parmesan-Crusted Grouper (page 253) or even our Not Your Momma's Meatloaf (page 203) to round out a complete meal. This is a quick and easy recipe and will take 30 minutes or less to make.

- 1 pound sugar snap peas, ends trimmed
- 2 tablespoons extra-virgin olive oil
- ¼ cup julienned or thinly sliced yellow onion
- 1 tablespoon minced garlic
- ½ teaspoon dried marjoram
- ½ teaspoon dried thyme
  Salt and freshly ground black pepper

1. Preheat the oven to 400°F.

2. In a large mixing bowl, combine all the ingredients and toss so that the snap peas are evenly covered with the olive oil, garlic, and herbs.

3. Spread the mixture into an 8-inch square baking dish. Bake for 30 to 40 minutes, or until the peas are tender but still firm and the onions are soft. Serve.

EASY PILAU RICE

  MAKES 4 SERVINGS

THIS PILAU RICE CAN ONLY MEAN ONE THING: CURRY! THIS IS the perfect partner to any tasty Indian curry, but especially our addictive One-Pot Chicken Jalfrezi (page 232). The rice is the perfect thing to soak up all of that spicy, tangy, flavor-packed curry sauce. We love that, like so many Indian dishes, this rice is packed with fragrant, warm spices like cloves and cardamom. We recommend using whole cardamom pods in this dish while boiling your rice. If for some reason you have trouble finding whole cardamom pods in your spice aisle, you can substitute ¼ teaspoon ground cardamom. This proves Jilly's motto: "A spicy Indian curry a day will keep the doctor away." This is a quick and easy recipe and will take 30 minutes or less to make.

1¾ cups water

1 cup basmati rice

6 whole cloves

8 whole cardamom pods (or ¼ teaspoon ground cardamom if you can't find pods)

½ teaspoon ground turmeric

Pinch of salt

1. In a medium saucepan, bring the water to a boil over high heat.

2. Once boiling, add the rice, cloves, and cardamom pods to the pan.

3. Stir well and turn the heat down to low. Cover and simmer for 15 to 20 minutes, or until the water has been absorbed and the rice is cooked through.

4. Add the turmeric and a pinch of salt to the pan and stir well.

5. Pick out the cloves and cardamom pods and discard. Serve immediately.

GREEN BEAN CASSEROLE WITH CRISPY ONIONS

MAKES 6 TO 8 SERVINGS

GREEN BEAN CASSEROLE JUST SEEMS TO BE ONE OF THOSE Thanksgiving staples, and we were used to having it every year, as sure as we'd have turkey and gravy. Once we were diagnosed with our gluten issues, we thought the green bean casserole was a dish of our past. That is, until we revolted and created our own version. Now the green beans are back on our Thanksgiving table! This dish does require some time and various steps, but it is well worth it. The onions are just as crispy and delicious as we remember, and the homemade cream of mushroom soup is pretty good on its own, too.

CASSEROLE

- 2 pounds fresh green beans, trimmed and cut into bite-size pieces (1½ to 2 inches)
- 1 pound mushrooms (we like button or baby bella), roughly chopped
- 1 tablespoon extra-virgin olive oil
- 2 tablespoons unsalted butter
- ½ cup diced yellow onion
- 1 teaspoon minced garlic
- 3 tablespoons gluten-free flour blend (we like Arrowhead Mills Gluten Free All Purpose Baking Mix)
- 1 cup chicken stock
- 1 cup whole milk
  Pinch of cayenne pepper
- ¼ teaspoon salt
  Freshly ground black pepper

CRISPY ONIONS

  1   **medium yellow onion, halved**
       Egg whites from 2 large eggs
 ¼   **cup cornstarch**
       Pinch of salt
       Pinch of freshly ground black pepper
       Vegetable oil, for frying

1. Preheat the oven to 350°F.

2. Bring a large stockpot of water to a boil. Blanch the green beans in the boiling water for 4 to 5 minutes to soften them but not cook them completely. They should be al dente with some crunch remaining after blanching. Drain and rinse under cold water to stop the cooking process. Spread them evenly in the bottom of a 13 x 9-inch baking dish.

3. In a large, nonstick stockpot over medium heat, sauté the mushrooms in the olive oil for 3 to 4 minutes. Remove them from the pan and set aside.

4. In the same pan, melt the butter over medium heat. Sauté the onions in the butter until they start to soften, about 4 to 6 minutes.

5. Add the garlic and sauté for 30 seconds to 1 minute, or until the garlic is fragrant.

6. Stir in the flour to make a roux, making sure the onions are coated with the flour and butter mixture. The texture of the roux will remain slightly crumbly as opposed to smooth and liquidy. Cook for another 2 to 3 minutes.

7. Whisk in the chicken stock, milk, cayenne, salt, and black pepper to taste, being sure that the flour mixture dissolves into the liquid. Add the mushrooms back in at this point. As the liquid heats, it will thicken quickly, usually after 2 to 4 minutes. Once it is thick, remove it from the heat and pour it over the top of the green bean layer.

8. Bake for 25 to 30 minutes, or until the beans are soft and the soup mixture is bubbly.

9. While the casserole is baking, prepare the crispy onions. Using a mandoline, slice each half of your onion on a thin setting so that it produces shoestring-style onion pieces. If you don't have a mandoline, you can slice the onions by hand as thinly as possible.

10. Whisk the egg whites together in a small bowl. In another small bowl, mix your cornstarch, salt, and pepper together.

11. You can use a deep fryer to cook your onions if you have one. If not, fill a large, heavy-bottomed skillet with approximately ½ inch of vegetable oil. Heat the oil over medium-high heat until it is hot and shimmering. Ideally, you should heat the oil to between 350°F and 375°F. Use a candy/deep-fry thermometer to verify the oil temperature if you have one. If you don't, you can also test the oil's readiness by dropping one onion piece in. If it sizzles and cooks when it hits the oil, the oil is ready. If there is no sizzle, let the oil heat some more and test again.

12. Once the oil is ready, working in batches if necessary, dip your onions into the egg white mixture and then transfer them to the cornstarch mixture and toss to coat. Drop the coated onions into the prepared oil and fry briefly, about 2 to

3 minutes, or until the batter turns golden brown.

13. Remove the onions with a large slotted spoon and set on a paper towel–lined plate to absorb any excess oil.

14. Once the beans are cooked, remove the casserole from the oven. Sprinkle your fried onions evenly on top. If the onions have gotten cool since frying, pop the casserole with the onion topping back into the oven for another 5 minutes, or just until the onions are heated through again. Serve.

$\mathcal{P}$ERFECT AU GRATIN POTATOES

MAKES 6 TO 8 SERVINGS

WE KNOW IT'S DIFFICULT NOT TO LIKE ANY FOOD THAT IS drenched with ooey gooey, melty cheese, but these potatoes give all those other cheese-laden dishes a run for their money. The cheese sauce uses a roux as its base, so its consistency is extra creamy. Jessie's family likes these potatoes with a bit of bite, so she uses a lot of cayenne pepper. If your group is not such a fan of spice, then you can use a dash or two of the cayenne instead. We love to pair these potatoes with our Not Your Momma's Meatloaf (page 203) or our Slow Cooker Pot Roast (page 224), but many of our other entrées taste great next to these babies as well.

3   pounds similarly sized potatoes (preferably red potatoes)
6   tablespoons unsalted butter, plus more for the pan
¼   cup gluten-free flour blend (we like Arrowhead Mills Gluten Free All Purpose Baking Mix)
3   cups whole milk
1   teaspoon minced garlic
1   teaspoon salt
    Generous pinch of cayenne pepper (up to ¼ teaspoon)
2   cups shredded sharp Cheddar cheese

1. Preheat the oven to 375°F. Grease a 13 x 9-inch glass baking dish with nonstick cooking spray or butter.

2. First, peel your potatoes if desired. We usually do, unless the potatoes are too small to make that practical. Next, thinly slice the potatoes into ⅛-inch thick

174 BIG FLAVOR, BOLD TASTE—AND NO GLUTEN!

slices and put them in a bowl of cold, salted water. Set aside until the cheese sauce is ready.

3. In a large saucepan, melt the butter over medium-high heat.

4. Add in the flour and stir until well blended. Continue stirring and cook the roux for 2 to 3 minutes.

5. Whisk in the milk, garlic, salt, and cayenne. Continue whisking until the mixture becomes a thick-ish sauce. It will start to bubble slightly, and, when it coats a wooden spoon, it is ready. This usually takes us about 5 to 7 minutes.

6. Once the desired consistency has been achieved, remove the pan from the heat. Stir in the Cheddar and mix it until the cheese has been incorporated and the mixture is homogeneous.

7. Drain the potatoes and gently pat them dry with paper towels. Layer about half of the potatoes into the bottom of the prepared dish as evenly as possible.

8. Pour about half of the cheese mixture over the potatoes in the pan. Then, working carefully as the cheese sauce is hot, layer the remaining potatoes into the baking dish. Top with the remaining cheese sauce and season with additional salt and cayenne pepper, if desired. Bake for 50 to 60 minutes, or until the potatoes are tender, the dish is lightly browned on top, and the sides are bubbly.

9. Remove the dish from the oven and let it sit for about 5 minutes before serving. This gives the cheese mixture a bit of time to set.

DUCK FAT ROASTED POTATOES (A.K.A. ROASTIES)

DF MAKES 4 TO 6 SERVINGS

PLEASE DO NOT BE INTIMIDATED WHEN YOU READ "DUCK FAT." If anything, get excited because once you taste a piping hot potato roasted in this yumminess, you'll start asking yourself, "I wonder what else I can fry in this magic?!" Now, we have to say, you probably can't walk into your local grocery store and find this, but it is widely available. It usually comes in a small tub—one that will last you ages—and you can find it at your specialty food market, butcher, or Whole Foods store. You could use lard or oil instead, but it just won't be the same. This recipe will serve six well, but if you serve four, you'll have leftovers, which you can use as the tasty potato base in our Crispy Cod Fish Cakes with Horseradish Sauce (page 48). Also, we want to stress how important it is to melt the fat and get it nice and hot before adding in the potatoes. Cook these babies until they are golden brown and crispy on all sides.

3   pounds baking potatoes, peeled, halved lengthwise, and cut into thirds lengthwise (depending on size, you may have to cut into fourths)

3   tablespoons duck fat
    Salt and freshly ground black pepper

1. Preheat the oven to 400°F.

2. Place the potato chunks in a large pot and cover with COLD water. Bring to a boil over high heat.

3. Once boiling, salt the water and boil the potatoes until fork-tender, about 6 to 8 minutes. You want them to be soft but not too mushy.

4. Drain in a large colander and then forcefully shake the colander to roughen the potatoes up. The edges will look fluffy and starchy. Alternatively, you can put the drained potatoes back into the pot, cover with a lid, and shake roughly for a few seconds. You can be a bit aggressive with this!

5. Place the duck fat into a large roasting pan and put the pan in the preheated oven to melt the fat and get it nice and piping hot. This should only take a minute or two.

6. Take the roasting pan out of the oven and CAREFULLY add the drained, roughened-up potatoes. Be advised that the fat is VERY hot, so take caution here. The potatoes should sizzle slightly when added.

7. Generously salt and pepper the potatoes and give them a good stir to coat all the sides in the melted fat and seasoning. Place back into the oven and roast for 50 to 60 minutes, or until golden brown and crispy, flipping the potatoes at least twice throughout cooking to evenly brown all sides. This can take up to an hour (or even longer), so do not prematurely take them out of the oven. They should be deep GOLDEN brown and crispy on all sides.

8. Remove from the oven and immediately season with a bit more salt and pepper.

9. Transfer to a paper towel–lined plate or baking sheet and let the potatoes de-grease slightly before serving immediately.

ROASTED SWEET POTATOES AND SQUASH

DF   **MAKES 6 TO 8 SERVINGS**

GROWING UP, ONE THANKSGIVING DISH THAT WAS ALWAYS on the table was a sweet potato casserole. Mashed sweet potatoes mixed with brown sugar, marshmallows, butter, and pecan pieces made for tasty first and second servings every time. In a twist on that classic, Jessie tried to lighten it up for her family so that it could be enjoyed more often during the year. This version requires a long bake time in order to get the potatoes and squash tender, but it is so delicious that it is worth the wait!

   2   pounds sweet potatoes, peeled and cut into 1-inch cubes
   1   (1- to 2-pound) butternut squash, peeled, seeded, and cut into 1-inch cubes
  ¼   cup extra-virgin olive oil
  ¼   cup firmly packed dark brown sugar
  ½   teaspoon ground cinnamon
      Pinch of cayenne pepper

1. Preheat the oven to 400°F. Generously grease a 13 x 9-inch baking dish with nonstick cooking spray.

2. In a large mixing bowl, toss all the ingredients together so that the sugar, spices, and oil cover the potato and squash pieces evenly.

3. Transfer the mixture to the baking dish and bake for 50 to 60 minutes, or until the squash and potatoes are tender.

4. Remove from the oven, let sit for 5 to 10 minutes, and serve.

JESSIE'S FAVORITE POTATO SALAD

 DF MAKES 6 TO 8 SERVINGS

EVERY YEAR FOR OUR BIRTHDAYS, OUR DAD LET US CHOOSE what we wanted him to make us for our special days. Our wishes changed from year to year—sometimes it was baked stuffed shrimp, sometimes gumbo, maybe hamburgers with all the fixings. One of Jessie's recurring favorites, though, was always his potato salad. Super bacony with crisp onions mixed in, it was always a perfectly balanced mouthful of tasty potato goodness. This delicious version is the one Jessie now makes for her family, and it is always a hit! Naturally gluten-free, potato salad is a versatile accompaniment to many meals, from burgers to ribs to fried chicken. Or, if you like it as much as Jessie does, you'll eat it all by itself! This is a quick and easy recipe and will take 30 minutes or less to make.

2	pounds small red potatoes, cut into bite-size pieces
½	teaspoon salt
½	teaspoon freshly ground black pepper
⅓	cup finely diced celery
½	cup finely diced red onion
¾	cup mayonnaise
¼	cup Creole or spicy brown mustard
6	large hard-cooked eggs, cooled, peeled, and roughly chopped
1	pound bacon, cooked until crisp and roughly chopped

1. Put the cut potatoes into a stockpot filled with cool water and bring to a boil. Cook the potatoes until they are fork-tender (that is, soft enough to eat but still firm enough to maintain their shape). You don't want them mushy and falling apart. Depending on the size of your potato chunks, this could take 10 to 20 minutes, but usually the shorter the better.

2. When the potatoes are cooked to your desired tenderness, drain them and transfer to a large salad or serving bowl.

3. Add the salt, pepper, celery, red onion, mayonnaise, and mustard and stir until all the ingredients are evenly distributed and well mixed.

4. Add the chopped egg and bacon and gently fold these ingredients into the mixture. Serve the potato salad warm or chill until ready to serve.

Ms. LEYTHA'S HOT WATER BREAD

Q·E **DF**   MAKES 12 SLICES

OUR STEPMOTHER, ALDEN, HAS A COUSIN WHOM WE ALL CALL
Meme. Meme is one of the most amazing cooks you'll ever hope to meet and,
like many good cooks, says that she learned most of her cooking skills from her
grandmother, Ms. Leytha. You still with us? Ms. Leytha cooked from the heart
and always hosted the weekly Sunday dinner. As long as Meme can remember,
this hot water bread was a big part of those Sunday meals and something EVERY-
ONE looked forward to eating, hot right out of the skillet. (If you're not familiar
with hot water bread, it's basically an easy, tasty corn grits cake.) These can take
a bit of patience to get the consistency just right, but they are well worth it. They
shouldn't be too liquidy, so just add the water gradually and keep in mind that
the end goal is to be able to form them into patties with your hands. These are
truly delicious served with anything, but we love to pair them with our Baked
Pork Chops with Apple Rosemary Chutney (page 207) or our Slow Cooker Pot
Roast (page 224). This is a quick and easy recipe and will take you 30 minutes or
less to make.

1½	cups fine yellow cornmeal
¾	teaspoon salt
2	tablespoons vegetable shortening (such as Crisco), divided
1	cup boiling water (a bit more or less depending on your cornmeal)
	Butter, for serving (optional)

1. Preheat the oven to 350°F.

2. In a medium glass bowl, add the cornmeal, salt, and 1 tablespoon of the vegetable shortening.

3. Slowly pour the boiling water over the cornmeal mix and, with a wooden spoon, stir constantly until all of the cornmeal is moist and appears to stick together. You do not want it soupy. You need to be able to shape it into a patty, so it can't be too moist or it won't form. You may need a bit less or a bit more water with this, depending on the cornmeal you use, so add the water GRADUALLY until you get the desired consistency, then stop. Take the time to stir well to incorporate all the water and to let the fat melt and absorb before adding more water. We used just shy of the full cup of water for the desired consistency.

4. Let the mixture cool slightly in the bowl while you prepare your skillet. In a large cast-iron or heavy skillet, heat the remaining 1 tablespoon of vegetable shortening over medium-high heat.

5. As that is melting, use your hands to scoop a large handful of the warm cornmeal mixture and make a large, palm-size patty. You want four patties as evenly shaped as possible.

6. Carefully place the patties in the skillet with the hot shortening and cook for 2 to 3 minutes on each side, or until they are nice and brown.

7. Place the skillet in the oven and bake for 25 to 30 minutes, or until golden brown and hard and crispy on the outside.

8. Slice each patty into thirds and serve with a bit of butter on top, if desired.

GRANDPA KIEF'S PORK, APPLE, AND SAGE STUFFING   MAKES 6 TO 8 SERVINGS

AS CHILDREN, THANKSGIVING WAS ONE OF OUR MOST TREA-sured holidays. We usually drove from Massachusetts up to our grandparents' house in Saranac Lake, New York, to see all of our cousins, aunts, and uncles. Many of our fondest memories from childhood seem to involve Thanksgiving and the accompanying joy, laughter, and love that came with those times. This stuffing is one of our favorites. For this gluten-free version, we use premade GF baguettes like the ones made by Against the Grain. The baguettes and GF stuffing cubes, which you can use in lieu of baguettes, tend to absorb the chicken stock a bit differently than their gluteny counterparts. So, you might need to use a little more or a little less stock to get the desired wetness for your stuffing. Also, if you want to make this recipe dairy-free, simply use your favorite dairy-free baguettes.

16	ounces gluten-free baguettes, cut into bite-size cubes (see note)
1	pound pork breakfast sausage (in bulk or removed from casings if using links)
2	cups diced yellow onion
1	cup diced celery
2	Granny Smith apples, peeled, cored, and chopped
¼	cup chopped fresh sage
1	tablespoon finely chopped fresh rosemary
2	teaspoons freshly ground black pepper
	Salt
1 to 2	cups chicken stock

1. Preheat the oven to 375°F. Grease a 13 x 9-inch baking dish with nonstick cooking spray or butter.

2. Place the cubed bread in a large mixing bowl and set aside.

3. In a large, nonstick skillet with high sides, sauté the sausage over medium-high heat until browned and cooked through, about 8 to 10 minutes. Be sure to crumble up the meat as it cooks.

4. Once the meat is browned, use a slotted spoon to transfer it to a bowl or plate and set aside. You want the drippings to remain in the pan.

5. In the remaining pork drippings in the pan, sauté the onions, celery, and apples until they have softened somewhat, about 8 to 10 minutes.

6. Stir in the sage and rosemary and let cook for an additional 1 to 2 minutes. Mix in the sausage until all the ingredients are incorporated and then transfer it all to the bowl containing the bread cubes. Be careful, as the sausage mixture is still hot!

7. Gently fold the sausage mixture evenly into the bread cubes. Add in the black pepper and some salt to taste. Next, add the chicken stock until you've achieved your desired stuffing consistency. Some of the moisture will bake out but not too much, so be mindful of what texture you prefer your cooked stuffing as you are adding stock.

8. Transfer the stuffing mixture into the prepared baking dish and bake for 35 to 40 minutes, or until the top of the stuffing is lightly browned and crunchy and the center is the consistency you prefer.

9. Remove from the oven, let cool slightly, and serve.

NOTE: Against the Grain baguettes come in a 15-ounce bag. That is sufficient for this recipe; just shoot for 14 to 16 ounces of whatever kind of bread you choose to use.

GRAMMA HILDA'S TRADITIONAL PORTUGUESE STUFFING

OUR GRAMMA HILDA USED TO MAKE THIS STUFFING WHEN WE were kids growing up in Massachusetts. As a child, Jessie wasn't such a fan of the mushier texture, but she couldn't get enough of the chorizo, so she'd eat it anyway. Once she grew up, she found that she craved this stuffing, texture and all, and was lucky enough some years ago to have Gramma teach her how to make it. Ideally, try to make this stuffing using a gluten-free baguette or French-style loaf like Against the Grain's version. If you can't find those, the store-bought gluten-free stuffing cubes work well, or you can even make your own cubes if you have a gluten-free bread you like. The texture isn't quite the same as the original French bread version, but the wonderful taste is still there! And if you want to get this recipe as close to authentic as possible, see the note below about the chorizo.

2	tablespoons extra-virgin olive oil, divided
9 to 10	cups (½-inch cubes) stale gluten-free French-style bread, or 6 to 8 cups gluten-free stuffing cubes
3	cups milk (or favorite dairy-free version)
¼	pound ground beef
¾	pound chorizo, roughly chopped (see note)
1	cup chopped yellow onion
¾	cup diced green bell pepper
½	cup diced celery
½	teaspoon salt
½	teaspoon crushed red pepper flakes

½	teaspoon freshly ground black pepper
1	tablespoon minced garlic
2	large eggs, lightly beaten
3	tablespoons chopped fresh parsley

1. Preheat the oven to 350°F.

2. Using 1 tablespoon of the olive oil, grease a 13 x 9-inch baking dish and set aside.

3. In a large mixing bowl, combine the bread and milk. The bread will soak up most of the milk and get soft and squishy.

4. Heat the remaining tablespoon olive oil in a large skillet with high sides over medium-high heat. Add the ground beef. If you are using freshly made chorizo, remove the contents of the casings and add to the pan along with the beef. Brown the meat until fully cooked through and crumbly.

5. If you are using a hard chorizo that is suited for chopping, add it now and sauté for 3 to 5 minutes, or until the outer sides start to brown.

6. Add the onions, bell peppers, celery, salt, crushed red pepper, and black pepper. Cook until the vegetables are softened, about 4 to 6 minutes.

NOTE: The original recipe, as Gramma Hilda authentically cooked it, called for Portuguese chouriço, a unique blend of herbs, spices, and meat that produces a hard, chop-able sausage. This kind of chorizo is widely available around southeastern Massachusetts and can be found nationwide in some, but not many, grocery stores. Although any kind of chorizo or even andouille sausage will suffice for this recipe, you can order the authentic Fall River, Massachusetts, version online at www.gasparssausage.com if you'd like to try it.

7. Incorporate the garlic and let it cook for another 1 to 2 minutes before removing the mixture from the heat.

8. Add the meat and vegetable mixture to the bread and milk mixture and stir until it is mixed evenly.

9. Finally, add the eggs and parsley, mixing until all the ingredients are distributed evenly throughout the stuffing.

10. Using a spatula or wooden spoon, transfer the stuffing into the prepared baking dish. Try to level out the top so that it all cooks evenly.

11. Bake until the top is golden brown and crunchy looking but the interior is still soft, about 45 minutes to 1 hour. You want the inside stuffing to remain rather moist and not dry out, so use your judgment on cooking time.

12. Remove from the oven and serve with your favorite holiday meal or weeknight specialty. Yum!

Mookie's Three-Cheese Mac

OUR LITTLE SISTER, MERIL, A.K.A. MOOKIE OR THE MOOKSTER, loves anything with cheese—and the stinkier the cheese, the more she likes it. We couldn't quite bring ourselves to make a super stinky mac and cheese out of fear of offending the majority of the population, but we did come up with a nice little three-cheese combo in her honor. The Havarti, Gruyère, and Cheddar combine for a rich, tangy taste. Here's to you, Mookie! This is a quick and easy recipe and will take 30 minutes or less to make.

- 1 pound gluten-free macaroni or shells
- 2 tablespoons unsalted butter
- 3 tablespoons gluten-free flour blend (we like Arrowhead Mills Gluten Free All Purpose Baking Mix)
- 2 cups whole milk
- 8 ounces white Cheddar, shredded
- 6 ounces Havarti, sliced thin and broken into the smallest possible pieces
- 6 ounces Gruyère, shredded
  Generous pinch of cayenne pepper
  Salt and freshly ground black pepper

1. Preheat the oven to 350°F.

2. In a large stockpot, cook the pasta until al dente, about 8 to 12 minutes, depending on the pasta shape you've chosen. Drain, return it to the pot, and set aside.

3. In a large saucepan, melt the butter over medium heat. Add the flour and cook for 3 to 4 minutes, constantly stirring, to blend the butter and flour into a roux.

4. Next, add the milk and whisk until the roux is dissolved into the milk. Whisking often, cook until the sauce thickens and begins to boil.

5. Once the sauce has thickened up, remove the pan from the heat and stir in all three cheeses, along with the pinch of cayenne and salt and pepper to taste. As soon as all of the cheese is melted and the sauce is ooey-gooey cheesy thick, pour it over the pasta. Gently stir the mixture together until all of the cheese sauce is evenly distributed in the pasta.

6. Pour the mixture into a 13 x 9-inch baking dish and bake for 15 to 20 minutes, or until the cheese on top is beginning to brown.

7. Remove from the oven, let the pan sit for 3 to 5 minutes, and then serve with your favorite entrée or lunch selection.

TRUFFLE PARMESAN RISOTTO

MAKES 4 TO 6 DECADENT SERVINGS

THIS RISOTTO WAS ONE OF JESSIE'S MOST SOUGHT-AFTER splurges. It is very rich, so you can probably get away with smaller portions than you would expect. The salty Parmesan with the rich truffle oil, all blended in with the creamy risotto, make the constant stirring worth it! Truffle oil can be expensive, but it's great to have on hand—and a little goes a long way.

- 1 tablespoon unsalted butter
- 1 teaspoon minced garlic
- 3 cups chicken or vegetable stock
- 8 ounces arborio rice
- 2 tablespoons half-and-half
- 1 tablespoon white truffle oil (the higher quality, the better)
- ½ cup grated Parmesan cheese
  Salt and freshly ground black pepper

1. In a medium stockpot, melt the butter over medium heat. Add the garlic and sauté briefly, about 30 seconds to 1 minute.

2. Add the stock and bring the mixture to a boil. Once the stock is boiling, add the rice and, stirring constantly, cook until the mixture is creamy and the liquid has been absorbed. This should take about 16 to 18 minutes.

3. Stir in the half-and-half and truffle oil and cook for another 2 to 4 minutes. The risotto should be creamy, and the rice should be cooked with a slight al dente texture.

4. Stir in the Parmesan, season with salt and pepper to taste, and serve immediately.

CHEDDAR CHEESE SOUFFLÉ

MAKES 4 TO 6 SERVINGS

WE WERE ALWAYS A LITTLE INTIMIDATED WHEN IT CAME TO making soufflés, as we thought they were difficult and could easily be ruined. But, we are now here to say, just about everyone can make a beautiful, fluffy soufflé without too much work or stress! Be sure to whip the egg whites sufficiently and fold the egg white mixture into the cheese mixture GENTLY. If you do that, your soufflé will be airy and light but very flavorful and rich at the same time. It also helps to have all of your ingredients and equipment at the ready so no time is wasted while putting the soufflé together. We love pairing this with our Crispy Parmesan-Crusted Grouper (page 253) to compliment all the yumminess. Good luck!

Unsalted butter, at room temperature, for the pan

2 tablespoons plain gluten-free breadcrumbs

3 large egg yolks

3 tablespoons gluten-free flour blend (we like Arrowhead Mills Gluten Free All Purpose Baking Mix)

½ teaspoon garlic powder

¼ teaspoon ground nutmeg

¼ teaspoon salt

2 tablespoons unsalted butter

1⅓ cups HOT whole milk

8 ounces Cheddar cheese of your choice, shredded and at room temperature

5 large egg whites (make sure no yolk gets included here)

½ teaspoon cream of tartar

1. Preheat the oven to 375°F.

2. Using your room-temperature butter, grease an 8-cup soufflé mold. Sprinkle in the breadcrumbs and toss around to coat the inside of the dish. Shake out any excess crumbs and discard. Set the mold aside.

3. In a small bowl, whisk the egg yolks until creamy. Set aside.

4. In another small bowl, sift together the flour, garlic powder, nutmeg, and salt until evenly distributed.

5. In a medium stockpot or large saucepan, melt the butter over medium heat. Whisk in the flour mixture and let the roux cook for 2 to 3 minutes. Stir it frequently so it heats evenly and doesn't burn. The roux will appear almost crumbly and seem too dry, but it is correct the way it is.

6. Whisk in the hot milk, turn the heat up to high, and bring the mixture to a boil. It will thicken as it heats. Once it boils and has thickened, remove it from the heat.

7. Temper the yolks into the mixture by constantly stirring the mixture while adding the yolks slowly. Once the yolks are incorporated, mix in the cheese and stir until no lumps of unmelted cheese remain. Set this aside while you prepare the egg whites.

8. Using an electric mixer, beat the egg whites and cream of tartar on medium speed until the egg whites are thick and glossy and make stiff peaks when you remove the beater blades. This should take 4 to 5 minutes.

9. Gently FOLD about a third of the egg white mixture into the cheese mixture. Once that is incorporated, repeat with another third of the egg whites and then finally with the final third. You want the egg whites incorporated evenly and mixed in well, but you need to do it gently.

10. Pour the mixture into the prepared soufflé dish. Place it on a baking sheet in case of overflow and bake for 35 to 40 minutes. The top will brown, the edges should appear dry and not raw, and the center should be fully set.

11. Remove from the oven and serve immediately.

Mains

ALK ABOUT SOMETHING HERE FOR EVERYONE! YOU LIKE chicken? We've got that! Prefer lamb? We've got that, too. Craving some Spanish flavors? Check. How about a nice warm curry? Absolutely! As you'll see from this chapter's contents, our taste buds have multiple personalities and crave all different flavors and textures, depending on the day or mood. From talking with friends and family, we found that many other people experience the same thing. Their menus vary depending on the season, the weather, the time of day—nothing is static here. So, in keeping with that vibe, we created a diverse, vibrant entrée chapter guaranteed to contain something to hit the mark on most any day or for any craving! We also tried to offer some different cooking options. You'll find a few one-pot meals, like the Quick and Easy Enchilada Pie (page 272), some baked options, like the Dijon Chicken, Leek, and Mushroom Pot Pie (page 268), and some pan-fried choices, like the Seared Salmon with Warm Lentil, Tomato, and Mint Salad (page 250). That way, if you have an hour or even an entire day to prepare dinner, there is something here you can make that will taste great and be, as always, wonderfully gluten-free!

Quick and Easy Enchilada Pie, page 272

KINDA LIKE MAW-MAW'S SLOPPY JOES

 MAKES 6 TO 8 SERVINGS

MAW-MAW PATSY, JESSIE'S MOTHER-IN-LAW, MAKES DELICIOUS sloppy joes. They are spicy but sweet, sloppy but not too drippy. They are so tasty that Jessie wanted to put a version of the recipe in this book. This one here substitutes Maw-Maw's classic Manwich addition with a simple blend of tomatoes, apple cider vinegar, and brown sugar. The vinegar gives this recipe a certain tang that becomes less pronounced with cook time, so let it simmer away until your desired taste is achieved. We recommend 20 minutes of simmering, but feel free to adjust to your preference. This is a quick and easy recipe and will take 30 minutes or less to make.

- 1 tablespoon extra-virgin olive oil
- 2 pounds lean ground beef
- 1 medium-size yellow onion, diced
- 1 small red bell pepper, diced
- 1 small green bell pepper, diced
- 1 teaspoon minced garlic
- ¼ cup apple cider vinegar
- 1 tablespoon gluten-free Worcestershire sauce
- ¼ cup firmly packed light brown sugar
- 2 (10.5-ounce) cans tomato purée
- ½ teaspoon freshly ground black pepper
- 1 teaspoon garlic powder
- 1 tablespoon Dijon mustard
- Salt

Gluten-free hamburger buns, corn chips, or vessel of your preference, for serving

1. Heat a medium stockpot (we used a 6-quart here) over medium-high heat. Place the oil and meat in the pan and sauté until the meat is browned. Be sure to break it up into crumbles as it cooks.

2. Once the meat is brown and crumbly, add the onions, bell peppers, and garlic and sauté the vegetables in the meat for 3 to 4 minutes, or until they start to soften.

3. Mix in the vinegar, Worcestershire, sugar, tomato purée, black pepper, garlic powder, Dijon, and salt to taste. Stir until everything is evenly distributed.

4. Reduce the heat to a simmer and cook, uncovered, for approximately 20 minutes, or until the flavors have melded and some of the vinegary taste has cooked out. The final mixture should be slightly sweet with a lingering hint of acidity and tang from the vinegar.

5. Serve on fresh gluten-free hamburger rolls, if desired, or with corn chips for dipping or any other accompaniment you prefer.

NEW ENGLAND CLAM CHOWDER

CHOWDER, OR "CHOWDA," AS THEY SAY IN MASSACHUSETTS, IS a staple there, a common indulgence as ubiquitous as red beans and rice is in New Orleans. After Jessie had moved down to New Orleans, she'd occasionally get these "chowda" cravings. To help, our dad taught Jessie how to make his favorite kind. Funny enough, despite our dad's affection for "pork fat," Jessie now uses more bacon in her version of the recipe than he does! This chowder relies on a roux, the mix of fat and flour that creates the thick sauce-like consistency. Depending on the amount of bacon grease your bacon produces, you may have to add a little more or a little less flour. Just aim for a roux texture similar to the thickness of peanut butter. Also, we created this recipe using canned clams since fresh clams are quite hard to come by in some areas. Feel free to use fresh if you have them available. Be warned: this is a rich soup, so a little will go a long way. This is a quick and easy recipe but will take 45 minutes to make instead of the usual Q&E time of 30 minutes or less.

½	pound bacon, diced
2	cups chopped leeks (white bulb part only; thinly slice before chopping)
½	cup diced celery
¼ to ½	cup gluten-free flour blend (we like Arrowhead Mills Gluten Free All Purpose Baking Mix), depending on amount of rendered bacon fat
4	cups clam juice (see note)
	Salt and freshly ground black pepper
2	bay leaves

1 tablespoon chopped fresh thyme, or 1 teaspoon dried thyme

1 pound white potatoes, peeled and medium diced (try to keep the size consistent)

4 (6.5-ounce) cans of clams with liquid (see note)

½ cup half-and-half

1. In a large stockpot, render the bacon over medium-high heat until crispy, about 10 to 15 minutes.

2. Add the leeks and celery and sauté in the bacon grease for 3 to 5 minutes, or until the vegetables start to get soft.

3. Stir in ¼ cup of the flour and cook for 2 to 3 minutes. The flour will bind with the bacon grease and form a paste-like mixture. If the roux seems too loose, like it is still liquidy, add some additional flour until the peanut-butter-ish consistency is achieved. If it is too thick, we will correct that in the next step, so don't panic!

4. Stir in the clam juice along with salt and pepper to taste, the bay leaves, and the thyme. Bring the mixture up to a boil while stirring frequently. This will help the roux thicken up the liquid. If the soup is too thick for your taste, you can add some additional clam juice, chicken stock, or water.

NOTE: If you would like to use fresh clams, you should shoot for about 2 pounds of fresh little neck clams. Be sure to clean them well before chopping. Also, increase the amount of clam juice you use to 5 to 6 cups, as you won't have the additional clam juice from the canned clams.

5. Once thickened, reduce the heat to a simmer, add the potatoes and the canned clams with their juice, and cook on medium low until the potatoes are fork-tender, about 15 to 20 minutes, depending on the size of your diced potatoes.

6. Once the potatoes are ready, stir in the half-and-half.

7. Re-season with salt and pepper if necessary. Remove the bay leaves and serve.

NOT YOUR MOMMA'S MEATLOAF WITH HOMEMADE BROWN GRAVY

MAKES 6 TO 8 SERVINGS

OKAY, SO WE KNOW MEATLOAF IS JUST ONE OF THOSE DISHES that makes everyone say their mom made the best one. And everyone has had a great variety of meatloaves over the years. Since meatloaf seems to be so personal, we decided to make no claims about our mom's meatloaf except to say that it is our favorite version! We prefer to toast some gluten-free bread and make our own breadcrumbs, but packaged Italian-style breadcrumbs work just as well in this recipe. You can also use whatever flavor mustard you like, although we unanimously choose Dijon when given the option. The brown gravy is tasty and thick with that nice hint of sherry flavor. It goes well with other meats, too, so don't be afraid to try it on non-meatloaf nights! To enjoy this recipe if you are dairy-free, simply omit the homemade brown gravy and use dairy-free breadcrumbs.

MEATLOAF

2	pounds lean ground beef
1	cup finely diced yellow onion
2	large eggs
4 to 5	pieces gluten-free sandwich bread, toasted and then processed into crumbs, or 1 cup Italian-style gluten-free breadcrumbs
¼	cup ketchup
2	tablespoons mustard of your choice
2	teaspoons minced garlic
½	teaspoon freshly ground black pepper
	Salt

GRAVY

- ¼ cup (½ stick) unsalted butter
- ½ cup gluten-free flour blend (we like Arrowhead Mills Gluten Free All Purpose Baking Mix)
- 3 cups beef stock
- 1 teaspoon mustard (preferably the same used in the meatloaf)
- ½ teaspoon ground sage
-   Salt and freshly ground black pepper
- 1 to 2 tablespoons sherry (depending on your preference)

1. Preheat the oven to 400°F. Grease a 13 x 9-inch baking dish with nonstick cooking spray.

2. Using your hands, mix all the meatloaf ingredients together in a large mixing bowl until the ingredients are evenly distributed throughout the meat.

3. Shape the mixture into a loaf shape, trying to keep the ends the same thickness as the bulk of the loaf so that it cooks evenly. Place it in your baking dish.

4. Bake for 45 to 60 minutes, or until a meat thermometer inserted into the middle of the loaf reads 160°F. Times will vary depending on your loaf thickness, so just keep an eye on it after about 45 minutes of cook time.

5. Meanwhile, about 10 minutes before you anticipate the meatloaf to come out of the oven, make the gravy. In a medium saucepan, melt the butter over medium heat. Add the flour and cook, stirring, for 4 to 5 minutes, or until the mixture is golden brown.

6. Whisk in the beef stock, mustard, and ground sage. Bring to a simmer while whisking, and the gravy will thicken as it heats up. Once thick, remove the pan from the heat, season with salt and pepper, and stir in the sherry. Set aside, covered, until the meatloaf is ready to serve.

7. Once the meatloaf is cooked, remove it from the oven and let it sit for 10 minutes.

8. Cut and serve the meatloaf with a generous ladleful of gravy. There should be enough gravy to use over the top of your rice or mashed potatoes, too!

BAKED PORK CHOPS WITH APPLE ROSEMARY CHUTNEY

 **MAKES 4 SERVINGS**

PORK IS A WEEKLY DINNER MEAT AT JESSIE'S HOUSE. SHE HAS to change up her preparations often or else face the harsh criticism of her five-year-old son, Jude (think, "Mom, you just made this the other night!"). One of the acceptable repeat performances, though, is this pork chop version with a sweet, flavorful apple chutney on top. Everyone loves this one, so there are no complaints when she makes it often. Try to keep a close eye on your meat thermometer and pull the chops out as soon as they reach that magical 145°F. This will help keep them from getting dried out. This is a quick and easy recipe and will take 30 minutes or less to make.

PORK CHOPS

- 4 bone-in thick-cut pork chops
- 2 tablespoons extra-virgin olive oil
- ¾ teaspoon garlic powder
- ½ teaspoon freshly ground black pepper
   Salt

CHUTNEY

- 4 strips bacon, diced
- ½ cup finely diced yellow onion
- 3 medium-size sweet apples (like Gala or Fuji), cored and finely diced
- 1 tablespoon honey

2 sprigs fresh rosemary

1 tablespoon freshly squeezed lemon juice

⅓ cup chicken stock

¼ teaspoon freshly ground black pepper

Salt

1. Preheat the oven to 400°F. Grease a large baking sheet with nonstick cooking spray.

2. Season each side of your four pork chops with the olive oil, garlic powder, pepper, and some salt and place on the baking sheet. Bake for 20 to 30 minutes, or until your meat thermometer registers a 145°F internal temperature. Once cooked, remove from the oven immediately.

3. While the pork chops are baking, prepare your chutney. Begin by cooking the bacon in a medium saucepan over medium-high heat until the pieces become crispy but not burned, about 7 to 10 minutes.

4. Once the bacon is crispy, add the onion and sauté, stirring frequently, until tender, about 3 to 4 minutes.

5. Add the apples, honey, rosemary, lemon juice, chicken stock, black pepper, and salt to taste. Reduce the heat to medium and simmer, covered, for 15 to 20 minutes, or until the apples are tender and the sauce has kind of thickened from the breaking down of the apples.

6. Remove the rosemary sprigs and discard. Re-season the chutney if necessary. Transfer your pork chops to individual plates and top with a generous portion of the apple chutney. Serve.

HOME-STYLE CHILI WITH GLUTEN-FREE BEER

DF MAKES 4 TO 6 SERVINGS

BACK WHEN JESSIE LIVED ALONE AND SHE HAD TIME TO indulge in couch lazing and football watching, one of her favorite Sunday meals was chili with chips. This chili is one of those dishes that gets better day after day. So, if you can't finish it all by the end of Sunday night football, you can eat it for Monday night football, too, and it'll be even better than the day before! It also freezes very well, so you can always go that route if you get chili burnout before eating the whole pot. This recipe does require a gluten-free beer, of which there are many tasty choices these days. We think it goes best with a lager-style beer, so look for that description when choosing a beer for this recipe.

½ pound bacon, diced

1 pound lean ground beef

1 tablespoon extra-virgin olive oil

1 cup diced yellow onion

½ cup diced celery

1 cup diced green bell pepper

1 tablespoon minced garlic

6 ounces gluten-free lager-style beer

½ cup freshly brewed strong coffee

½ teaspoon chili powder, or more to taste

2 teaspoons ground cumin

1 (15-ounce) can tomato purée

1 (15-ounce) can diced tomatoes (preferably petite diced)
Salt and freshly ground black pepper

1 (15-ounce) can red kidney beans, drained and rinsed

1. In a large sauté pan or skillet over medium-high heat, cook the diced bacon until crisp. Drain, transfer the bacon to a bowl, and set aside.

2. In the same pan, brown the ground beef. Once cooked, drain if necessary.

3. Meanwhile, in a large stockpot over medium heat, heat the olive oil. Sauté the onions, celery, and bell peppers until soft, about 8 to 10 minutes. Add the garlic and sauté for another 1 to 2 minutes.

4. Add the cooked beef, the bacon, and all the remaining ingredients except the kidney beans. Reduce the heat to medium low and simmer the chili, uncovered, for 45 to 50 minutes. Stir the mixture often to ensure no pieces are sticking to the bottom and burning.

5. Gently add the kidney beans and let cook for an additional 5 to 10 minutes.

6. If too much liquid remains at the end of this cooking time for your preference, you can ladle some of it off the top. Just remember that the chili will thicken slightly and absorb some additional liquid as it cools.

7. Re-season the chili if necessary and serve with your favorite chili accompaniments.

E.J.'S CRUNCHY FRIED CHICKEN

MAKES 4 SERVINGS

WHENEVER OUR LITTLE BROTHER, E.J., COMES TO NEW Orleans, we can usually find him at our dad's restaurant Emeril's, cozying up to a big ole plate of fried chicken and waffles. He never really makes it to the waffles, but he can almost eat his own body weight in fried chicken. We came up with this recipe just for him, and it seems everyone agrees that this may be the best fried chicken ever! And, yes, it happens to be gluten-free. You can make this recipe two ways: crispy or super crispy by either battering the chicken once or twice. If you do go for the double batter, you may need to increase your fry time slightly and try to not chip a tooth! You'll need to have both a candy/deep-fry thermometer to ensure your oil is at the peak frying temperature and also a meat thermometer to make sure the internal temperature of the chicken is 165°F and fully cooked. Feel free to use any cuts of chicken you prefer, keeping in mind your fry time may vary depending on bigger and thicker pieces and cuts.

2	cups buttermilk
8 to 10	dashes hot sauce (we like Tabasco or Crystal)
2	pounds chicken pieces (wings, thighs, breasts)
2⅔	cups superfine white rice flour
1⅓	cups cornstarch
2	tablespoons garlic powder
2	tablespoons salt
3	tablespoons Emeril's Original Essence seasoning or Cajun seasoning of your choice
½	teaspoon cayenne pepper
	Vegetable oil, for frying

1. In a large resealable plastic bag, combine the buttermilk and hot sauce. Add the chicken pieces and seal the bag firmly. Place the bag in a bowl and refrigerate for at least 3 hours but no more than 24 hours.

2. When the chicken is done marinating, carefully transfer the buttermilk and chicken mixture into a large mixing bowl. Discard the plastic bag.

3. Prepare the batter. In a large shallow bowl or casserole dish, combine the rice flour, cornstarch, garlic powder, salt, Essence, and cayenne. Mix them together with a fork or spoon until well combined.

4. Set up a cooling rack or baking sheet on which to lay your battered chicken. Work piece by piece. Remove a piece of chicken from the buttermilk mixture and let the excess buttermilk drip off slightly before laying the chicken in the dry batter mixture.

5. Coat the entire piece with a layer of the dry batter as evenly and as well as possible before laying the breaded chicken piece on either the cooling rack or the baking sheet. Repeat this process until all the chicken has been battered.

6. If you want the regular one-breaded version, stop here. If you want the super-crunchy double-breaded version, repeat the battering process once more so that each chicken piece gets dipped into the buttermilk and dry batter a total of two times. Discard any remaining batter and buttermilk.

7. Let your battered chicken sit at room temperature for 20 to 25 minutes while you prepare your frying station. If you are using a deep fryer, heat the oil and cook as directed according to manufacturer's instructions.

8. If frying on the stove, fill a large, deep frying pan or cast-iron skillet halfway with vegetable oil. Using a candy/deep-fry thermometer, heat the oil until it is between 350°F and 375°F. Once the temperature has been reached, carefully drop in a few pieces of the battered chicken, making sure not to overcrowd the pan. Fewer is better. After about 4 to 5 minutes, depending on the cuts of chicken you've used, carefully use tongs to turn the chicken pieces over and fry the other side for another 4 to 5 minutes. You MUST be sure the chicken is cooked through to an internal temperature of 165°F. Remove a test piece, check the temperature,

and return the chicken to the pan to continue cooking, if necessary. We do not recommend trying to test the temperature while the chicken is immersed in the oil.

9. Once fully cooked, remove the pieces by using tongs and place on a large, paper towel–lined plate or baking sheet to cool.

10. Repeat the frying process until all the chicken pieces have been fried. Keep an eye on the thermometer and try not to let the oil temperature dip below the 350°F mark, paying special attention to the temperature right after you remove the finished chicken pieces and are getting ready to add new pieces.

11. Let cool a few minutes before serving.

CHICKEN AND DUMPLINGS

 MAKES 6 TO 8 SERVINGS

WHEN WE WERE KIDS AND WE'D VISIT EMERIL'S RESTAURANT, we'd always hope Mr. Lou, the pastry chef, would be there and that maybe, just maybe, he'd made some of his famous and nearly irreproducible chicken and dumplings. Like so many of his other recipes, he never revealed just how he made his version. So, we were left trying and trying at home to replicate it. After years and years of attempts, and then years and years of adjusting those attempts to be GF, we finally settled on this version. A thick and rich sauce, chock-full of veggies and chicken, is interspersed with fat, dense little drop dumplings. Although we admit our recipe will never come close to Mr. Lou's, we know he would approve of our best effort. This is a quick and easy recipe and will take 30 minutes or less to make.

BASE

1½	pounds boneless, skinless chicken breasts
¼	cup (½ stick) unsalted butter
1½	cups diced yellow onion
½	cup diced carrot
¾	cup diced celery
2	teaspoons minced garlic
½	cup gluten-free flour blend (we like Arrowhead Mills Gluten Free All Purpose Baking Mix)
4	cups chicken stock
4	sprigs fresh thyme
2	bay leaves
½	teaspoon Emeril's Original Essence or Cajun spice of your choice

¼ teaspoon salt, or more to taste

¼ teaspoon freshly ground black pepper

½ cup frozen peas

DUMPLINGS

1 cup gluten-free flour blend (we like Arrowhead Mills Gluten Free All Purpose Baking Mix)

1 tablespoon baking powder

Pinch of salt

½ teaspoon xanthan gum

½ cup whole milk

2 tablespoons unsalted butter, melted

1. First, make the chicken base. In a medium saucepan, boil the chicken breasts in water until cooked through. Drain them and set them aside to cool. Once cooled, use your hands or two forks to gently shred the chicken meat. Set aside.

2. Melt the butter in a large stockpot over medium heat. Sauté the onion, carrot, and celery until they start to soften, about 5 to 6 minutes. Add the garlic and stir until fragrant, for 30 seconds to 1 minute. Add the flour and stir so that the vegetables are coated with the butter and flour roux. Cook for 2 to 3 more minutes.

3. Stir in the chicken stock, thyme, bay leaves, Essence, salt, and pepper. As the mixture heats up, it will thicken. Once it has thickened, add in the shredded chicken meat and the peas. Cover and let it cook for about 10 to 15 minutes, stirring often to ensure it doesn't stick to the bottom and burn.

4. While the chicken base is cooking, make your dumpling batter. In a small mixing bowl, sift together the flour, baking powder, salt, and xanthan gum. Add the milk and melted butter and stir until a dough forms.

5. Once the chicken base has cooked for its 10 to 15 minutes, remove the cover and turn the heat down to low. Using a teaspoon, spoon the dough into a rough ball and drop it carefully into the simmering mixture. Using a spoon, gently push the dumpling down into the liquid so it can fully cook and so you have room to spoon the rest of the dough in. Repeat with the rest of the dough. The dumplings will want to float, so you'll need to carefully push them down into the pan as you drop them in.

6. When all the dough has been dropped and immersed in the liquid, cover the pot again and cook for an additional 5 to 10 minutes, or until the dumplings are puffy and cooked through. During this time, stir the mixture occasionally and very carefully so as not to break the dumplings apart. They will remain slightly doughy in the middle but should not be raw.

7. Remove from the heat and serve.

MEME'S EGGPLANT AND RICOTTA LASAGNA

MAKES 4 TO 6 SERVINGS

OUR STEPMOTHER ALDEN'S COUSIN, MEME, IS NOT ONLY AN important part of our family, but she is also one of the most incredible women we know. She is always up for trying out new recipes and giving anything a go if it means she could put a smile on someone's face. When Meme learned just how severe Jilly's celiac disease and reactions were, she would often make special gluten-free meals and treats for her when she would come home to visit. She never once flinched at trying to learn about, understand, and master this interesting disease and its many reactions and symptoms. This recipe is one of Jilly's favorite and most often requested Meme meals. It is incredibly quick and easy, and, like so many of Meme's meals, it is also quite healthy, too. The secret ingredient? Eggplant as a stand-in for noodles. You can serve this simply on its own with your favorite gluten-free roll or baguette, or, for a more filling meal, serve it with your favorite gluten-free pasta. So, go make Meme proud and have fun cooking!

1	pound eggplant, ends trimmed and discarded, cut into ¼-inch-thick slices
	Salt and freshly ground black pepper
1	(15-ounce) container ricotta cheese (preferably low-fat)
½	teaspoon minced garlic
2	teaspoons Italian seasoning
	Pinch of crushed red pepper flakes
1	medium egg, lightly beaten
3	cups high-quality tomato-based pasta sauce
1	cup shredded mozzarella cheese

1. Preheat the oven to 375°F.

2. Lay all the slices of eggplant on a large, paper towel–lined baking sheet and season both sides generously with salt and pepper. The salt will help to extract the moisture from the eggplant, and the paper towel will absorb the excess moisture. Loosely lay a piece of paper towel over the top of the eggplant slices as well, to help absorb some more moisture. Set aside until ready to layer the slices in step 5.

3. In a medium bowl, place the ricotta, garlic, Italian seasoning, and crushed red pepper flakes. Add a bit of salt and pepper and the lightly beaten egg and mix together well.

4. In a 13 x 9-inch glass baking dish, spoon a quarter of the tomato sauce on the bottom of the dish and spread out to cover as evenly as possible.

5. Lay a third of the eggplant slices over the sauce, with the pieces slightly overlapping each other.

6. Spread another quarter of the tomato sauce over the eggplant, followed by half of the ricotta mixture. Spread it out as evenly as possible with a spoon.

7. Layer another third of the eggplant slices on top of the ricotta mixture, followed by another quarter of the sauce. Spread gently over the top.

8. Layer the remaining third of the eggplant slices over the sauce, overlapping them slightly, followed by the remaining half of the ricotta mixture.

9. Finish with the remaining quarter of the sauce and spread it out to cover the ricotta evenly. Sprinkle the shredded mozzarella all over the top.

10. Bake uncovered for 45 minutes to 1 hour, or until the eggplant is very soft and easy to cut into and the cheese is nice and bubbly. The time may vary depending on the thickness of the eggplant. Be sure to place a baking sheet on the rack below to catch anything that bubbles over. Serve immediately on its own or alongside your favorite gluten-free baguette or pasta.

SLOW COOKER POT ROAST

SINCE HAVING HER KIDS, JESSIE HAS FALLEN IN LOVE WITH her slow cooker. She's gotten to where she can make almost any course in her trusty Crock-Pot . . . even dessert! This recipe is one of her go-to weekday meals. It is healthy, easy to put together, and delicious. We don't rely on a lot of additional spices here; we lightly season the meat with salt and pepper, choosing instead to let the flavor of the meat itself be the star. However, you can always add whatever spices you'd like to personalize the recipe.

2	tablespoons minced garlic
3 to 4	medium-size carrots, chopped
2	small yellow onions, chopped
4 to 5	medium-size potatoes (we like Yukon gold here), peeled and chopped into bite-size pieces
4 to 5	stalks celery, chopped
1	(4-pound) beef chuck roast
	Salt and freshly ground black pepper
1	tablespoon extra-virgin olive oil
2	cups beef stock, divided
	Pinch of crushed red pepper flakes
2 to 3	tablespoons cornstarch

1. Layer the garlic and vegetables in the bottom of your slow cooker.

2. Season the roast with salt and pepper as desired. In a large skillet, heat the olive oil over high heat. Make sure your pan is piping hot so that your meat gets a good sear on it. Brown all sides of the roast. Usually a few minutes on each side is sufficient.

3. Transfer the roast into the slow cooker, add 1 cup of the beef stock and the pinch of crushed red pepper flakes, cover, and cook on the low setting for 8 to 10 hours.

4. About 20 minutes before the roast should be done, mix the cornstarch with the remaining cup of beef stock. If you like a thinner gravy, 2 tablespoons of cornstarch should suffice. If you prefer a thicker gravy, use 3 tablespoons. Add the mixture to the slow cooker, stirring gently to incorporate it. The liquid in the slow cooker should thicken just in time to serve it.

5. When the roast is done, turn off your slow cooker, uncover the roast, and serve.

EMERIL'S SPAGHETTI À LA CARBONARA

Q+E MAKES 4 TO 6 SERVINGS

SPAGHETTI CARBONARA, FOR JESSIE ANYWAY, IS ANALOGOUS to indulgence and cheesy deliciousness! The pancetta adds a nice crunch and rich bacony flavor, while the shallots add the oniony dimension. Perfect. Our dad prefers to use a quinoa pasta for this recipe. We also tried it using a rice-based pasta, and it tasted fantastic. What type you use really depends on your preference. Regardless of the type of pasta you choose, beware of the over-cooked, mushy pasta syndrome. Err on the al dente side to avoid oddly textured carbonara! This is a quick and easy recipe and will take 30 minutes or less to make.

6	quarts water
1	tablespoon fine sea salt
8	ounces pancetta, diced into ¼-inch cubes
2	tablespoons minced shallots
1	pound quinoa spaghetti (we like Ancient Harvest)
2	large whole eggs
3	large egg yolks
½	cup grated Parmesan cheese
½	cup grated Pecorino Romano or Grana Padano cheese
2	tablespoons minced fresh parsley
½	teaspoon freshly ground black pepper

1. Bring the water to a boil in a large pot and add the salt.

2. Meanwhile, in a medium sauté pan over medium heat, cook the pancetta until the fat has rendered and the pancetta is crisp, for about 5 minutes. Add the shallots and continue to cook until the shallots are tender, for about 3 minutes. Remove from the heat and set aside.

3. Cook the spaghetti in the boiling water for 8 minutes, or until just al dente. Reserve ¼ cup of the cooking liquid and set aside. Drain the pasta in a colander and set aside, keeping warm.

4. In a large heat-proof bowl, add the eggs, egg yolks, Parmesan, Pecorino, parsley, and black pepper and whisk until the mixture is well combined. Add the hot pasta and the reserved cooking liquid and toss to coat. Add the pancetta and shallot mixture and toss to combine.

5. Serve immediately.

HERB, SAUSAGE, AND TOMATO PENNE

Q+E MAKES 4 SERVINGS

THIS IS A SUPER-EASY AND QUICK ENTRÉE TO THROW
together on a weeknight. The sausage provides a lot of the seasoning for this
dish, so you'll notice we don't add that much to it. Make sure you taste the cooked
version before adding any additional salt because we have found lots of Italian
sausage to be very salty. Also, fresh herbs work great in this recipe, so feel free
to substitute the fresh equivalent for the dried measurements below (the generally accepted rule is 1 teaspoon dry = 1 tablespoon fresh). This is a quick and easy
recipe and will take 30 minutes or less to make.

8   ounces gluten-free penne pasta
1   pound Italian sausage (sweet, mild, or spicy), casing removed
1   cup diced yellow onion
2   teaspoons minced garlic
2   cups diced fresh tomatoes
2   teaspoons dried basil, or 2 tablespoons roughly chopped fresh
    basil
½   teaspoon dried oregano, or 1½ teaspoons fresh oregano leaves
¾   cup white wine (remember, if you wouldn't drink it, don't cook
    with it!)
    Salt and freshly ground black pepper
½   cup grated Parmesan cheese (omit if dairy-free)

1. In a large pot of salted boiling water, cook the penne until tender but firm. Drain and return to the pot.

2. While the pasta is cooking, cook the sausage in a large, nonstick skillet over medium heat until cooked through. Be sure to break it up into crumbles as it cooks. Drain any fat if necessary.

3. Add the onions into the skillet and cook until tender, about 3 to 5 minutes. Add the garlic and cook for another 1 to 2 minutes.

4. Stir in the tomatoes, basil, oregano, and white wine. Simmer, uncovered, for 10 to 12 minutes. The tomatoes will start to break down and soften.

5. Once the sauce mixture is ready, pour it over the reserved pasta and stir to incorporate. Season with salt and pepper as desired. Stir in the Parmesan cheese, if using, and serve immediately.

J.P.'S BAKED ZITI

JESSIE'S SON J.P. ABSOLUTELY LOVES THIS ZITI DISH. IT WAS one of his first "real" solid meals and continues to be one of his favorites still. There are different schools of thought about precooking the pasta for this dish, and Jessie has tried it both ways several times. While it is possible to use dried pasta, the consistency is sometimes not as uniform as one would like. It also takes a lot longer to cook! So, below we've included the precooked-pasta version, but you are welcome to try it the other way if you prefer. Just add some cook time and possibly some additional liquid or sauce! Also, if you use the precooked-pasta method, you can make this dish the night before, pop it in the fridge, and then take it out and bake it the next day for the same great flavors but less prep time before dinner. If you're a busy mom or dad, you'll love this time-saver!

1 pound gluten-free pasta of your choice (we like to use ziti)
1 tablespoon olive oil
1 cup diced yellow onion
1 pound lean ground beef
1 pound sweet or mild Italian sausage, casing removed
2 teaspoons minced garlic
2 (25-ounce) jars favorite tomato-based pasta sauce
   Salt and freshly ground black pepper
1 pound mozzarella cheese, shredded, divided
½ cup shredded Parmesan cheese, divided

1. Preheat the oven to 375°F.

2. In a large pot of salted boiling water, cook your pasta until it is still a bit crunchy but mostly cooked. It will finish cooking while it bakes. The cook time varies with the type of pasta you choose, so just start testing the texture after about 5 to 6 minutes. Once cooked, drain and set aside.

3. Meanwhile, in a large skillet with high sides, heat the olive oil and sauté the onions until they begin to soften, about 3 to 5 minutes. Next, add the ground beef and the Italian sausage. Cook the meat until cooked through, breaking it up into crumbles as it cooks.

4. Stir in the garlic and cook for 1 to 2 minutes more. Remove from the heat.

5. Transfer the meat mixture to a large mixing bowl. Add the tomato sauce and mix it together thoroughly. Next, add the pasta and gently fold it into the mixture. Season with salt and pepper to taste.

6. In a large baking dish (we used a 13 x 9-inch), spread approximately half of the mixture evenly in the pan. Cover with half of the mozzarella and half of the Parmesan cheese.

7. Top this layer with the remaining pasta mixture and finish with a top layer of the remaining mozzarella and Parmesan cheese.

8. Bake uncovered for 30 to 45 minutes, or until the pasta is fully cooked, the mixture is heated through, and the cheese is gooey and melty. Cook time will vary depending on pasta shape and brand, so use the texture of the pasta as the determining factor and just use the suggested cook time as a guide.

9. Remove from the oven and serve with your favorite accouterments.

ONE-POT CHICKEN JALFREZI

 **MAKES 4 SERVINGS**

WHAT'S NOT TO LOVE ABOUT THE SPICY, FRAGRANT, AWAKENING-
every-sense culinary experience that IS Indian cuisine? It is especially near
to Jilly's heart because through those first few years of her celiac diagnosis, it seemed that Indian restaurants were one of the few safe havens where
she could actually enjoy a meal with a group of people and not be THAT girl
asking, "Are you SURE it doesn't have any wheat flour in it? Really?!" This
is a pretty common curry that can range in heat from a nice medium heat, which
we've done here, to as fiery as one can take (by adding in extra chiles or using
a hot curry powder). As when handling any chile, though, we recommend you
wear gloves, so just keep a box of disposable gloves handy. You'll need them
because, once you try this curry the first time, you'll be currying it up on a
weekly basis! This is perfectly paired with our Easy Pilau Rice (page 169). A
dairy-free tip: Jilly likes to use coconut cream in this, which is a bit thicker
than coconut milk and is great if you can't easily find a dairy-free yogurt. You
should be able to find coconut cream in most stores; it's usually in a can and
found where all the ingredients are for making piña coladas. This is a quick and
easy recipe and will take 30 minutes or less to make.

CHICKEN

- ⅓ cup dairy-free plain yogurt or coconut cream (or full-fat plain or Greek-style yogurt)
- ½ teaspoon curry powder (mild or medium)
- 1 pound boneless, skinless chicken breasts or thighs, cut into bite-size pieces

2   tablespoons sunflower or vegetable oil

1   cup quartered, then roughly sliced yellow onion

1   cup roughly chopped green bell pepper

1   green jalapeño pepper or Thai chile, seeded and roughly chopped

1½   teaspoons minced garlic

1   tablespoon minced fresh ginger or ginger purée (from a jar)

1   (15-ounce) can tomato sauce

2   medium fresh tomatoes, cut into wedges (halve the tomato before cutting into wedges; aim for 1 cup)

2½   teaspoons curry powder (mild or medium, not vindaloo)

1½   teaspoons garam masala

   Pinch of salt

⅓   cup dairy-free yogurt, coconut cream, or coconut milk (or full-fat plain or Greek-style yogurt)

¼   cup roughly chopped fresh cilantro

1. First, prepare the chicken. In a small bowl, combine the yogurt and curry powder and mix well to make a paste. Add the chicken chunks to this, stir well, and set aside.

2. For the curry, heat the oil in a large sauté pan with high sides or a medium saucepan over medium heat. Add the onion, bell pepper, chiles, garlic, and ginger and cook until the vegetables soften slightly, about 6 to 7 minutes.

3. Add the marinated chicken to the pan (discard any marinade that hasn't been absorbed by the chicken), stir well, and cook for another 6 to 7 minutes, or until the chicken is almost cooked through, stirring occasionally.

4. Add the tomato sauce, tomato wedges, curry powder, garam masala, and a pinch of salt to the pan. Stir well, turn the heat down to low, and cook for 20 minutes, covered, stirring occasionally.

5. Once all the chicken is cooked through, turn off the heat. Stir in the yogurt and cilantro. Mix well and serve immediately with our Easy Pilau Rice (page 169).

JAMAICAN JERK CHICKEN WITH RICE AND PEAS

DF **MAKES 6 SERVINGS**

THIS IS A CARIBBEAN DISH THAT JILLY'S BEST FRIEND IN London, Sareta, used to regularly make and one that Jilly couldn't get enough of. This recipe makes a big batch of food, but it is perfect for your next summer barbecue or game day get-together (added bonus: leftovers people actually want to eat!). The chicken is delicious on the grill, too. The marinade ensures the chicken stays nice and juicy. Use a meat thermometer to ensure your chicken is cooked through; the internal temperature you are looking for is about 165°F. And we strongly recommend that you wear gloves whenever handling chiles. Just use the disposable, nonpowdered plastic variety you can find in stores. Oh, and don't rub your eye after . . . or touch anything else! Trust us.

MARINADE AND CHICKEN

- 2 Scotch bonnet or habanero chiles, seeded
- 3 garlic cloves
- 1½ teaspoons minced fresh ginger or ginger purée (from a jar)
- 1 cup roughly chopped yellow onion
- 2 teaspoons pumpkin pie spice blend (blend of ground cinnamon, ginger, nutmeg, and allspice)
- 1 teaspoon ground allspice
- 1 tablespoon fresh thyme leaves
  Pinch of salt
- ¼ cup apple cider vinegar
- 1 (8-ounce) can crushed pineapple, slightly drained of juice
- 2 tablespoons loosely packed light brown sugar
- ¼ cup gluten-free soy sauce or gluten-free tamari

3   tablespoons vegetable or sunflower oil

2   pounds chicken thighs (we used boneless and skinless)

1½   cups basmati rice

1   (14-ounce) can coconut milk

1½   cups vegetable stock (preferably low-sodium)

½   teaspoon ground allspice

    Pinch of salt

1   (14-ounce) can red kidney beans, drained and rinsed

⅓   cup finely chopped green onions (white and green parts), plus
    more for garnish

1. Put all of the marinade ingredients (everything but the chicken) into a blender and blend until nice and smooth.

2. Pour three quarters of the marinade into a large bowl and add the chicken thighs. (If using skin-on thighs, score each piece two to three times with a sharp knife before marinating.) Cover the bowl with plastic wrap and marinate in the fridge for at least 1 hour but no more than 24 hours. Reserve the remaining marinade mixture for an extra bit of sauce to serve.

3. After the marinating time, preheat the oven to 350°F. Alternatively, you can prepare a grill and cook the chicken that way.

4. Using a slotted spoon, transfer the chicken thighs into an oven-safe baking dish. Discard the remaining marinade. Bake for 35 to 45 minutes, depending on the cut and thickness of your chicken, until cooked through. You want an internal temperature of 165°F.

5. While the chicken is baking, prepare the rice and peas. In a medium saucepan, combine the rice, coconut milk, stock, allspice, and salt, stirring well.

6. Over medium-high heat, bring to a boil. Once boiling, turn the heat down to low, cover, and simmer for about 20 minutes, or until the rice is cooked through but not mushy.

7. Add the kidney beans and green onions to the pan and stir well until all is well mixed. Turn off the heat and keep warm.

8. Once the chicken is done, scoop a generous spoonful of the rice and peas onto a plate. Top with one or two chicken thighs and finish with a spoonful of the reserved sauce over top. Garnish with a bit more green onion, if desired.

MS. JACKIE'S THAI GREEN CHICKEN CURRY WITH JASMINE AND KAFFIR LIME RICE

Q+E DF **MAKES 4 SERVINGS**

A STEAMING HOT BOWL OF SPICY, COCONUTY THAI CURRY ON A cold day is one of life's simple pleasures . . . especially if you've got a sore throat. There is something so soothing about these combinations of flavors. This is another dish that Jilly learned to make from her mum-in-law, Ms. Jackie, and it's proven to be one of Jilly's favorites. She usually adds some boiled potatoes to the curry to make it an even more filling meal. Feel free to try shrimp or tofu as the protein if you'd prefer, or even lobster for a decadent twist. This is a quick and easy recipe and will take 30 minutes or less to make.

- 1½ tablespoons vegetable oil
- 10 mini pearl onions, ends trimmed, peeled, and left whole (see note)
- 1 pound boneless, skinless chicken breast tenders, diced into bite-size chunks
- ½ teaspoon minced fresh ginger or ginger purée (from a jar)
- 2 ounces Thai green curry paste (we like Thai Kitchen brand; see note)
- 1 (14-ounce) can coconut milk (light if preferred)
- ¾ cup vegetable or chicken stock
- 1 tablespoon loosely packed light brown sugar
- 1 red bell pepper, julienned
- 1½ tablespoons roughly chopped fresh cilantro
- ¼ cup finely sliced green onions (white and green parts)
- 1 recipe Jasmine and Kaffir Lime Rice (recipe follows), for serving
- 2 tablespoons roughly chopped fresh basil, for garnish (optional)

1. In a large sauté pan or skillet with high sides, heat the oil over medium heat and fry the onions until slightly softened, about 5 minutes. Be careful of the oil splattering and, if desired, use a splatter shield.

2. Using a slotted spoon, carefully remove the onions and transfer to a bowl. Set aside.

3. Add the chicken and ginger to the pan and cook until the chicken is browned on all sides and the meat is almost cooked through, about 5 to 6 minutes, depending on size, stirring often.

4. Add the curry paste, coconut milk, stock, and brown sugar to the pan and mix well.

5. Add the onions back into the pan, turn the heat down to medium low, and cook for 5 to 6 minutes, stirring occasionally.

6. Add the sliced bell peppers, cilantro, and green onions to the pan, turn the heat down to low, and gently simmer for 8 to 10 minutes, stirring often. You don't want it to boil, just simmer.

7. Check to ensure the meat and the pearl onions are cooked through. Once they are, turn off the heat and serve immediately with the rice and garnish with chopped basil, if desired.

NOTE: The mini pearl onions are quite small and almost resemble cloves of garlic. If you can't find them, you can substitute small shallots— you may just need to halve them in size. You should be able to find a jar of Thai green curry paste in the international section of most local grocery stores. If you can only find Thai red curry paste, it will work just as deliciously well. And if you're brave enough to handle the heat, feel free to use the whole jar of curry paste (we warn you though!).

JASMINE AND KAFFIR LIME RICE

MAKES 4 SERVINGS

FRAGRANT JASMINE AND KAFFIR LIME-INFUSED RICE MAKES the perfect partner to our Thai green chicken curry. What's better to soak up all the delicious spicy, coconuty broth? Kaffir lime leaves are a staple ingredient and spice in Thai cuisine that add a wonderful fragrant, citrusy depth to curries, soups, fish cakes, and stir-fries. Of course, if you can't find these little flavoring gems, you can simply make the jasmine rice on its own. Although we provide some specific measurements for cooking the rice below, we suggest following the instructions on your rice package since there are some variations depending on brands and types of rice.

1½   cups jasmine rice, rinsed under cool water
2¼   cups cold water
      Few kaffir lime leaves, dried or fresh (if in a jar, you need a very small forkful; see note)

||||||||||||||||||||||||||||||||||||||||||||||||||||||||||||||||||||||||||||||||||||||||||

NOTE: You'll find kaffir lime leaves either in dry- or fresh-leaf form, or preserved in saltwater in a jar. Look in the international section of your regular grocery store or in your favorite spice market or specialty Asian grocer. It adds such a unique citrus taste to lots of dishes and, since a little goes a long way, your one jar will last you ages!

1. Combine the rice, cold water, and kaffir lime leaves in a medium saucepan and bring to a gentle boil over medium-high heat.

2. Once gently boiling, turn the heat down to low and cover. Simmer until the water is well absorbed, about 18 to 20 minutes. Avoid the urge to keep uncovering or fiddling with the rice. You want the lid to remain on in order to build up moisture and steam the rice. This can take only 15 minutes depending on the brand of rice and your stove, so after 15 minutes, check to see if the rice is already fully cooked.

3. After the 18 to 20 minutes, turn off the heat and LEAVE COVERED for 10 minutes.

4. Uncover and fluff the rice with a fork. Serve immediately.

EMERIL'S PORK MEDALLIONS WITH CABBAGE AND APPLES

IT IS HARD TO DENY THAT PORK AND APPLES PAIR VERY WELL together. Although we include another pork and apple dish here in this book, the Baked Pork Chops with Apple Rosemary Chutney (page 207), we think this one is different enough to also merit inclusion! This wonderful main course makes use of two unexpected pork-pairing ingredients: heavy cream and hard apple cider. The cider enhances the apple flavor of the dish terrifically, while the cream gently mellows the whole thing out.

2	(1-pound) pork tenderloins
2	cups hard apple cider (such as Crispin), divided
1	stick cinnamon
3	whole cloves
¼	cup Creole mustard or other whole grain mustard
3	teaspoons salt, divided
1	teaspoon freshly ground black pepper, divided
3	tablespoons olive oil
3	tablespoons unsalted butter
¼	cup finely chopped shallots
1	teaspoon fresh thyme leaves
4	quarts thinly sliced green cabbage
2	apples (preferably Honeycrisp or Pink Lady), peeled, cored, and cut into ⅓-inch-thick slices
1	cup heavy whipping cream

½ cup apple juice
2 tablespoons freshly squeezed lemon juice

1. Place the pork tenderloins in a large resealable plastic bag with 1 cup of the hard apple cider, the cinnamon stick, and the cloves and allow to marinate at room temperature for at least 1 hour and up to 3 hours.

2. Transfer the tenderloins to a platter or a cutting board and pat dry. Using a spatula, spread the mustard all over the tenderloins. Season each tenderloin with ½ teaspoon salt and ¼ teaspoon black pepper. Cut the tenderloins crosswise into 2-inch-thick medallions.

3. Heat a large, nonstick sauté pan over medium-high heat and add the olive oil. Working in batches, sear the medallions for 2 minutes and then turn and sear for 2 minutes longer on the second side.

4. Transfer the pork to a clean platter or baking sheet and set aside, loosely tented with aluminum foil.

5. Heat a large Dutch oven over medium heat. When hot, add the butter and shallots and cook, stirring, until the shallots are translucent, about 2 to 3 minutes. Add the thyme and cabbage and cook, covered, for 10 to 12 minutes, stirring occasionally.

6. Add the remaining 1 cup of hard cider and cook until it is almost completely reduced, for about 4 minutes.

7. Add the apples, cream, and apple juice and continue to cook until the cream has slightly thickened, usually for 5 to 6 minutes.

8. Season with the lemon juice and the remaining 2 teaspoons salt and remaining ½ teaspoon pepper.

9. Transfer the pork and any juices to the pan, nestling it in the cabbage. Cook for several minutes longer, just until the pork is completely warmed through. Serve.

Moroccan Lamb Tagine

MAKES 4 SERVINGS

NOT ONLY IS THIS ONE-POT DISH BURSTING WITH WARM, comforting, aromatic spice, it's wonderfully easy to throw together and perfect for a chilly midweek night. Like many Moroccan dishes, this recipe uses a blend of meat and fruit along with the trusty ras el hanout seasoning to create a delicious dance of spicy sweetness on your palate. The aroma that this dish emits as you are cooking will bring neighbors you didn't even know you had knocking on your door! While lamb is really suited to this recipe, you could substitute chicken if you prefer. Also, though we call for dried apricots, you still want them to be a bit moist and juicy, not parched and withered. We really hope you give this dish a go and enjoy something deliciously new on this tasty gluten-free journey we are on.

1	pound lean lamb, deboned and cut into bite-size pieces
2	tablespoons plus ½ teaspoon ras el hanout seasoning, divided
2	tablespoons olive oil
1	cup chopped yellow onion
1½	cups diced carrot (halve lengthwise before dicing into bite-size chunks)
1½	teaspoons minced garlic (about 2 cloves)
⅛	teaspoon ground cinnamon
	Salt and freshly ground black pepper
1	(14.5-ounce) can diced tomatoes (preferably low-sodium)
1	(15-ounce) can chickpeas, drained and rinsed
1	cup dried apricots, halved
2½	cups vegetable stock

244 BIG FLAVOR, BOLD TASTE—AND NO GLUTEN!

2 tablespoons roughly chopped fresh cilantro
2 tablespoons roughly chopped fresh mint
Cooked quinoa or rice, for serving (optional)

1. If using a Dutch oven, preheat the oven to 350°F. If cooking on the stove top, proceed without preheating. Either way is fine and will end in the same delicious result, so the choice is yours.

2. Season the lamb pieces with ½ teaspoon ras el hanout, making sure all sides of the lamb are equally seasoned.

3. Either in a heavy enamel Dutch oven or a 6-quart stockpot, heat the olive oil over medium heat and add the seasoned lamb to the pot. Brown all sides of the lamb, about 4 to 5 minutes, then scoop out with a slotted spoon and place into a medium bowl.

4. Add the onions, carrots, and garlic to the pan and cook for 5 minutes to soften the vegetables.

5. Add the remaining 2 tablespoons of the ras el hanout, the cinnamon, salt and pepper to taste, and the tomatoes, chickpeas, and apricots. Stir well.

6. Add the lamb back into the pan along with the stock. Stir and turn the heat up to medium high until the mixture reaches a gentle bubble. If cooking the dish

NOTE: Ras el hanout is a seasoning that can contain a mix of up to thirty different spices. Each blend or maker has their own recipe, but most commonly it contains a blend of cinnamon, anise, cardamom, ginger, turmeric, coriander, black pepper, cayenne pepper, allspice, and cloves. You should be able to find this magical, aromatic mix in your local grocery store's spice aisle. If not, check out your nearest international market or go online (check out our Resources section on page 333). Trust us, you'll be glad you did.

on the stove top, turn the heat back down to low and simmer for 1 hour, covered. If cooking in the oven, put the lid on your Dutch oven, place in the preheated oven, and cook for 1 hour.

7. If, after the hour, your lamb isn't tender, cook for another 10 to 20 minutes, covered, until sufficiently tender.

8. Taste and re-season with more salt and pepper, if desired. Sprinkle the chopped cilantro and mint into the pot, stir well, and serve warm with either cooked quinoa or rice, if desired.

EMERIL'S LAMB T-BONES WITH BALSAMIC ONIONS, BABY KALE, AND FINGERLING POTATOES

MAKES 4 SERVINGS

IF YOU ARE A LAMB LOVER LIKE WE ARE, YOU ARE GOING TO freak for this! Everything about this dish screams warmth and earthy comfort. The lamb is marinated in a slathering of herbs, warming red wine, garlic, and tangy Worcestershire sauce and then cooked to a medium-rare perfection. This dish is bursting with earthiness from the warm potatoes and perfectly seasoned kale. To bring this meal into the tasty stratosphere, we serve it with sweet and tangy balsamic onions. We recommend making the balsamic onions first to simplify things a bit, and you can always marinate the lamb in advance as well.

8	(4-ounce) lamb T-bones
1½	cups red wine (something full bodied, like a Merlot or Cabernet)
1	tablespoon gluten-free Worcestershire sauce
2	garlic cloves, smashed
4	sprigs fresh rosemary
2	sprigs fresh thyme
2	pounds fingerling potatoes, scrubbed well and cut into ½-inch-thick rounds
4	tablespoons olive oil, divided
3	teaspoons salt, divided
1	teaspoon freshly ground black pepper, divided
2	tablespoons unsalted butter
10	ounces baby kale
1	recipe Balsamic Onions (recipe follows)

1. Preheat the oven to 400°F.

2. Place the lamb in a gallon-size resealable plastic bag.

3. Add the wine, Worcestershire, garlic, sprigs of rosemary, and thyme and marinate at room temperature for at least 1 hour.

4. In a medium mixing bowl, toss the potatoes with 2 tablespoons of the oil, 1 teaspoon of the salt, and ¼ teaspoon of the pepper.

5. Transfer the potatoes to a baking sheet and roast in the oven until golden brown, for about 20 minutes.

6. Transfer the lamb from the marinade to a platter and season with 1 teaspoon of the salt and ½ teaspoon of the pepper.

7. Heat a large sauté pan over medium-high heat and add the remaining 2 tablespoons of the oil. When hot, sear the lamb for 2 minutes per side. If necessary, cook the lamb in two batches.

8. Transfer the lamb to a baking sheet and place in the 400°F oven for 3 to 4 minutes for medium-rare.

9. Remove the lamb from the oven and set aside to rest for at least 5 minutes before serving.

10. Meanwhile, in a large sauté pan over medium heat, melt the butter. When hot, add the kale in batches, stirring as it begins to wilt. Continue to stir and add more kale.

11. Once the kale has completely wilted, add the remaining 1 teaspoon salt and ¼ teaspoon pepper and cook for 2 minutes longer.

12. Serve the lamb with the kale, potatoes, and onions.

BALSAMIC ONIONS

MAKES 2 CUPS

- 2 tablespoons olive oil
- 6 cups thinly sliced red onion (about 4 small onions)
- 2 teaspoons loosely packed light brown sugar
- 1 teaspoon kosher salt
- ½ teaspoon freshly ground black pepper
- ½ cup balsamic vinegar
- ½ cup port
- 3 tablespoons cold unsalted butter, diced into small cubes

1. In a large sauté pan with high sides, heat the oil over medium heat. When hot, add the onions, sugar, salt, and pepper.

2. Cook the onions, stirring occasionally, until they are very soft and tender, for about 20 minutes.

3. Add the balsamic vinegar and port, reduce the heat to medium low, and cook for 40 minutes longer, or until the onions are coated with the balsamic glaze.

4. Just before serving but while the onions are still warm, stir in the butter. Serve warm or at room temperature.

SEARED SALMON WITH WARM LENTIL, TOMATO, AND MINT SALAD

 **MAKES 4 SERVINGS**

YEARS AGO, OUR DAD USED TO MAKE A SALMON AND LENTIL Sunday dinner that we both enjoyed every time he served it. This version has been adapted over the years and is now much more herby than his original. But it is still just as delicious and healthy! Be sure to slightly undercook your lentils so they don't get mushy when mixed with the herbs and tomatoes. They should be tender but slightly al dente. Also, please remember to look for salmon fillets that are close to the same thickness. This will ensure that everyone gets a hot plate at the same time. This is a quick and easy recipe but will take about 45 minutes to make instead of the usual Q&E time of 30 minutes or less.

1	cup lentils of your choice, rinsed (Jilly likes to use black, Jess uses green)
	Chicken or vegetable stock, for cooking lentils (quantity varies depending on lentil variety)
3	tablespoons extra-virgin olive oil, divided
¼	cup diced yellow onion
1	cup grape tomatoes, quartered (if large enough) or just halved if small
¼	cup chopped fresh parsley
¼	cup chopped fresh mint
	Salt and freshly ground black pepper
2	tablespoons freshly squeezed lemon juice
4	(6-ounce) salmon fillets, skin on
½	lemon

1. In a small saucepan over medium-high heat, bring the lentils and the necessary amount of stock to a boil. (Use the lentil package instructions to determine the proper proportion of stock to lentils.) Cook the lentils until they are tender but al dente. The timing can vary greatly depending on the variety of lentil you choose, so keep a close eye on them. You don't want them mushy, and they should keep their shape. Once cooked, remove from the heat and set aside.

2. Once the lentils are cooked, heat 2 tablespoons of the olive oil in a large skillet over medium-high heat. Add the onion and sauté until they are translucent, about 3 to 4 minutes. Add the lentils, tomatoes, parsley, mint, and salt and pepper to taste and stir gently to evenly incorporate. Let the mixture cook for 2 to 3 minutes, stirring often so that it doesn't burn.

3. Remove from the heat and stir in the lemon juice. Set aside.

4. Now it is time to sear your salmon. First, season your fillets with salt and pepper as desired.

5. Over high heat, heat the remaining 1 tablespoon of olive oil in a large, nonstick skillet. Once the oil is hot, place the salmon fillets skin-side down in the pan. Reduce the heat to medium low and cook until the salmon looks to be about three quarters of the way cooked through, about 5 to 8 minutes. The timing of this depends on the thickness of your fillets, so focus more on the color of the fish than the time on the clock. You will see the flesh change from pink to a whitish-pink color as it cooks. Try not to mess with the fillets during this time. Just let them cook away.

6. Right before you anticipate your fish to be done, spoon a generous portion of lentils onto each of four plates. Top each serving of lentils with a portion of the salmon. (First remove the skin of the fish and discard, if desired.) Squeeze a few drops of lemon juice from the lemon half on top of the salmon and serve immediately.

CRISPY PARMESAN-CRUSTED GROUPER

Q+E   MAKES 4 TO 6 SERVINGS

JESSIE'S HUSBAND, STEVEN, LOVES TO FISH—DEEP SEA, POND, stream, or side-of-the-road puddle. If there's a body of water, he'll try to fish in it! When he does catch something—and it's legitimately edible—Jessie loves trying to cook up the fresh bounty in different ways. This recipe is one of her experiments that has become a family staple. The crispy panko-style bread-crumbs give this fish a great crunch that her kids love, and the subtle season-ing is present but not overpowering. It is versatile, too, because you can use any firm, white-fleshed fish in place of the grouper (we like it with cod and pollock especially). As with most of our recipes, feel free to adjust the seasoning to your preference if you happen to like it spicier or milder than we do! This is a quick and easy recipe and will take 30 minutes or less to make.

    2   large eggs
    1½ cups gluten-free breadcrumbs, preferably panko-style
        (we like Ian's)
    1   tablespoon chopped fresh parsley
    1   teaspoon garlic powder
    1   teaspoon freshly ground black pepper
        Salt
    ½   cup grated Parmesan cheese
    1½ pounds grouper or other mild-flavored, firm white-fleshed fish
        (pollock, haddock, cod, etc.), divided into 4- to 6-ounce pieces
        depending on number of servings being made
    1   large lemon, halved

1. Preheat the oven to 425°F. Grease a large baking sheet with nonstick cooking spray.

2. In a large, shallow bowl, beat the 2 eggs to break them up. In a second large, shallow bowl, mix together the breadcrumbs, parsley, garlic powder, pepper, salt to taste, and Parmesan cheese until evenly incorporated.

3. Dip a piece of the fish first in the bowl of eggs, making sure to coat the fish completely. Then, dip the egg-coated fish into the breadcrumb mixture, turning the fish as necessary to ensure an even coating.

4. Place the fish on the baking sheet and repeat step 3 until all the fish is breaded. Before baking, squeeze half of the lemon over the fish pieces.

5. Bake for 20 to 25 minutes, or until the fish is cooked through but not dried out.

6. Squeeze the remaining lemon half over the cooked fish and serve with your favorite accompaniments.

Easy Seafood Paella, page 256

EASY SEAFOOD PAELLA

THIS IS OUR FAVORITE VERSION OF THE ICONIC SPANISH paella, brimming with fresh seafood and that traditional paella flavor combination of saffron and smoked paprika. The nice thing about this dish is that it is versatile and can be tweaked to your preference. You can use different seafood combinations, going with whatever is fresh or whatever you like most. Swap clams for mussels, throw in some firm white-fleshed fish, use sea scallops instead of bay scallops . . . the possibilities are almost endless. Just remember, in order to get that signature crispy, crusty bottom layer, you have to keep yourself from stirring the dish once the rice has come to a boil (it's harder to resist than you might think). Don't worry, it shouldn't burn!

6	cups clam or seafood stock
1	teaspoon saffron threads
2	tablespoons extra-virgin olive oil
1	cup diced yellow onion
½	cup chopped green onions (white and green parts)
1½	cups diced red bell pepper
1	(14.5-ounce) can diced tomatoes
3	tablespoons chopped fresh parsley
2	teaspoons minced garlic
1	tablespoon minced fresh thyme leaves
2½	teaspoons smoked paprika
2	cups bomba paella rice
	Salt

12 large shrimp, in shells with heads removed
 1 dozen clams or mussels, cleaned well
½ pound small bay scallops
    Finely chopped fresh parsley, for garnish (optional)

1. In a large stockpot over medium heat, heat the clam stock. Stir in the saffron and bring the liquid to a boil. Once the stock begins boiling, remove it from the heat and let the saffron infuse into the stock.

2. In a 15-inch paella pan or 15-inch sauté pan, heat the olive oil over medium heat. Sauté the yellow onion, green onion, and red bell pepper until they are slightly softened, about 6 to 8 minutes. Add the tomatoes and cook it all together until the tomato breaks down and becomes almost sauce-like, about 3 to 5 minutes.

3. Stir in the parsley, garlic, thyme, and paprika and cook briefly, about 30 seconds to 1 minute, being sure to mix well so everything is incorporated.

4. Now add the reserved hot broth and bring the mixture to a boil.

5. Once the mixture is boiling, add the rice by sprinkling it evenly into the pan. Bring the mixture back up to a boil and let it remain at a boil for 2 to 3 minutes.

6. At this point, add salt to taste and re-season as necessary because you will not stir the mixture again until it is served.

7. Once the seasoning is to your liking, reduce the heat to low and simmer until the rice starts to thicken and has absorbed some of the liquid, for about 10 minutes.

8. Now, arrange your shrimp, clams or mussels, and scallops over the rice, being sure to place the edges of the clams or mussels facing up. Continue cooking, uncovered, for another 15 to 20 minutes, or until the rice is al dente but cooked through.

9. Remove the pan from the heat and cover the whole thing with foil. You want to try to keep the steam inside the pouch, so secure it tightly. Let it sit for 10 to 15 more minutes under the foil. Remove the foil and discard any clams or mussels that didn't open during cooking. Sprinkle with some finely chopped parsley, if desired, and serve.

BEEF STEWPOT WITH THYME BISCUIT CRUST

 MAKES 4 TO 6 SERVINGS

NOW THIS IS FOOD THAT CAN HAPPILY FILL UP ANY FAMILY, even those "Ohhh is this gluten-free again?!" partakers you may have to please. What's not to love about a warm, hearty meat-and-gravy filling deliciously topped off with hot, fresh thyme-infused crusty biscuits?! The great thing, too, is you can put your own twist on this. Perhaps try using ground turkey, lamb, or buffalo instead of the beef. If dairy isn't an issue, try using our divine Savory Cheddar Scones (page 62) instead of the thyme biscuits here. Also, if you do not have a dairy issue, the biscuits will work deliciously well using unsalted butter and regular whole milk. If you don't have cooking sherry, you can use water to dissolve the cornstarch, but the sherry really adds a nice depth to the dish. No matter how you make it, we challenge you to try this and not go back for more!

STEWPOT

- 2 tablespoons olive oil
- 1 cup chopped yellow onion
- 1 cup chopped carrot
- 1 cup chopped celery
- ½ teaspoon minced garlic
- 1 pound lean or extra-lean ground beef (or ground turkey, buffalo, etc.)
- 1 tablespoon fresh thyme leaves (preferably lemon thyme)
- 1 tablespoon chopped fresh parsley
- 1 (15-ounce) can tomato sauce (preferably low-sodium)

⅔ cup beef or vegetable stock

1 tablespoon cornstarch dissolved in 3 tablespoons cooking sherry

   Pinch of cayenne pepper

   Salt and freshly ground black pepper

1½ cups gluten-free flour blend (we like Arrowhead Mills Gluten Free All Purpose Baking Mix)

1 teaspoon baking powder

½ teaspoon salt

¼ cup coconut oil (or cold unsalted butter, cubed)

1½ teaspoons fresh thyme leaves

½ cup cold dairy-free whole milk (or regular whole milk), plus more for brushing

1 medium egg, lightly beaten

1. First, make the stewpot. In a large sauté pan with high sides, heat the oil over medium heat.

2. Add the onion, carrot, celery, and garlic to the pan and sweat the vegetables until slightly softened, about 5 to 6 minutes.

3. Add the ground beef and, as it's browning, break it up into crumbles with a wooden spoon. Cook until the meat is brown and cooked through, about 5 to 6 minutes.

4. Add the thyme, parsley, tomato sauce, stock, cornstarch/sherry mixture, and cayenne to the pan and season with a bit of salt and pepper. Stir well. Turn the heat down to low and simmer uncovered for 10 to 15 minutes. Turn off the heat and set aside.

5. Preheat the oven to 400°F.

6. Now make the biscuit crust. Sift the flour, baking powder, and salt into a medium bowl.

7. Add the coconut oil to the bowl and, with your hands, blend the fat into the flour mix until it resembles fine breadcrumbs.

8. Add the thyme, milk, and egg to the bowl and mix well. The dough will be thick and a bit lumpy, almost resembling oatmeal.

9. Pour the beef mixture into a 13 x 9-inch ovenproof dish, like a Pyrex or a similar-sized casserole dish.

10. Using a ¼-cup measuring cup, scoop ¼ cup of the biscuit dough and use your hands to slightly flatten it out, almost like you're making a hamburger patty. Place on top of the beef mixture. Repeat until you have eight ¼-cup biscuits on the top, forming the crust. They should all fit edge to edge and mostly, if not entirely, cover the top of the meat mixture. Depending on your casserole dish, you may only fit six or seven biscuits on top.

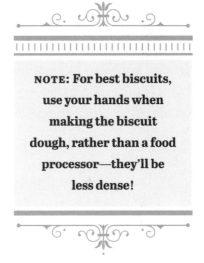

NOTE: For best biscuits, use your hands when making the biscuit dough, rather than a food processor—they'll be less dense!

11. With a pastry brush, brush a bit more milk on top of each biscuit and then bake for 20 to 25 minutes. The biscuits should be golden brown, and the sides of the filling should bubble slightly.

12. Serve immediately, scooped into bowls, making sure each person gets a good bit of the biscuit topping.

SHEPHERD'S PIE WITH PARSNIP MASH

THIS IS PURE ENGLISH COMFORT FOOD AT ITS FINEST . . .
meat, gravy, and, of course, potatoes—plus extra veggies for a healthy kick! We
added one of Jilly's favorites, parsnips, to give the mash a little something extra.
Parsnips are in the carrot family but have a sweet, almost anise-like flavor and
are packed with potassium and fiber. So, really, you are doing your body good by
eating that second helping! Traditionally, a shepherd's pie would be made with
ground lamb like we've done here, but you can use ground beef. To elevate this
humble pie even further, try sprinkling some of your favorite shredded cheese
on top of the green onions.

FILLING

1	tablespoon olive oil
½	teaspoon minced garlic
1⅓	cups chopped yellow onion
1	pound ground lamb (preferably lean)
¾	cup finely diced carrot
	Salt and freshly ground black pepper
	Generous pinch of ground cinnamon
1	tablespoon fresh thyme leaves (preferably lemon thyme)
2	tablespoons chopped fresh parsley
1	cup frozen peas
1⅓	cups vegetable or beef stock (preferably low-sodium)
2	tablespoons gluten-free flour blend (we like Arrowhead Mills Gluten Free All Purpose Baking Mix)
2	tablespoons tomato paste

1½ pounds baking potatoes (we like russet), peeled and cut into equal-
      size chunks
1½ pounds parsnips, peeled and cut into equal-size chunks
¼   cup (½ stick) salted butter, plus more for the pan
      Salt and freshly ground black pepper

1   cup sliced green onions (white and green parts)
¼   cup sharp Cheddar cheese (optional)

1. Grease a 13 x 9-inch baking dish well with nonstick cooking spray or butter and set aside.

2. First, make the filling. In a very large sauté or frying pan over medium heat, heat the olive oil. Add the garlic and onion and cook until slightly softened, stirring occasionally, about 6 to 7 minutes.

3. Add the ground lamb to the pan and brown for about 7 to 8 minutes, or until all the meat is cooked through. Use a wooden spoon to help break the meat up into crumbles as it browns.

4. Once the meat is fully cooked, add the carrots, a bit of salt and pepper, the cinnamon, and the fresh herbs and cook until the carrots start to soften, about 3 to 4 minutes.

5. Add the frozen peas to the pan and stir well.

6. In a measuring cup, add the stock, flour, tomato paste, and a bit of black pepper. Whisk well until the flour dissolves and add this mixture to the pan.

7. Stir well, raise the heat to medium high, and let gently bubble for 1 to 2 minutes to allow the sauce to thicken.

8. Once thickened, turn the heat down to low and simmer for 5 minutes, stirring often. Taste and re-season with a bit more salt and pepper, if desired. Turn off the heat and set aside.

9. Preheat the oven to 400°F and position an oven rack in the middle.

10. Now make the mash. Place the potato and parsnip chunks into a pot and fill with enough cold water to cover the pieces. Bring to a boil over high heat. Cook until fork-tender and cooked through, about 16 to 18 minutes, depending on size.

11. Once cooked, turn off the heat, drain, and return the vegetables to the pot. Add the butter. With either a masher or an electric mixer, mash well until as few lumps remain as possible.

12. Season with salt and pepper to taste and stir well.

13. Now for the assembly. Spoon the meat mixture into the prepared baking dish and level out with the back of a spoon.

14. Using a clean spoon, scoop the mash over the top of the meat mixture and gently spread it evenly over the meat.

15. Drag the back of a fork over the top of the mash to form little peaks or criss-crosses and then scatter the sliced green onions on top. If using shredded cheese, sprinkle it over the green onions.

16. Bake on the middle rack for 35 to 40 minutes, or until the top is golden and the sides are slightly bubbly. Allow to cool for a few minutes before serving warm.

NOTE: Jilly learned from her English mum-in-law that you should always begin to cook root vegetables in cold water—never drop them into already boiling water. This will keep the vegetables from getting mealy in texture, and it helps them cook through evenly. Also, when making the mash, avoid the urge to add any liquid. You want it to be pretty thick and solid so it doesn't get too moist when added atop the filling.

Steven's Crawfish Pie, page 266

STEVEN'S CRAWFISH PIE

JESSIE'S HUSBAND, STEVEN, LOVES TO COOK. HE CAN AND WILL spend all day creating all kinds of wonderful foods. One of Steven's favorites, crawfish bread, takes forever to make, so Jessie tried to capture most of its flavors in an easy-to-make pie instead. The key here is to blind bake your crust first; you don't want a soggy bottom underneath all this fantastic seafood deliciousness. There are two ways to try this one: the first is to make one large 9-inch pie. The second, as you see here, is to divide the crust and filling between two smaller baking dishes. Either way tastes the same and cooks pretty much the same, so it is purely up to you to decide how to try it. If you want to add a top crust to contain all this yumminess, please feel free to do so. Just make two recipes of the Basic Pie Crust and roll out the second one for a top. Bonus: If you happen to have some filling left over, it is delicious served over rice!

1	recipe Basic Pie Crust (page 70)
¼	cup (½ stick) unsalted butter
6	tablespoons gluten-free flour blend (we like Arrowhead Mills Gluten Free All Purpose Baking Mix)
¾	cup chopped yellow onion
¾	cup chopped red bell pepper (or any color you prefer)
½	cup chopped celery
1	tablespoon minced garlic
2	cups fish stock
1	pound crawfish tail meat (usually widely available frozen but not fresh)
½	cup canned diced tomatoes (preferably petite diced)
½	teaspoon salt, or more to taste

½ teaspoon cayenne pepper

Freshly ground black pepper

1. Follow the directions on page 70 to prepare and then blind bake one recipe of the Basic Pie Crust. This will be your pie shell. If you are preparing two separate pies, as shown in the photos, simply divide the pie crust dough roughly in half and follow the same instructions for preparing and blind baking the single pie. Your blind-bake time might be slightly shorter with two pies, but it really depends on your oven. Just keep an eye on it and be ready to remove the crusts a few minutes sooner if making two crusts.

2. Once the crust is blind baked and cooled, prepare the filling. Melt the butter in a large stockpot over medium heat. Add the flour to make a roux and let it cook for 3 to 4 minutes, stirring frequently to keep it from burning.

3. Add the onion, bell pepper, and celery and sauté in the roux until the vegetables are tender, about 8 to 10 minutes. Stir it often so that the roux and veggies don't burn and stick to the pan bottom.

4. Add the garlic and cook briefly, about 30 seconds to 1 minute, or until fragrant.

5. Stir in the fish stock, making sure the roux dissolves completely in the stock. As the mixture heats up, it will thicken.

6. Once the mixture has thickened, stir in the crawfish tail meat, tomatoes, salt, cayenne, and pepper to taste. Let cook for 4 to 5 minutes. Then remove from the heat and let cool for 25 to 30 minutes.

7. While the filling cools, preheat the oven to 400°F.

8. Once the filling has cooled slightly, transfer it into your blind-baked crust(s). Place the pie or pies on a baking sheet in case of any bubble-overs and bake for 30 to 40 minutes, or until the crust has browned. Again, cook time may vary slightly if cooking two smaller crusts instead of one, but it shouldn't change by more than 5 minutes or so. The color and crispness of the crust is what you're looking for, so please don't just go by time alone.

9. Remove from the oven and let cool for 5 to 10 minutes before serving.

DIJON CHICKEN, LEEK, AND MUSHROOM POT PIE

MAKES 4 SERVINGS

THIS CHICKEN, LEEK, AND MUSHROOM POT PIE IS A THING OF beauty. As with any pot pie, this is truly a comfort dish, just snazzied up with that ole Lagasse Girls touch. We have elevated this pot pie with tangy Dijon mustard, the warm anise-like taste of fresh tarragon, and earthy leeks and mushrooms, all cooked in a creamy and fragrant sauce. This recipe can take some time, so if time is an issue, feel free to use a store-bought premade gluten-free pie crust dough and work the whole grain mustard into it. The short cut's only in the timing—the end result will still be absolutely delicious.

CRUST

- 1 cup gluten-free flour blend (we like Arrowhead Mills Gluten Free All Purpose Baking Mix)
- 6 tablespoons cold, salted butter, diced into small cubes
- 1½ teaspoons whole grain mustard
- 2 tablespoons cold water
- 2 tablespoons milk (any %), for brushing

FILLING

- 1 pound boneless, skinless chicken thighs or breasts, diced into bite-size chunks
- 1½ teaspoons Emeril's Original Essence seasoning or Cajun seasoning of your choice
- 2 tablespoons olive oil
- 1 teaspoon minced garlic

1½ cups thinly sliced leeks (discard green leaves and clean leeks before slicing)

1½ cups thinly sliced baby bella mushrooms

2 tablespoons roughly chopped fresh tarragon leaves

Pinch of ground or freshly grated nutmeg

Pinch of cayenne pepper

Salt and freshly ground black pepper

2 tablespoons Dijon mustard

1 tablespoon cornstarch dissolved in 3 tablespoons cooking sherry

⅔ cup crème fraîche

1. First, make the crust. In a medium bowl, mix the flour and butter together, either with your hands or a pastry cutter, until you have a breadcrumb consistency. Alternatively, you can use a food processor.

2. In a small bowl, combine the mustard and cold water and mix together. Add this to the flour and, with a fork, mix well until a dough ball forms. Wrap the dough ball in a bit of plastic wrap and refrigerate for 30 minutes.

3. In the meantime, make the filling. In a small bowl, combine the chicken and Essence together and stir to ensure all pieces are well coated. Set aside.

4. In a large sauté pan with high sides, heat the oil over medium heat.

5. Add the garlic, leeks, and mushrooms to the pan and cook down until the mushrooms are wilted and softened, about 4 to 6 minutes.

6. Add the chicken, tarragon, nutmeg, and cayenne, along with a bit of salt and pepper, and cook until the chicken is cooked through, for about 6 minutes, stirring frequently.

7. Turn the heat down to low and add the mustard and cornstarch mixture; stir well. Cook for 2 minutes and then turn off the heat.

8. Stir in the crème fraîche. Taste and re-season with a bit more salt and pepper, if desired.

9. Preheat the oven to 400°F.

10. Spoon the warm chicken mixture into a 3-cup round Pyrex baking dish, Dutch oven, or oven-safe enamel dish and set aside.

11. Take the dough ball out of the fridge. Lay a large piece of plastic wrap on a cutting board or countertop. Unwrap the dough and place it on the plastic wrap. Place another large piece of plastic wrap over the top. Use a rolling pin to roll the dough out just slightly larger than whatever dish you are using.

12. Remove the top piece of the plastic wrap and carefully flip the dough on top of the baking dish. Peel off the other piece of plastic wrap and press the dough down into the dish so there isn't much overhang. Alternatively, using a pizza cutter, you can cut the dough into long strips and then lay the pieces in a crisscross fashion over the top of the pie.

13. Using a pastry brush, brush the milk on top of the crust and, using a nice, sharp knife, slice a few slits into the crust for ventilation. Place onto a baking sheet to catch any drippings.

14. Bake for 25 to 30 minutes. You want the crust to be nice and golden brown, and the sides should be bubbling up slightly. Serve immediately.

$\mathcal{Q}$UICK AND EASY ENCHILADA PIE

WHEN JESSIE FIRST BROUGHT HER OLDEST SON, JUDE, HOME from the hospital, Jilly came from London to stay with them. She helped with the night shift, kept the house livable, and cooked for Jessie and Steven during those first few difficult but wonderful weeks. This dish was one of Jilly's go-to casseroles that she made during her stay. You can cook a big ole batch and then slice and freeze it in individual servings for later (on second thought, this dish is so tasty, there might not be many leftovers for freezing!). Feel free to substitute a premade enchilada sauce from the grocery store if it is easier for you and to really make this a quick meal. Most of the varieties we found were all gluten-free and tasted great in this recipe, too. This tasty dish is dairy-free if you omit the cheese.

SAUCE

- 1 tablespoon olive oil
- 1 tablespoon gluten-free flour blend (we like Arrowhead Mills Gluten Free All Purpose Baking Mix)
- 2 tablespoons chili powder
- 3 tablespoons apple cider vinegar
- 1 cup beef stock (preferably low-sodium)
- 1 (6-ounce) can tomato paste
- ½ teaspoon garlic powder
- ½ teaspoon ground cumin
- ¼ teaspoon salt

     1   tablespoon olive oil
     1   pound lean ground turkey or beef
     1   cup chopped yellow onion
     1   cup chopped red bell pepper
    1¼   cups chopped zucchini (trim ends and halve lengthwise before
         chopping)
     2   teaspoons ground cumin
     1   teaspoon freshly ground black pepper
     1   (10-ounce) can diced tomatoes with green chiles (we like Ro-Tel)
     1   (15-ounce) can black beans, drained and rinsed
About 1 cup homemade enchilada sauce (recipe above) or store-bought
         variety
     1   (2.5-ounce) can sliced black olives, drained
     1   tablespoon roughly chopped fresh cilantro
    18   (5- to 6-inch) small corn tortillas, white or yellow
     2   cups Mexican cheese blend (omit for dairy-free)
         Sour cream and chopped fresh cilantro, for garnish (omit sour
         cream for dairy-free)

1. First, make the enchilada sauce. If using a store-bought variety, skip to step 4. In a small saucepan over medium-high heat, heat the oil. Add the flour and stir until smooth, cooking only briefly, about 1 to 2 minutes.

2. Add the chili powder and stir to incorporate. Next, add the remaining sauce ingredients and stir to combine.

3. Bring the mixture to a boil and then reduce the heat to low and cook for 10 minutes. Remove from the heat and set aside until assembly.

4. Preheat the oven to 350°F. Grease a 13 x 9-inch baking dish with cooking spray and set aside.

5. Now make the pie. In a large skillet with high sides, warm the olive oil over medium-high heat. Add the meat and cook until it is fully cooked through and browned, crumbling it with a wooden spoon as it cooks.

6. Once the meat is fully cooked, add the onion, bell pepper, and zucchini and sauté until softened, about 5 to 7 minutes, stirring frequently.

7. Add the cumin, black pepper, diced tomatoes with chiles, black beans, and enchilada sauce. Reduce the heat to low and cook for 5 to 6 minutes, stirring often.

8. Stir in the sliced olives and cilantro. Cook for another minute or two and then turn off the heat.

9. Assemble the pie by layering six tortillas in the bottom of the prepared dish so they are slightly overlapping. Ladle a third of the meat mixture over the top of the tortillas, making sure to spread it out evenly so that all the tortillas are covered and moist. If using cheese, sprinkle approximately half of your cheese evenly over the top of the meat mixture.

10. Layer six more tortillas over the top of the cheese and meat mixture in the same slightly overlapping fashion. Ladle another third of the meat mixture over the top, ensuring all the tortillas are covered and moist.

11. Layer the final six tortillas, followed by the final third of the meat mixture, spreading well so all the tortillas are covered and moist.

12. Sprinkle the remaining half of the cheese, if using, evenly over the top of the pie.

13. Cover the dish with aluminum foil and bake for 25 minutes. Remove the foil and cook uncovered for a final 5 minutes.

14. Remove from the oven and let cool for 3 to 5 minutes before slicing and garnishing with sour cream and cilantro, if desired.

DADDY'S DUCK AND ANDOUILLE SAUSAGE CHRISTMAS GUMBO

DF   MAKES 6 TO 8 SERVINGS

THIS CHRISTMAS GUMBO IS A TRUE LAGASSE FAMILY TRADI-
tion for us during the holidays, though it is delicious anytime of the year. For
us, it is perfect for Christmas, when we all seem to give in to a bit of decadence
a bit more willingly. The rich duck with the spicy andouille sausage makes this
a very decadent gumbo indeed. We have fond memories of a big ole pot of this
gumbo bubbling away on the stove on Christmas Eve, which was a big night in
our house. There would be Christmas music playing, kids running around and
lots of our friends and family popping in for a cocktail or two, a bit of present
exchanging and, of course, a little bowl of this true delight. I'm not sure what
everyone was looking forward to more, the gifts or this gumbo! We hope you and
your family will try this during the holiday season, or just for your next Sunday
get-together, and make some new memories and traditions of your own.

1½ to 2	pounds domestic duck breasts
1½	teaspoons Emeril's Original Essence seasoning or Cajun seasoning of your choice
1	cup vegetable oil
1⅓	cups gluten-free flour blend (we like Arrowhead Mills Gluten Free All Purpose Baking Mix)
1½	cups finely chopped yellow onion
¾	cup finely chopped green bell pepper
¾	cup finely chopped red bell pepper
1	cup finely chopped celery
1	teaspoon minced garlic

¼	teaspoon cayenne pepper, or more to taste
¼	teaspoon salt
	Freshly ground black pepper
1	pound gluten-free andouille sausage or smoked sausage, halved lengthwise and cut into bite-size slices (we like Wellshire Farms andouille)
1	tablespoon fresh thyme leaves
2	bay leaves
10	cups chicken or vegetable stock
⅓	cup finely sliced green onions, plus more for garnish
2	tablespoons finely chopped fresh parsley, plus more for garnish
1½ to 2	cups cooked wild rice

1. Using a sharp knife, in a crisscross fashion, slice the fatty skin on the duck breasts to score the meat, being mindful not to fully cut through the breasts. Season all sides of the duck breasts with the Essence.

2. In either a large Dutch oven or a 6- to 8-quart heavy stockpot, heat the oil over medium-high heat. Once the pan is piping hot, add the seasoned duck breasts, scored-skin-side down first, and cook for 6 to 7 minutes, or until the skin becomes nice and crispy.

3. Once the skin is crispy, gently flip the duck breasts and cook for another 5 minutes. Remove the breasts from the oil and place on a large plate or baking sheet, loosely cover with foil, and set aside.

4. Add the gluten-free flour mix to the same pot over medium heat to make a roux. Stir constantly and cook for 20 minutes.

5. After 20 minutes, add the onions, bell peppers, celery, garlic, cayenne, salt, and pepper to taste. Cook until the vegetables soften, about 8 to 10 minutes, stirring constantly.

6. Next, add the andouille sausage and fresh thyme to the pot, stir, and cook for 5 minutes.

7. Add the bay leaves and stock, turn the heat up to medium high, and bring to a gentle boil.

8. Once boiling gently, turn the heat down to low and simmer for 1 hour, uncovered, stirring frequently.

9. After the hour, add the whole duck breasts into the pot and simmer on low for another hour, stirring frequently.

10. After this hour, use a slotted spoon to remove the bay leaves and discard them. Also, if any fat/oil has risen to the top, skim it off and discard it now as well.

11. Using tongs or a fork, gently remove the whole duck breasts from the pot and place on a cutting board. If there are any large, loose pieces of duck fat, remove and discard them. The meat should be very tender. Either chop the breasts into bite-size chunks, or, as we prefer, let the breasts cool slightly until you can handle them and shred the breasts with your hands. Wearing disposable plastic gloves is helpful here.

12. Once your duck meat is chopped or shredded, add the meat back to the pan, along with the green onions and parsley. Stir and taste for seasoning. If you'd like to add a bit more cayenne, salt, or pepper, do so now. Cook for a final 30 minutes, stirring frequently.

13. Serve the gumbo over the cooked wild rice in deep bowls, garnishing with a bit more green onion or parsley, if desired. Serve immediately.

For Afters

MMMMM. JUST THE WORD "DESSERT" CAUSES OUR MOUTHS to start watering in anticipation of some fantastically decadent sweet closure to a meal well made and greatly enjoyed. Or, if you're like Jessie, you think there's never an inappropriate time for dessert! As it goes for most topics and traits with us, we are very different when it comes to our preferred dessert foods. That's a bonus for you because this resulting dessert chapter is as diverse and eclectic as we are. You can go traditional, like Jessie tends to, and stick to Classic Apple Pie (page 316) and Old-Fashioned Oatmeal Raisin Cookies (page 308). Or you can take Jilly's more adventurous path and try a Greek Yogurt Cheesecake with Fig Swirls and Pistachio Crust (page 299) or a Fragrant Coconut Rice Pudding with Vanilla Caramelized Pineapple (page 314). One terrific thing about this dessert journey, though, is that there is NO wrong path to take (or to cake!). No matter which direction you try, you'll end up at a deliciously rewarding gluten-free destination!

Sugar Cookie Jam Thumbprints, page 305

MOMMA'S STRAWBERRY SHORTCAKE WITH HOMEMADE BISCUITS

 MAKES 8 SERVINGS

ONE OF OUR FAVORITE DESSERTS GROWING UP WAS OUR MOM'S
strawberry shortcake. She'd make the whipped cream from scratch, and we'd
all sit outside enjoying the Massachusetts summer and the strawberry bounty
she'd made even better with homemade biscuits. When we went gluten-free,
we had to make our adjustments to the biscuits. But this recipe results in delicious, tender biscuits that soak up all the strawberry juices just perfectly. As
with most of our recipes, you can adjust this one to suit your preferences. Make
the strawberries sweeter, the whipped cream less so—whatever you like best.
This recipe is quick and easy and will take 30 minutes or less to make.

1½	cups gluten-free flour blend (we like Arrowhead Mills Gluten Free All Purpose Baking Mix)
1	teaspoon baking powder
½	teaspoon xanthan gum
¼	teaspoon salt
¼	cup coconut oil
½	cup cold whole milk
1	medium-size egg, lightly beaten
1	pound strawberries, washed and sliced
1	tablespoon granulated sugar
1 to 2	tablespoons water
1	pint heavy whipping cream
1	tablespoon confectioners' sugar
1	vanilla bean pod, sliced and seeds scraped

1. Preheat the oven to 425°F. Grease a large baking sheet with nonstick cooking spray.

2. Sift the flour, baking powder, xanthan gum, and salt together in a medium bowl.

3. Add the coconut oil and use your hands to mix until similar-size fine crumbles form. If the coconut oil is solid, it will melt naturally with your body heat and help to form the crumbles. Blend this as smoothly as you can, keeping in mind it will still be a bit lumpy.

4. Add the cold milk and egg and with a wooden spoon stir well to make a dough. It should be quite thick and cohesive.

5. Using a ¼-cup measuring cup, measure out eight servings of dough and place them on the prepared baking sheet.

6. Bake for 14 to 16 minutes, or until the biscuits are golden brown on top.

7. While the biscuits are baking, mix the sliced strawberries with the granulated sugar and the water in a small bowl and give it all a good stir. You want the strawberries to retain their shape and allow the sugar mixture to coax the fruit's natural juices out so you have enough juice to spoon over your biscuits. If your strawberries are super ripe, you may only need 1 tablespoon of water. Set aside while you make the whipped cream.

8. In another medium bowl, whip the heavy cream, confectioners' sugar, and vanilla bean seeds with an electric mixer until stiff peaks form.

9. Once your biscuits are cooked, split each one in half and place them in small bowls. Scoop a generous spoonful of strawberries with juice over each. Top with a few heaping spoonfuls of whipped cream and dig in.

Meyer Lemon Meringue Icebox Pie, page 286

MEYER LEMON MERINGUE ICEBOX PIE

MAKES A 9-INCH PIE

IF YOU MADE OUR SCRUMPTIOUS LEMON POPPY SEED CAKE (page 91), you know that Jessie loves just about anything with lemon. Anything. And that includes a good lemon meringue pie. So, Jilly took on the challenge of creating the most delicious, most incredible lemon meringue pie recipe she could for this book. After a lot of trial and error (mostly error! Who knew it was so hard to master the art of lemon curd filling?), Jilly came up with a pie that goes beyond the typical lemon meringue pie you might be expecting. We used Meyer lemons, which are a delightful cross between a lemon and a mandarin orange, because they are less tart and a bit sweeter than your traditional lemon. You can always use regular lemons, if necessary—just taste your filling and adjust it for tartness before using in the pie! We also made our pie into an icebox version of the original by freezing it briefly for 2 hours before serving. What that leaves you with is a pie so delightfully refreshing, you may want two slices on that hot summer day. And if there's one slice left? It truly is a pie so good, you may fight your sister for it! There are now premade gluten-free graham cracker pie crusts on the market, so feel free to take that time-saving step if desired.

CRUST

16 ounces gluten-free graham cracker cookies (we like Kinnikinnick S'moreables Graham Style Crackers)

3 tablespoons unsalted butter, melted

FILLING

1 cup Meyer lemon zest

1 cup freshly squeezed Meyer lemon juice

<table>
<tr><td align="right">5</td><td>tablespoons cornstarch</td></tr>
<tr><td align="right">1</td><td>cup water</td></tr>
<tr><td align="right">6</td><td>large egg yolks (reserve the whites for the meringue)</td></tr>
<tr><td align="right">1½</td><td>cups granulated sugar</td></tr>
<tr><td></td><td>Pinch of salt</td></tr>
<tr><td align="right">2</td><td>tablespoons unsalted butter, diced into small cubes</td></tr>
</table>

MERINGUE

<table>
<tr><td align="right">6</td><td>egg whites</td></tr>
<tr><td align="right">½</td><td>teaspoon cream of tartar</td></tr>
<tr><td align="right">1</td><td>teaspoon vanilla extract</td></tr>
<tr><td align="right">½</td><td>cup sugar (either confectioners' or granulated)</td></tr>
</table>

1. First, make the crust. If using a premade gluten-free graham cracker crust, skip to step 4. If not, roughly break up the cookies and place them into a food processor along with the melted butter. Pulse until the mixture forms crumbs. You want a breadcrumb texture here, but it should stick together when pinched between your fingers.

2. Using your fingertips, press the cookie crumb mixture firmly into the bottom and up the sides of a 9-inch pie pan. Spread it out as evenly and firmly as possible. A helpful trick is to cover the flat bottom of a spice bottle or small measuring cup tightly with plastic wrap and use it like a mini flattening tool.

3. Place the crust in the fridge to set for 30 minutes, uncovered.

4. Meanwhile, make the filling. In a medium bowl, mix the lemon zest, juice, and cornstarch together well.

5. In a medium, nonstick saucepan, bring the water to a boil over medium-high heat.

6. Once boiling, turn the heat down to medium and quickly add the lemon mixture to the pan. Whisk constantly until the mixture thickens, for about 1 minute, and then turn off the heat and leave to rest for a moment.

7. In another medium bowl, mix together the egg yolks, sugar, and pinch of salt until it forms almost a thick yellowy paste. Working in three batches, SLOWLY add a third of this mixture at a time to the warm lemon mixture in the pan. Whisk constantly so you don't break or curdle the eggs. Repeat until all the egg yolk mixture is whisked in well.

8. Turn the heat back on to medium high and cook the mixture until it has thickened, stirring constantly, about 2 to 3 minutes. You want it thick enough so that when whisking, it is almost a bit hard to stir. Once thickened, turn the heat down to low and add the diced butter to the pan. Whisk constantly until all the butter has melted and the mixture is nice and thick, about 1 to 2 minutes. Turn off the heat. Let cool slightly (to room temperature at least) before proceeding.

9. Once the filling is slightly cooled, remove the pie crust from the fridge. Gently pour the lemon filling into the prepared pie shell and set aside. You will only need roughly 3 cups of the lemon filling for a standard 9-inch pie pan, so you may have leftover lemon filling. Not to worry, this is homemade lemon curd! So, either store refrigerated in an airtight container and use for jam tarts or thumbprint cookies (see page 305), or you can simply just discard.

10. Preheat the oven to 350°F.

11. Now it's time to make the meringue. In a large, clean, and dry bowl, combine the egg whites, cream of tartar, and vanilla. Beat on high with an electric mixer until soft peaks form. It is very important that you use a clean bowl and beaters and that NO yolk gets into your egg whites! These are all reasons why your meringue might not work or stiffen.

12. Add ¼ cup of the sugar and beat until slightly stiffer peaks form. Add the remaining ¼ cup sugar and beat until very stiff peaks form.

13. Gently spoon the meringue over the top of the lemon filling in the pie shell. With either your clean fingers or a spatula, spread the meringue to the edge of the pie so it completely covers the filling, being mindful not to accidentally sweep any crust crumbage into the meringue. Using either your finger or a spoon, create little swirls and peaks all over the top. Kids love helping with this job, and you can get as creative as you'd like.

14. Bake for 15 to 17 minutes, or until the meringue peaks are golden brown and the meringue is not too jiggly. Let cool fully to room temperature before freezing the pie whole for at least 2 hours before serving.

15. When ready to serve, take the pie out of the freezer and let thaw for a few minutes before slicing and serving. Any leftover pie can be stored in a food container with a lid and put back in the freezer for future use. We recommend storing for only 4 to 5 days, after which time the lemon curd filling tends to get a bit liquefied.

CHOCOLATE LAVA SOUFFLÉS

MAKES 4 (6-OUNCE) SOUFFLÉS

GLUTEN-FREE CHOCOLATE LAVA SOUFFLÉS WITH DELICIOUSLY warm, dark chocolate oozing out from the center. This recipe is insanely good. There's really not much else to say. Except that we do like serving this with a sprinkling of confectioners' sugar and some fresh raspberries. And we strongly recommend that you grease your ramekins generously, almost obscenely, so that the lava soufflés turn out with ease. Also, since every oven varies, you really need to keep an eye on these babies and pull them out when the desired look is achieved as directed . . . so no calling your girlfriend to chat or painting your nails while these are baking, okay? We say this from experience (Jilly!). Good luck, and may the chocolate soufflés' love be with you.

- 10 ounces semisweet chocolate chips
- ¼ cup (½ stick) unsalted butter, plus more for the ramekins
- 1½ teaspoons vanilla extract
  Pinch of salt
- 4 large eggs, at room temperature
- ¼ cup granulated sugar
  Confectioners' sugar and fresh raspberries, for garnish (optional)

1. Generously grease the four 6-ounce ramekins or small oven-safe bowls with butter and set aside. If you are generous with the greasing here, you'll be thankful when you try to free these soufflés later.

2. Preheat the oven to 375°F.

3. Fill a medium saucepan halfway full of water and bring to a boil over medium-low heat. Once boiling, turn the heat down to low so the water simmers gently.

4. Combine the chocolate chips, butter, vanilla, and salt in a large, heatproof glass bowl. The bowl needs to fit on top of the saucepan of simmering water, but it also needs to be large enough to contain the egg mixture from step 6 that you will have to add in.

5. Place the bowl over the saucepan and, using a spatula, stir constantly until all the chocolate and butter has melted and the mixture is smooth and well combined. It helps to have an oven mitt to hold the bowl still while stirring. Once fully melted, turn off the heat and place the bowl on a heatproof surface to cool slightly.

6. In a separate bowl, add the eggs and granulated sugar. With an electric mixer, beat the eggs and sugar on high until they have at least doubled in size and become light and frothy. Have patience here, as this can take 4 to 5 minutes.

7. Once whipped, slowly add half of the egg mixture into the bowl of the warm chocolate mixture, whisking CONSTANTLY and firmly so the eggs don't curdle and break. Once the first half of the egg mixture has been well mixed and everything is smooth, add the remaining half and whisk constantly until incorporated and smooth.

8. Evenly distribute the batter into the four prepared ramekins and place them onto a baking sheet.

9. Bake for 12 to 15 minutes. The soufflés should rise up out of the ramekins, and the edges should look cooked but the center may look a bit undercooked. Pull out of the oven immediately when they reach this appearance.

10. As soon as the soufflés come out of the oven, set out whatever small serving plates you'll be using and put on some oven mitts. Holding a ramekin as close over the plate as possible without actually touching it, carefully but SWIFTLY turn the ramekin over. If you greased them well, the soufflés should just pop out of the ramekin. If you have any trouble, try running a butter knife around the edges of the ramekin. Repeat until all of the lava cakes are out and plated.

11. Quickly dust the tops of each cake with a bit of confectioners' sugar and scatter a few berries around the plate, if so desired. Serve immediately! These are delicate desserts that can deflate quickly, so you must serve straightaway. The centers should still be soft, gooey, and oozy.

CHOCOLATE RASPBERRY LAYER CAKE WITH CHOCOLATE BUTTERCREAM FROSTING

MAKES 8 TO 10 SERVINGS

IF YOU LOVE DESSERTS, SCRUMPTIOUS, MOIST, OOEY GOOEY cake may be one thing you thought you'd miss the most when you went gluten-free. Well, have we got a recipe for you. We thought about calling it *Mmmmmm*. Because there is no better descriptor for this one than that. *Mmmmmm*. It is moist and chocolaty with hints of raspberry throughout. The buttercream frosting just makes it that much more irresistible. The yogurt and half-and-half give this cake its terrific moistness, reminiscent of our pre-gluten-free Betty Crocker Devil's Food Cake days. We recommend ¼ cup of raspberry preserves be spread between the layers. Feel free to increase that amount to create a thicker layer of jam if you prefer. Ask for this cake by name. Or just say *Mmmmmm*.

CAKE

2	cups gluten-free flour blend (we like Arrowhead Mills Gluten Free All Purpose Baking Mix)
1¾	cups granulated sugar
¾	cup unsweetened cocoa powder
2	teaspoons baking powder
1	teaspoon baking soda
1	teaspoon xanthan gum
½	cup full-fat plain yogurt
1	(12-ounce) bag frozen unsweetened raspberries, thawed and puréed (should yield about 1 cup)
1½	teaspoons vanilla extract

1¼   cups half-and-half
  2   large eggs

FROSTING

  1   cup (2 sticks) unsalted butter, at room temperature
  3   cups confectioners' sugar
  ½   cup unsweetened cocoa powder
  2   teaspoons vanilla extract
  ¼   cup half-and-half

  ¼   cup raspberry preserves
      Fresh raspberries, for garnish (optional)
      Chocolate shavings, for garnish (optional)

1. Preheat the oven to 350°F. Grease two 9-inch cake pans well with butter or nonstick cooking spray and set aside.

2. First, prepare the cake. Sift the flour, sugar, cocoa powder, baking powder, baking soda, and xanthan gum in a large mixing bowl and stir to combine. Stir in the yogurt, raspberry purée, vanilla, half-and-half, and eggs to make a thick-ish batter.

3. Divide the batter, by eye, evenly between the two prepared cake pans. Bake for 30 to 35 minutes, or until a toothpick inserted into the center comes out clean.

4. Cool in the pans for 5 to 10 minutes and then gently transfer to a cooling rack to cool completely.

5. Once the cake is almost completely cooled, prepare the frosting. Using an electric mixer, cream the butter to mix it to an even consistency, for 2 minutes or so. Add in the remaining frosting ingredients. Beat on low speed until the dustiness of the sugar and cocoa is eliminated and a frosting consistency starts to form. Then, increase the mixer speed to medium and beat until the mixture is an even frosting thickness, about 2 to 3 more minutes.

6. Place one of the cooled cakes onto your serving plate or cake stand. This will be the bottom layer. Gently spread the raspberry preserves in an even layer across the top of the cake.

7. Once you have a nice, even raspberry layer, place the second cake layer on top.

8. Frost the entire cake with as even a layer of chocolate frosting as possible. Garnish with some fresh raspberries or chocolate shavings, if desired. Slice and serve with a nice big glass of cold milk! Store any leftover cake in the refrigerator.

VANILLA POACHED PEARS WITH CARDAMOM GOAT CHEESE CREAM

MAKES 4 SERVINGS

JILLY THOUGHT OF THIS DISH AFTER SHE REALIZED THE BEST part of going out to dinner for her was the fruit and cheese board after the meal! There is something so inviting about delicious pears and fragrant vanilla, and sweet fruits and tart cheese belong together like Sonny and Cher or like Ross and Rachel or like, well you get the idea. We tried making this using two different varieties of pears: Bartlett and Bosc. Hours of toil later led us to this: the Bartlett variety is much firmer, so it takes a bit more time to cook and a bit more effort to core. But, it is delicious in this dish since it keeps its pear flavor even after cooking. The Bosc variety is a bit easier to core and a bit less dense, so it cooks quicker, but it is more mild in taste. Try any variety you like and give this a go for your next fancy dinner party. See how many compliments you get for your genius take on the fruit and cheese plate with this one!

PEARS

- 5 cups water
- 2 cups granulated sugar
- ½ of a whole, fresh vanilla bean pod (store the other half in an airtight container for later use)
- 4 pears, any variety (Bartlett, Bosc, etc.)
- 2 tablespoons freshly squeezed lemon juice

8 ounces high-quality goat cheese, at room temperature

2 teaspoons confectioners' sugar

¼ teaspoon ground cardamom

1. First, prepare the pears. In a medium, 3.5-quart, saucepan, combine the water and sugar and set aside.

2. Take the vanilla bean pod half and, using a small paring knife, slice the pod in half down the middle lengthwise so you expose all the tiny little vanilla bean seeds.

3. With the back of the small paring knife, scrape out the inside of each vanilla pod half as much as possible. It will be sticky and look like a bunch of tiny specks. These are the vanilla bean seeds.

4. Add all the scraped out seeds to the pan with the water and sugar and bring to a gentle boil over medium heat.

5. Using an apple corer and/or melon baller, carefully core out the seeds from each whole pear, leaving the stems attached and working from the bottom. You want to keep the pears whole, so just remove the seeds, being careful to not core away too much of the pear.

6. Using a vegetable peeler, peel the cored pears. Brush each peeled pear generously with the lemon juice.

7. Gently add the prepared pears to the simmering water and sugar mixture, either by hand or with a large slotted spoon.

8. Turn the heat down to low and simmer uncovered, turning the pears occasionally so all sides are cooked.

9. Cook until a toothpick can be easily inserted into the pears' flesh. For the Bosc, this is usually 10 to 15 minutes. For the Bartlett, 20 to 25 minutes. Depending on the size of your pears, this step can take a bit longer, so use the softness of the pear as your guide rather than the suggested cook time.

10. Once cooked, turn off the heat and allow the pears to fully cool in the pan.

11. Once completely cooled, gently remove the pears from the liquid and place in a large bowl. Cover with plastic wrap and refrigerate for at least 1 hour but no longer than 24 hours.

12. Save 1½ cups of the poaching liquid and store in an airtight container in the fridge until needed. Discard the remaining liquid.

13. When the pears are nearly ready to come out of the fridge, begin to make the sauce and goat cheese cream to serve.

14. Pour the reserved 1½ cups poaching liquid through a strainer into a small saucepan. Bring to a gentle boil over medium-high heat, uncovered, for 15 to 20 minutes, or until the liquid becomes thicker and syrupy. It should be able to coat the back of a spoon. If it starts to overly bubble, turn the heat down slightly. Once syrupy, turn off the heat and let cool fully.

15. While the syrup is cooling, pull the pears out of the fridge and allow them to come to room temperature.

16. In a medium bowl, combine the softened goat cheese, confectioners' sugar, and ground cardamom. With a fork, blend together vigorously until you have what looks like a whipped frosting.

17. Place one pear on each of four plates. Scoop a generous amount of the goat cheese cream alongside each pear.

18. To finish, drizzle a bit of the syrup all over both the pear and the cream. Serve immediately.

GREEK YOGURT CHEESECAKE WITH FIG SWIRLS AND PISTACHIO CRUST

MAKES A 9- OR 10-INCH CHEESECAKE

WE HAVE BEEN DIGGING THE WHOLE GREEK YOGURT, HONEY, pistachios, and figs thing long before it became so "in" and hip! Everyone loves a cheesecake, but wouldn't everyone love a healthier cheesecake even more? We wanted to combine all those scrumptious flavors into a healthy cheesecake, which actually doesn't have any cream cheese in it at all. The baked pistachio crust is the perfect base to encase this silky, creamy, and honey-infused Greek yogurt filling, all topped with delicious dollops of fig preserves swirled through for cheesecake perfection. You do need to use full-fat Greek yogurt, however, or the filling won't thicken properly. Hey, we all need a little bit of fat!

CRUST

- 2 cups raw, unsalted shelled pistachios
- ¼ cup (½ stick) unsalted butter, melted
- ¼ cup granulated sugar

FILLING

- 2 cups full-fat Greek-style yogurt
- ⅓ cup granulated sugar
- 2 large eggs
- 2 teaspoons vanilla extract
- 1 tablespoon plus 1½ teaspoons cornstarch
- 2 tablespoons honey

FIG SWIRLS

⅓ cup high-quality fig preserves

Fresh fruit, for garnish (optional)

1. Preheat the oven to 350°F.

2. Place all the crust ingredients into a food processor and blend until the pistachios are very fine, almost like breadcrumbs. You want as few chunks as possible.

3. Lightly grease a 9- or 10-inch springform pan and place the pistachio mixture into the pan. Using your hands or the back of a ¼-cup measuring cup, spread the mixture across the bottom and up the sides as much as you can and pat down firmly and as evenly as possible to make the crust.

4. Bake the crust for 10 minutes, remove it from the oven, and set aside. Leave the oven on and position an oven rack in the middle.

5. While the crust is baking, place all the filling ingredients except the cornstarch and honey into a large bowl. Beat with an electric mixer on medium-high speed until all is blended well and is light and fluffy.

6. Add the cornstarch and stir well. Add the honey and mix together with the electric mixer on medium speed until no lumps of cornstarch remain.

7. Pour the filling mixture evenly into the baked crust. Gently drizzle or spoon the fig preserves all over the top of the filling.

8. Using either a metal skewer or the tip of a sharp knife, drag it back and forth through the fig and the filling to create little swirls. Get as creative as you'd like!

9. Bake on the middle rack for 30 to 35 minutes. The center will still be a bit jiggly but should be cooked through. The edges of the cake should be brown and pulling away slightly from the pan.

10. Cool to room temperature and then place in the fridge uncovered to set for at least 3 hours before releasing the springform and slicing. For ease of slicing, try running your sharp knife under hot water first. Rinse and wipe before each slice. Garnish with a bit of fresh fruit on top, if desired.

PUMPKIN CHEESECAKE

YEARS AGO, A COWORKER OF JESSIE'S SHARED A VERSION OF this recipe with her. It became a Thanksgiving constant and was also one of her go-to recipes for parties and potlucks. That is . . . until she couldn't have the gluteny crust anymore. To solve that problem, Jessie reformulated the crust by substituting the gluteny graham cracker crust with one made of crumbled up gluten-free sugar cookies and by adjusting the filling ingredients slightly so that it could still be made and enjoyed just like before. This version really is delicious and quite easy to make. We hope your family likes it as much as ours does!

CRUST

- 2½ cups gluten-free crunchy cookie crumbles, preferably sugar or graham flavored (you'll most likely have to use your food processor to crumble whole cookies)
- 3 tablespoons unsalted butter, melted

FILLING

- 16 ounces cream cheese, at room temperature
- ¾ cup canned pumpkin purée
- ½ cup granulated sugar
- 1 teaspoon vanilla extract
- ½ teaspoon ground cinnamon
  Pinch of ground nutmeg
  Pinch of ground cloves
- 2 large eggs

Whipped cream, for garnish (optional)
Chopped pecans, for garnish (optional)

1. Lightly grease the bottom and sides of a deep-dish 9-inch pie pan with butter or nonstick cooking spray.

2. Put the cookie crumbles and the melted butter into a food processor and pulse until the two ingredients are evenly blended. You can test this by pinching the mixture in your fingers. If the mixture stays together when you squeeze it, it is ready.

3. Using a flat-bottomed cup, firmly press the mixture evenly into the bottom and up the sides of the pie pan. Use your fingers to press the crust along the edges of the pan as evenly as possible.

4. Put the pressed crust into the refrigerator uncovered for 30 minutes to allow it to set.

5. Meanwhile, preheat the oven to 350°F.

6. Next, let's prepare the filling. In a large bowl, add the cream cheese, pumpkin purée, sugar, vanilla extract, cinnamon, nutmeg, and cloves. Using an electric mixer, mix on medium-high speed until well blended.

7. Add the eggs and mix again until well blended.

8. Pour the filling into your chilled crust.

9. Bake for 40 to 50 minutes, or until a toothpick inserted into the middle comes out clean and the pie appears slightly jiggly but not uncooked.

10. Cool completely, cover with plastic wrap, and refrigerate for a minimum of 3 hours before serving.

11. When you are ready to serve the pie, garnish with the whipped cream and chopped pecans, if desired, and slice.

SUGAR COOKIE JAM THUMBPRINTS

MAKES ABOUT 30 COOKIES

EVERY YEAR, JESSIE'S MOTHER-IN-LAW, MAW-MAW PATSY, HAS a Christmas-Cookie Exchange party. There are a few strict rules for this event. Namely, no store-bought cookies, and you must bring a minimum of six dozen cookies. Every year, someone makes a version of the jam thumbprint, and every year Jessie wishes she had a good GF version of them because they are so tasty. Finally, this past year, Jessie decided to crack the GF jam thumbprint code, and this is her result. These cookies hold together well, and the jam flavor can be changed to suit your preference. Make them for your next cookie exchange—or whenever you need a little bit of crumbly, fruity goodness.

2	cups gluten-free flour blend (we like Arrowhead Mills Gluten Free All Purpose Baking Mix)
1	teaspoon baking powder
¼	teaspoon salt
½	teaspoon xanthan gum
1	cup (2 sticks) unsalted butter, at room temperature
¾	cup granulated sugar
2	large eggs
1	teaspoon vanilla extract
⅔	cup favorite fruit jam (smooth varieties without fruit pieces work best; we like apricot or raspberry)

1. In a medium mixing bowl, sift together the flour, baking powder, salt, and xanthan gum. Set aside.

2. In a large mixing bowl, using an electric mixer, beat the butter and sugar on medium-high speed until smooth. Add the eggs and beat until fluffy, about 2 to 3 minutes. Then beat in the vanilla.

3. Gradually mix in the dry ingredients, using either an electric mixer on medium-low speed or doing it by hand with a wooden spoon. Mix until just incorporated before adding additional flour mixture. The dough will be somewhat firm, so you'll have to use some muscle to mix it!

4. Once the dough is formed, divide it into two chunks, flatten each one into a disk, wrap in plastic wrap, and refrigerate for at least 30 minutes.

5. Once the dough is chilled, preheat the oven to 350°F.

6. Grease a large baking sheet with butter or nonstick cooking spray. Remove one disk of dough from the refrigerator. Using a tablespoon as a guide, scoop out approximately 1 tablespoon of dough. Roll it into a ball and place it on the baking sheet. These cookies don't expand much, so you can leave 1 inch or so between FLATTENED balls (see the next step). Repeat this process until the baking sheet is full or you have used all of the disk of dough. If you have extra space on your baking sheet, you can always steal some of the dough from your second disk to fill out the tray. Refrigerate any remaining dough until it is time to scoop and roll it for the next round.

7. Using your thumb, press each ball down so that a well is formed in the middle of each flattened dough ball. This is where you'll put the fruit jam. Fill the wells with a portion of the ⅔ cup of jam.

8. Bake for 15 to 18 minutes, or until the cookie edges are just beginning to brown.

9. Cool slightly on the baking sheet before transferring the cookies CAREFULLY to a cooling rack. The cookies are slightly fragile when they first emerge from the oven (but firm up as they cool), so please be extra careful when transferring them so that they don't break.

10. Repeat steps 6 through 9 until all the dough has been used.

OLD-FASHIONED OATMEAL RAISIN COOKIES

G-F MAKES ABOUT 36 COOKIES

OH MY GOODNESS! THERE ARE HONESTLY NOT THAT MANY
foods in life that Jessie loves more than these chewy, raisiny cookies. If they could
provide all of her necessary nutritional requirements, she'd sustain herself on
oatmeal raisin cookies alone. Her boys are no different. They'd eat them by the
handful if allowed! This recipe is an easy one to have the kids help make. Jessie's
son Jude loves using the electric mixer, and J.P. loves doing the hand mixing.
This fantastic version of the traditional oatmeal raisin cookie maintains a great
chewiness without being too soft, and the dark brown sugar gives the cookies an
added depth of flavor. Although oats are not technically gluteny, they are very
often cross-contaminated during growth and harvest, so please be sure to look
specifically for oats labeled gluten-free. This is a quick and easy recipe and will
take 30 minutes or less to prepare.

- 1 cup (2 sticks) unsalted butter, at room temperature, plus more if needed for the pans
- ½ cup granulated sugar
- 1¼ cups firmly packed dark brown sugar
- 2 large eggs
- 2 teaspoons vanilla extract
- 1¾ cups gluten-free flour blend (we like Arrowhead Mills Gluten Free All Purpose Baking Mix)
- 1 teaspoon baking soda
- 1 teaspoon baking powder
- ½ teaspoon ground cinnamon
- ½ teaspoon ground or freshly grated nutmeg

½	teaspoon salt
3½	cups old-fashioned gluten-free oats
1½	cups raisins

1. Preheat the oven to 350°F and position an oven rack in the upper half of your oven. Grease two baking sheets with butter or nonstick cooking spray. (If your oven won't accommodate the two baking sheets on one rack, bake the cookies in batches, one tray at a time. The second sheet of cookies will be fine if it has to sit and wait its turn.)

2. Cream together the butter, sugars, eggs, and vanilla using an electric mixer on medium speed until the ingredients are light and fluffy. The color will change from dark brown to light brown when it is ready.

3. In a separate bowl, whisk together the flour, baking soda, baking powder, cinnamon, nutmeg, and salt until mixed well.

4. Stir the flour mixture into the wet ingredients until smooth and well blended. Then stir in the oats and raisins until all ingredients are evenly distributed.

5. Drop the dough by heaping tablespoonfuls (about 2 tablespoons per cookie) onto your baking sheets, leaving 2 to 3 inches between cookies.

6. Bake for 9 to 12 minutes, or until the edges are golden brown but the tops still appear a bit underdone. This will help them remain chewy.

7. Remove from the oven. Let the cookies sit on the baking sheets for 1 to 2 minutes before transferring them to a cooling rack.

ORANGE COCONUT MACAROONS

 MAKES 18 TO 20 MACAROONS

WE JUST LOVE A NICE AND SIMPLE SWEET TREAT THAT WE CAN whip up on the fly. We also love when it is easy and quick enough that we can sit back and let the kids do it all on their own! These macaroons are like little pillows of coconut heaven. Light, airy, and flavorful little orangey kisses. You get the idea! They really are a nice and light treat to savor with your favorite cup of tea. If you don't like the orange flavor, you can just use a full teaspoon of the vanilla extract or any other extract you prefer instead. They will still be delicious. Round up the kids and try these for your next tea party. This is a quick and easy recipe and will take 30 minutes or less to make.

>   3 large egg whites
> ⅛ teaspoon cream of tartar
> ⅛ teaspoon salt
> ½ cup granulated sugar or coconut sugar
> ½ teaspoon vanilla extract
> ½ teaspoon orange extract
> 1½ cups unsweetened shredded coconut (we like Bob's Red Mill)
> ½ cup sweetened coconut flakes

1. Preheat the oven to 350°F. Line two baking sheets with parchment paper.

2. In a medium clean bowl, beat the egg whites, cream of tartar, and salt with an electric mixer on high speed until stiff peaks form, almost like you're making a meringue.

3. Gently fold the sugar, the vanilla and orange extracts, and the shredded and flaked coconut into the egg white mixture.

4. Using a tablespoon, scoop a level tablespoon of the batter and drop it onto the lined baking sheet. Repeat until all of the batter has been dropped onto the baking sheets. With your fingers, slightly pinch the top of each macaroon to make a little peak and to keep them from spreading out too thin.

5. Bake for 10 to 15 minutes. The tops should turn a light golden-brown color. Let cool for a few minutes before serving. Serve either warm or at room temperature and store extras in an airtight container.

PEANUT BUTTER CHOCOLATE BROWNIES

PEANUT BUTTER. CHOCOLATE. WE KNOW A LOT OF PEOPLE WHO love this combo (okay, Jessie in particular). In this recipe, the peanut butter flavor is not overwhelming, and the yogurt really adds a nice moistness to the finished brownie without changing the taste. Have some fun using a knife or spatula to create neat designs in the peanut butter swirl!

BROWNIES

1	cup gluten-free flour blend (we like Arrowhead Mills Gluten Free All Purpose Baking Mix)
1	teaspoon baking powder
¼	teaspoon salt
1	cup granulated sugar
½	cup (1 stick) unsalted butter, sliced into pieces
8	ounces high-quality dark chocolate, roughly chopped
3	large eggs
¾	cup smooth peanut butter
½	cup full-fat plain yogurt
2	teaspoons vanilla extract

FILLING/TOPPING

3	tablespoons unsalted butter, melted
½	cup confectioners' sugar

¾   cup smooth peanut butter

¾   teaspoon vanilla extract

Vanilla ice cream or whipped cream, for serving (optional)

1. Preheat the oven to 325°F. Grease an 11 x 8-inch baking pan with butter or nonstick cooking spray.

2. First, make the brownie base. In a large mixing bowl, sift the flour, baking powder, salt, and sugar and mix until evenly combined.

3. In a medium saucepan, melt the butter over medium-low heat. Add the chopped chocolate and stir until the chocolate is melted. Be sure to stir it often so the chocolate doesn't burn. Remove from the heat as soon as the chocolate is fully melted.

4. Add the eggs one at a time and stir each one into the chocolate mixture before adding the next one. Then stir in the peanut butter, yogurt, and vanilla extract.

5. Pour the chocolate mixture into the mixing bowl with the dry ingredients and stir until a batter forms and all the ingredients are incorporated evenly.

6. Pour the batter into the pre-greased baking pan and set aside.

7. Now it's time to make the peanut butter topping/filling. Combine the melted butter, confectioners' sugar, peanut butter, and vanilla extract in a medium bowl and stir until it is a uniform consistency.

8. Using a spoon, scoop the filling evenly over the prepared batter. Then using the spoon or a butter knife (for prettier blending), gently run it through the batter so that the peanut butter filling spreads over the top and down into the batter. It doesn't have to be pretty or perfect. Just make sure the peanut butter finds its way down into the brownie batter.

9. Bake for about 1 hour, or until a toothpick inserted into the center of the brownies comes out clean.

10. Let cool completely in the pan. Slice and then serve with vanilla ice cream or whipped cream, or eat them as is.

FRAGRANT COCONUT RICE PUDDING WITH VANILLA CARAMELIZED PINEAPPLE

(DF) MAKES 4 SERVINGS

LIKE MANY OF US GROWING UP, WHEN OUR PARENTS SAID WE were having rice pudding for dessert, it didn't exactly make us want to finish our dinner any more quickly . . . I mean, rice pudding? Yeah, we know. But we can assure you that this updated, grown-up recipe is delicious enough to heal even the most scarred rice pudding eaters! It is packed with exotic flavors, from the cardamom-infused coconut milk to the heavenly vanilla-soaked pineapple grilled just warm enough to balance the cool pudding and the surprising crunch of the toasted coconut flakes. We recommend using only fresh pineapple for this, as the natural sugars just work better here as opposed to the canned variety. Sure, you probably wish you were dipping your feet into some exotic Tahitian ocean right now. If that's not in your immediate future, how about you take a lil' food trip to the exotic with this?

- ¼ cup unsweetened coconut flakes or shredded coconut
- 1¾ cups cold water
- 1 (14-ounce) can coconut milk (preferably light)
- ⅓ cup granulated sugar
- ¼ teaspoon ground cardamom
- 1 teaspoon vanilla extract, divided
- ⅔ cup jasmine rice, rinsed well
- 1 cup bite-size cubes FRESH pineapple (about ½ pound)
- 1 tablespoon firmly packed light brown sugar

1. Preheat the oven to 350°F.

2. Spread the coconut flakes evenly onto a baking sheet. Bake for 3 to 5 minutes, or until light golden brown, keeping a watchful eye not to burn them, which happens quickly! Set aside and let cool on the pan.

3. In a small saucepan, combine the cold water, coconut milk, sugar, cardamom, and ½ teaspoon of the vanilla extract.

4. Over low heat, warm gently and stir until the sugar dissolves, 4 to 5 minutes. Then turn the heat up to medium high and bring to a gentle boil. Once boiling, turn the heat down to low and simmer gently, stirring often, for a final 3 to 4 minutes.

5. In a medium saucepan, add the rice and ladle in half of the warmed coconut milk mixture. Over medium-low heat, bring this to a simmer, stirring until all the liquid has been absorbed, 6 to 8 minutes.

6. Once absorbed, repeat the process with the remaining half of the coconut milk mixture, stirring constantly, until the mixture has been absorbed. Continue cooking, uncovered, on medium-low heat until the rice is tender, for about 15 minutes. This can take a bit longer depending on the brand of rice you use. You want it to be similar to rice pudding or a gooey, risotto-like texture.

7. Once cooked through, turn off the heat, cover, and set aside to cool to room temperature. Once at room temperature, chill in the fridge for at least 20 minutes, covered.

8. Meanwhile, in a small bowl, combine the fresh pineapple chunks, the remaining ½ teaspoon of vanilla extract, and the brown sugar. Stir to coat the pineapple evenly.

9. In a medium, nonstick frying pan over medium heat, add the pineapple mixture and cook until warm and the sugar starts to caramelize, 4 to 6 minutes, flipping occasionally so all the sides are caramelized. Remove from heat.

10. Divide the cooled pudding among the bowls. Spoon a bit of the warmed caramelized pineapple on top and then sprinkle on a bit of the toasted coconut flakes. Enjoy slightly warm or chilled fully, if preferred.

CLASSIC APPLE PIE

ONE THING JESSIE MISSED TERRIBLY AT THANKSGIVING IN the years after she was diagnosed with her gluten intolerance was a simple, classic apple pie. Over time, she found suitable substitutes and eventually even some frozen gluten-free versions. They were tasty but never quite the same as what she remembered. So, finally, she decided to conquer the crust and come up with a GF version of her favorite. This is it—in all of its cinnamon-appley goodness. For this recipe, we do blind bake the bottom crust, but the top crust is not pre-baked. No worries, though, because the result is still a beautifully crispy crust with a gooey, tender filling. Just what a classic apple pie should be!

2	recipes Basic Pie Crust (page 70) (add 1 teaspoon sugar to each recipe), or 2 premade, store-bought gluten-free pie crusts (unbaked)
1	pound Granny Smith apples
1	pound sweet, crisp apples, such as Gala or Fuji
¼	cup orange juice
1	cup firmly packed light brown sugar
2	tablespoons cornstarch
½	teaspoon ground cinnamon, or more to taste
¼	teaspoon ground nutmeg
	Pinch of ground cloves
¼	teaspoon salt
1	large egg, beaten

1. Prepare and blind bake your bottom crust according to the recipe and instructions on page 70. Prepare your top crust and keep it unrolled in the refrigerator until rolling time. If you are using a premade crust, blind bake the bottom crust per the package instructions.

2. Preheat the oven to 375°F.

3. Peel and core your apples. Slice each one in half and then cut into ¼-inch-thick slices. Transfer them to a large mixing bowl and toss with the orange juice.

4. Add the brown sugar, the cornstarch, all the spices, and the salt to the apples. Toss to combine and distribute evenly.

5. Place your blind-baked bottom crust on a baking sheet to catch any yummy apple bubble-over. Now, fill your crust with the apple mixture. The apples should fit easily into the 9-inch pie pan but, if it seems extra full, pile the extra apples in the center as opposed to near the edges. That'll help reduce bubble-over.

6. Roll out your top crust, following the instructions on page 70. Once it is ready, we like to gently lift the bottom piece of waxed paper on which you rolled the crust and invert it directly on top of the apple mixture. Then, gently peel the waxed paper away so just the crust is left on top of the pie. If using a premade crust, roll it out to make your top crust and gently transfer it to the top of your pie.

7. Gently press the edges of the top crust down onto the edges of the bottom crust. Cut away or fold under any overhang and crimp the edges with your fingers to give the pie a nice decorative finish. Brush the top of the crust with the beaten egg. Cut a few slits in the pie top for venting.

8. Bake for 50 to 60 minutes, or until the crust is golden brown and the apple juices are bubbling and look thick. If the crust edges start to get too brown, cover them carefully with some foil for the duration of the cook time.

9. Remove the pie from the oven and let cool for at least 2 hours before serving. This helps all of the filling gel together better and makes it easier to serve the pie intact.

HOCOLATE PECAN PIE

HAPPY HOLIDAYS FROM THE SOUTH, HONEY! THAT IS ALL WE think about when we hear the words "chocolate pecan pie." This is one of the first desserts Jilly learned to make when she was younger, and it has since become a very steady Christmas tradition. This is truly a tradition-making pie, whether it's for a special holiday or any day you want to make a holiday. This pie can be made dairy-free by simply using dairy-free chocolate chips and a dairy-free pie crust.

CRUST

1 premade, store-bought gluten-free pie crust (we like Kinnikinnick or Whole Foods premade crusts), blind baked per package instructions, or 1 recipe Basic Pie Crust (page 70), blind baked per recipe instructions

FILLING

1½ cups pecan halves

½ cup semisweet chocolate chips (or dairy-free chocolate chips, if preferred)

4 large eggs, lightly beaten

½ cup granulated sugar

½ cup loosely packed light brown sugar

½ cup amber agave syrup (we used this in place of light corn syrup)

1 teaspoon vanilla extract

Vanilla ice cream or whipped cream, for serving (optional)

1. Preheat the oven to 375°F and position an oven rack in the middle.

2. Evenly spread the pecan halves and chocolate chips on the bottom of the blind-baked pie shell.

3. In a large bowl, add all the remaining filling ingredients and whisk well to combine.

4. Pour this mixture over the top of the pecans and chocolate chips in the pie shell. You want the pie shell to be full but not dripping over.

5. Place the pie on a baking sheet and bake on the middle oven rack for 50 to 60 minutes, or until the filling is set and not too jiggly.

6. Let cool for 15 to 20 minutes on the tray before slicing, to allow the filling to firm up a bit.

7. Serve warm or cool with a bit of vanilla ice cream or fresh whipped cream, if desired.

WARM BREAD PUDDING WITH RUM-SAUCE DRIZZLE   MAKES 8 SERVINGS

WARM BREAD PUDDING IS ONE OF THOSE FAMILIAR HOLIDAY dishes that we missed a lot when we were first diagnosed with gluten issues. This tasty version adds a sweet rum sauce to complement the pudding. When looking for a gluten-free bread to use in this recipe, try to get a thick, farmhouse-style bread. Although any type will work, the thicker bread lends itself to a smushier pudding, and that's just how we like it!

BREAD PUDDING

3	large eggs
1	cup granulated sugar
½	cup firmly packed light brown sugar
1	teaspoon ground cinnamon
¼	cup (½ stick) unsalted butter, melted
2	cups whole milk
8 to 10	slices gluten-free bread, toasted and cubed (about 5 to 6 cups of cubed bread)
½	cup raisins

RUM SAUCE

¾	cup firmly packed dark brown sugar
½	cup (1 stick) unsalted butter
¼	cup dark rum
1	teaspoon vanilla extract
1	tablespoon gluten-free flour blend (we like Arrowhead Mills Gluten Free All Purpose Baking Mix)

1. Preheat the oven to 375°F. Grease a 13 x 9-inch baking dish with butter or nonstick cooking spray.

2. First, make the bread pudding. In a large mixing bowl, whisk the eggs until slightly beaten. Add the sugars, cinnamon, butter, and milk and mix until all the ingredients are incorporated.

3. Gently fold in the bread cubes and raisins. Once all the bread is covered with the egg and sugar mixture, pour or spoon the mixture into the prepared baking dish.

4. Bake the bread pudding for 50 to 60 minutes, or until the top is browned and the middle is set and not jiggly or uncooked. Depending on your oven, you might want to cover the pan with foil after about 30 minutes to keep the top from becoming overly crunchy and brown. Remove from the oven and set aside.

5. Now it is time to make the rum sauce. In a small saucepan, combine all the rum sauce ingredients and heat over medium, whisking constantly, until the sauce thickens and coats the back of a spoon, about 6 to 8 minutes. At this point, remove the sauce from the heat. Depending on your preference, you can either transfer the sauce into a small serving bowl for everyone to pour themselves or you can pour the sauce directly from the saucepan over the top of the bread pudding. Personally, we think the sauce is very sweet, so we prefer to let everyone dole it out for themselves, but it is up to you!

HOLY COW TIRAMISU

WE NAMED THIS DESSERT HOLY COW TIRAMISU BECAUSE "holy cow!" was the most common response we received when we asked our testers to sample it. It really is super delicious, so we have to admit that we concur with the name! It does require a few steps and some time to chill the filling but, believe us, it is absolutely worth it. To make things a little easier, here are a couple of notes: Make sure your mascarpone is at room temperature. This ensures that the filling will be uniform in consistency and not have little chunks of mascarpone throughout it! Also, we use a loaf pan in which to assemble the tiramisu, just because it allows us to create a few layers. You can, however, use a baking dish if you prefer. It is still just as tasty, though not as tall for slicing.

1	cup plus 2 tablespoons heavy whipping cream, divided
¼	cup semisweet chocolate chips
4	large egg yolks
¼	cup dark rum
⅓	cup granulated sugar
	Pinch of salt
¼	cup plus 2 tablespoons confectioners' sugar, divided
1	(8-ounce) container mascarpone cheese, at room temperature
2½	cups strong-brewed coffee, at room temperature
21 to 24	crisp gluten-free ladyfinger cookies (we like Schar)
	Unsweetened cocoa powder, for garnish
	Semisweet chocolate chips, for garnish (optional)
	Confectioners' sugar, for garnish (optional)

1. First, make the chocolate sauce. Bring a saucepan of water to a boil and then reduce the heat to a simmer (you don't want a violent boil here).

2. Add 2 tablespoons of the whipping cream and the chocolate chips to a medium, heatproof glass bowl that fits atop the saucepan of simmering water but does not actually touch the water below. Place the bowl on top of the saucepan and heat over medium, stirring very often, until the chocolate chips are melted and the cream is mixed in with the chocolate uniformly. Set the chocolate mixture aside but keep warm. Let the water continue to simmer over medium heat.

3. Whisk the egg yolks, rum, granulated sugar, and salt in another medium or large, heatproof glass bowl until blended and creamy. Set the bowl carefully over the saucepan of simmering water to create a double-boiler setup, as you did with the chocolate mixture. The bottom of the bowl should not be touching the water. Whisk this mixture constantly until it gets thick and creamy, about 3 to 4 minutes.

4. Remove the rum mixture from the heat. Fold the reserved chocolate mixture into the rum mixture and stir until blended evenly. Cover with plastic wrap and refrigerate until completely cool, about 30 minutes to 1 hour.

5. Once the chocolate rum sauce is cool, you may begin preparing the rest of the tiramisu. Using an electric mixer, beat on high speed the remaining 1 cup cream and ¼ cup of the confectioners' sugar in a large mixing bowl until soft peaks form. Add the room-temperature mascarpone cheese and mix gently until the mixture is homogeneous and no clumps of cheese remain.

6. Next, fold in the chilled chocolate rum sauce and stir only until the mixture is evenly combined. Again, cover with plastic wrap and put it in the refrigerator to chill while you prepare the rest of the tiramisu.

7. In a small mixing bowl, dissolve the remaining 2 tablespoons confectioners' sugar in the room-temperature coffee. You want the bowl deep and wide enough so that it can accommodate a ladyfinger being submerged in the coffee. Set aside.

8. Line a standard loaf pan (9 x 5 x 2.75 inches) with plastic wrap, leaving enough plastic so that it hangs over the edge of the pan lengthwise. Gently spread a third of your mascarpone mixture into the bottom of the pan, holding the plastic in place to avoid it bunching up or clumping.

9. Working cookie by cookie, submerge a ladyfinger in the coffee. They should no longer be hard in the middle, but be careful not to oversoak them, or they will break apart. If you have a few extras in your store-bought package of ladyfingers, you can always experiment with one or two so you can gauge the right amount of time to dip them. If you don't have extras, just do your best on the first few until you hit your ladyfinger-soaking stride. No harm will come to the finished product if some are unevenly soaked.

10. Place the dipped cookies in a single layer atop the mascarpone mixture at the bottom of the loaf pan. You should be able to fit seven or eight, depending on the brand of ladyfinger you use.

11. Drizzle 1 tablespoon of the coffee mixture evenly over the cookies. Then gently spread another third of the mascarpone mixture over the cookies.

12. Follow this with another layer of ladyfingers, prepped as in step 10, and another layer of coffee drizzle as in step 11. Spread the remaining mascarpone gently on top. For the final layer, add another round of coffee-soaked ladyfingers, along with a final drizzle of the coffee mixture. Gently press the whole thing down in the loaf pan to compact the layers. Cover with plastic wrap and refrigerate at least 6 hours.

13. When the tiramisu is completely chilled and set, unwrap the plastic wrap cover and invert the tiramisu onto a serving platter, using the plastic wrap from inside the pan to help.

14. Gently peel off the plastic wrap bottom, which is now on the top, and spread the mascarpone to even it out if necessary.

15. Garnish with cocoa, chocolate chips, or confectioners' sugar, if desired. Slice and serve.

METRIC CONVERSIONS

The recipes in this book have not been tested with metric measurements, so some variations might occur. Remember that the weight of dry ingredients varies according to the volume or density factor: 1 cup of flour weighs far less than 1 cup of sugar, and 1 tablespoon doesn't necessarily hold 3 teaspoons.

GENERAL FORMULA FOR METRIC CONVERSION

Ounces to grams	multiply ounces by 28.35
Grams to ounces	multiply grams by 0.035
Pounds to grams	multiply pounds by 453.5
Pounds to kilograms	multiply pounds by 0.45
Cups to liters	multiply cups by 0.24
Fahrenheit to Celsius	subtract 32 from Fahrenheit temperature, multiply by 5, divide by 9
Celsius to Fahrenheit	multiply Celsius temperature by 9, divide by 5, add 32

VOLUME (LIQUID) MEASUREMENTS

1 teaspoon	= ⅙ fluid ounce	= 5 milliliters
1 tablespoon	= ½ fluid ounce	= 15 milliliters
2 tablespoons	= 1 fluid ounce	= 30 milliliters
¼ cup	= 2 fluid ounces	= 60 milliliters
⅓ cup	= 2⅔ fluid ounces	= 79 milliliters
½ cup	= 4 fluid ounces	= 118 milliliters
1 cup or ½ pint	= 8 fluid ounces	= 250 milliliters
2 cups or 1 pint	= 16 fluid ounces	= 500 milliliters
4 cups or 1 quart	= 32 fluid ounces	= 1,000 milliliters
1 gallon	= 4 liters	

WEIGHT (MASS) MEASUREMENTS

1 ounce	= 30 grams	
2 ounces	= 55 grams	
3 ounces	= 85 grams	
4 ounces	= ¼ pound	= 125 grams
8 ounces	= ½ pound	= 240 grams
12 ounces	= ¾ pound	= 375 grams
16 ounces	= 1 pound	= 454 grams

OVEN TEMPERATURE EQUIVALENTS, FAHRENHEIT (F) AND CELSIUS (C)

100°F	= 38°C
200°F	= 95°C
250°F	= 120°C
300°F	= 150°C
350°F	= 180°C
400°F	= 205°C
450°F	= 230°C

VOLUME (DRY) MEASUREMENTS

¼ teaspoon	= 1 milliliter
½ teaspoon	= 2 milliliters
¾ teaspoon	= 4 milliliters
1 teaspoon	= 5 milliliters
1 tablespoon	= 15 milliliters
¼ cup	= 59 milliliters
⅓ cup	= 79 milliliters
½ cup	= 118 milliliters
⅔ cup	= 158 milliliters
¾ cup	= 177 milliliters
1 cup	= 225 milliliters
4 cups or 1 quart	= 1 liter
½ gallon	= 2 liters
1 gallon	= 4 liters

LINEAR MEASUREMENTS

½ inch	= 1½ cm
1 inch	= 2½ cm
6 inches	= 15 cm
8 inches	= 20 cm
10 inches	= 25 cm
12 inches	= 30 cm
20 inches	= 50 cm

QUICK & EASY RECIPES Ⓠᴇ

FOR STARTERS

- Easy Artichoke Dip
- Easy Chicken Satay Skewers [close to 45 minutes]
- Maw-Maw's Deviled Eggs
- Roasted Veggie Dip à la Baba Ghanoush [close to 45 minutes]
- Savory Cheddar Scones with Red Onion Marmalade
- Shrimp-Stuffed Mushrooms
- Smoky Pea and Truffle Crostini with Goat Cheese, Grape Tomatoes, and Pea Shoots
- Spicy Crab Dip with Homemade Garlic Parmesan Crackers [close to 45 minutes]

BREAKFAST

- Fruit and Yogurt Parfaits with Homemade Granola
- Healthy Huevos Rancheros
- Perfect Blueberry Muffins
- Toad in the Hole with Bacon-Wrapped Asparagus Spears
- Traditional Breakfast Biscuits
- You-Won't-Taste-the-Veggies Zucchini Muffins

LUNCHTIME FAVORITES

- Broccoli and Cheese Soup
- Cuban Black Bean Soup [close to 45 minutes]
- Jilly's Ginger Sesame Pork Stir-Fry
- Kale and Apple Salad with Pine Nuts, Cranberries, and Goat Cheese
- Minestrone Soup à la Venus de Milo
- Mom's Pasta Salad

- Poached Egg, Arugula, and Bacon Salad
- Spicy Tomato Soup with Grilled Cheese Dippers
- Sun-dried Tomato Pesto Pasta Salad
- Warm Moroccan Spiced Quinoa Salad with Apricots

ACCOMPANIMENTS

- Easy Pilau Rice
- Herbed Sugar Snap Peas
- Jessie's Favorite Potato Salad
- Mookie's Three-Cheese Mac
- Ms. Leytha's Hot Water Bread

MAIN COURSES

- Baked Pork Chops with Apple Rosemary Chutney
- Chicken and Dumplings
- Crispy Parmesan-Crusted Grouper
- Emeril's Spaghetti à la Carbonara
- Herb, Sausage, and Tomato Penne
- Kinda Like Maw-Maw's Sloppy Joes
- Ms. Jackie's Thai Green Chicken Curry with Jasmine and Kaffir Lime Rice
- New England Clam Chowder [close to 45 minutes]
- One-Pot Chicken Jalfrezi
- Seared Salmon with Warm Lentil, Tomato, and Mint Salad [lentils might bring this closer to 45 minutes]

FOR AFTERS

- Mama's Strawberry Shortcake with Homemade Biscuits
- Old-Fashioned Oatmeal Raisin Cookies
- Orange Coconut Macaroons

DAIRY-FREE RECIPES DF

FOR STARTERS
- Crispy Cod Fish Cakes with Horseradish Sauce
- Crispy Sriracha and Lime Chicken Wings
- Easy Chicken Satay Skewers
- Maw-Maw's Deviled Eggs
- Pork and Mushroom Spring Rolls
- Roasted Vegetable Dip à la Baba Ghanoush

BREAKFAST
- Healthy Huevos Rancheros
- Perfect Blueberry Muffins
- Toad in the Hole with Bacon-Wrapped Asparagus Spears
- Traditional Breakfast Biscuits

LUNCHTIME FAVORITES
- Baked "Fried" Shrimp Tacos with Mango Salsa and Homemade Zingy Tartar Sauce
- Cuban Black Bean Soup
- Daddy's Split Pea Soup
- Gramma Cabral's Portuguese Kale Soup
- Jilly's Ginger Sesame Pork Stir-Fry
- Minestrone Soup à la Venus de Milo
- Poached Egg, Arugula, and Bacon Salad
- Red Pepper and Parsley Spanish Tortilla
- Warm Moroccan Spiced Quinoa Salad with Apricots

ACCOMPANIMENTS

- Duck Fat Roasted Potatoes (a.k.a. Roasties)
- Easy Pilau Rice
- Herbed Sugar Snap Peas
- Jessie's Favorite Potato Salad
- Ms. Leytha's Hot Water Bread
- Roasted Brussels Sprouts in Spicy Mustard Sauce
- Roasted Sweet Potatoes and Squash

MAIN COURSES

- Baked Pork Chops with Apple Rosemary Chutney
- Beef Stewpot with Thyme Biscuit Crust
- Daddy's Duck and Andouille Sausage Christmas Gumbo
- Easy Seafood Paella
- Home-Style Chili with Gluten-Free Beer
- Jamaican Jerk Chicken with Rice and Peas
- Kinda Like Maw-Maw's Sloppy Joes
- Moroccan Lamb Tagine
- Ms. Jackie's Thai Green Chicken Curry with Jasmine and Kaffir Lime Rice
- One-Pot Chicken Jalfrezi
- Seared Salmon with Warm Lentil, Tomato, and Mint Salad
- Slow Cooker Pot Roast

FOR AFTERS

- Fragrant Coconut Rice Pudding with Vanilla Caramelized Pineapple
- Orange Coconut Macaroons

RESOURCES

ONLINE RESOURCES FOR LOTS OF GREAT GLUTEN-FREE PRODUCTS WE USE THROUGHOUT THE BOOK AND BEYOND:

www.againstthegraingourmet.com or (802) 258–3838: We can't get enough of Against the Grain's insanely good products, especially their gluten-free baguettes, which we use throughout the book. They are making some of the finest rolls, bagels, pizzas, and baguettes that we have tasted. Unfortunately, though, they do not ship directly to customers, so if your local grocery store or Whole Foods Market doesn't already carry this brand, simply MAKE THEM! We mean, politely ask them to start carrying Against the Grain products.

www.amazon.com: Amazon's gluten-free product list seems to be growing each hour, and you can find most of the ingredients needed to make the recipes here, easily and quickly.

www.arrowheadmills.com or (800) 434–4246: This is your go-to for ordering their wonderful Gluten Free All Purpose Baking Mix, which we use throughout the book. They also carry a variety of beans, rice, seeds, nut butters, flours, and baking mixes.

www.blackbird-bakery.com: This is a beautiful website by Karen Morgan, the author of the fantastic cookbook *Blackbird Bakery: Gluten-Free*. Not only can you order her book, but you can also order her amazing flour blends, such as her tart + pie blend or her fab puff pastry blend. Her aim is "to make gluten-free better than what came before" and she is! You can also find recipes and her blog on this site.

www.bobsredmill.com: Bob's is truly a one-stop shop for your gluten-free baking needs and carries almond meal flour, xanthan gum, chickpea or gram flour, tapioca starch and flour, finely milled cornmeal, certified gluten-free oats, shredded coconut, and loads of other products we use in this book. This website could save you heaps of time going to the store.

www.celiac.com/glutenfreemall or (866) 575–3720: This is a great resource for all things gluten-free, everything from premade pizza crusts to gluten-free frozen foods.

www.clabbergirl.com or (812) 232–9446: Log on here to buy either Clabber Girl or Rumford gluten-free baking powder and cornstarch. Their products are produced in a peanut-free facility, which can be very handy if you have a strict peanut allergy, and they also allow you to buy in bulk. Bonus.

www.drlucys.com: This is our go-to for several delicious cookies that are the base for many of our dessert crusts.

www.emerils.com: This is where we go to order all of our dad's products, including the ever useful Emeril's Original Essence seasoning that we use throughout the book.

www.englishteastore.com or (877) 734–2458: This is one of Jilly's favorite sites to get all her English products and essentials, like proper teas and adorable tea sets, lemon curd and jams, Devon double cream and clotted cream, golden syrup and treacle, and more. They are one of the only places we know of in the United States that carries Sharwood's brand curry powders, puppodums, mango chutneys, and curry pastes, which happen to be her FAV!

www.foodforlife.com: This is where you can buy awesome tortillas, be it brown rice, exotic black rice, or their sprouted corn tortillas, which we use in our recipes. We also love their gluten-free English muffins.

www.gasparssausage.com: You can order their delicious chouriço and other spicy Portuguese sausages that we use throughout the book.

www.gilliansfoodsglutenfree.com: We could eat Gillian's French rolls for days; fortunately, she also offers many other delish products, such as croutons, brownies, cookie dough, baking mixes, garlic bread, pizza dough, and even frozen French bread pizzas! Yum.

www.glutino.com: Glutino makes so many fabulous products it's hard to list them all! Crackers, pretzels, cereals, cookies, pizzas, and even frozen meals! We particularly love their Genius by Glutino breads and use them in lots of recipes.

www.julianbakery.com: They are the makers of some delicious Paleo-style breads that are perfect for the gluten-free lifestyle and for those who are also following a Paleo diet. We can't get enough of their low-carb breads.

www.kalustyans.com or (212) 685–3451: Kalustyan's store in New York City is a sight to behold, but if you can't get there, just order online. They carry every type of spice imaginable, especially the exotic spices we use in our Moroccan dishes, like ras el hanout seasoning, and in our Indian recipes, like cardamom, madras curry paste, tandoori spice, curry powders, curry pastes, and more. They also carry a number of bean and rice flours, as well as several types of rice noodle. This truly is a fabulous specialty store in which you can find almost anything.

www.kinnikinnick.com: Kinnikinnick Foods has many amazing products, but we especially love their premade gluten-free frozen pie crusts, panko-style breadcrumbs, and graham cracker crumbs for pie-crust making. Oh . . . and they make DONUTS!

www.schar.com: Schar has a huge selection of delicious gluten-free products such as cookies, crackers, mixes, breads, pastas, pizzas, and frozen products, not to mention their gluten-free ladyfingers, which we use in our Holy Cow Tiramisu recipe.

www.triumphdining.com: Triumph Dining offers some really incredible guides, like their Essential Gluten-Free Grocery Guide and a restaurant guide of over 6,500 gluten-free restaurants and 100 gluten-free lists from your familiar chain restaurants. They also make the fantastic Triumph Dining Cards that are available in ten different languages, which list all the things you are not allowed to eat. These are great for all you world travelers, or, if you just like to eat your way around the world without leaving your own hometown, these cards cover every cuisine imaginable and only take a chef or waiter about a minute to read. Very cool!

www.udisglutenfree.com: Udi's makes everything from delicious bagels, baguettes, breads, brownies, muffins, cookies, cinnamon rolls, tortillas, pizza crusts, premade pizzas, granola, and granola bars. *Phew*, they've got something for everyone.

www.wholefoodsmarket.com: Did you know you could log on and order from a store near you? Yep, you can. Whole Foods Market consistently has a huge number of gluten-free products and is great for offering new products you haven't even heard of. This is also where we buy our duck fat, crème fraîche, flour blend, and other specialty products.

www.zatarains.com: Order crab-boil liquid or spice mix and their new gluten-free rice and jambalaya mixes.

FANTASTIC MAGAZINES FOCUSED ON GLUTEN-FREE OR ALLERGY-FRIENDLY LIFESTYLES:

www.allergicliving.com (click on the Celiac tab)

www.delightglutenfree.com

www.easyeats.com

www.glutenfreeliving.com

www.livingwithout.com

www.simplygluten-free.com/glutenfreemagazine

HELPFUL WEBSITES FOR YOUR GLUTEN-FREE JOURNEY:

American Celiac Disease Center

www.americanceliac.org

Celiac Disease Center at Columbia University

www.celiacdiseasecenter.columbia.edu

Celiac Disease Foundation

www.celiac.org

Celiac Sprue Association

www.csaceliacs.org

Center for Celiac Research

www.celiaccenter.org

Mayo Clinic

www.mayoclinic.com/health/celiac-disease

University of Chicago Celiac Disease Center

www.cureceliacdisease.org

SOME FAB GLUTEN-FREE AND CELIAC BLOGGERS WE LOVE. BIG TIME!!

With the new social media craze going on in our world (Facebook, Instagram, Twitter, Snapchat, and all the other things you folks are into), it seems everyone we know has a blog. So, we wanted to include a list of some of our favorite gluten-free and celiac bloggers out there who are really doing some great things and making a delicious impact in the gluten-free and celiac community. We salute you, you bloggers you! A big THANK YOU to all our fellow Celiac Soul Sisters and Brothers, you are amazing.

www.adventuresofaglutenfreemom.com: Heidi blogs about gluten sensitivity and celiac disease from a mom's perspective and has loads of tasty kid-friendly recipes and lots of helpful information.

www.anniesglutenfreegrub: Annie Proctor is a "gluten free foodie eating her way through a gluten free world" and doing one tasty job of it. Her blog is one of our faves, and she is doing so much for the gluten-free community. Thanks, Annie.

www.celiacandthebeast.com: Not only is this THE place to order some super rad gluten-free-themed T-shirts, this is a really fun lifestyle blog from the incredible Erica Dermer that is filled with product and restaurant reviews, informative articles, and info. She is a huge celiac-awareness advocate and has helped to make great progress for the gluten-free community.

www.glutenfreegeek.com: Gluten Free Geek hosts annual gluten-free awards, with awards for everything from the best bagel to the best blog! They also have a "Best Of" list for cities all over the country, so go check out your city today to see what gluten-free love you're missing out on.

www.glutenfreegirl.com: This is a witty, informative blog by a gluten-free girl and her chef hubby. Great recipes and information.

www.glutenfreeonashoestring.com: This is a comprehensive site with a blog, recipes, tips, and you name it by its incredible author, Nicole Hunn. Hey, gluten-free can be expensive! Nicole is the best at offering money-saving tips for this pricey, albeit tasty, gluten-free world.

www.glutenismybitch.wordpress.com: The insanely awesome April Peveteaux's website is always humorous and delicious, filled with tasty recipes, shopping and travel tips, and restaurant lists. This is one of our favorite blogs, plus you can order her hilarious book here, *Gluten Is My Bitch: Rants, Recipes, and Ridiculousness for the Gluten-Free*. Major fist bump to you, April, for all you are accomplishing!

www.healthnowmedical.com/theblogs/: Dr. Vikki Petersen's gluten-free blog is hosted by Health Now Medical Center, which specializes in digestive problems, gluten sensitivities, celiac disease, treatments, and diagnosis.

www.wheatwatchersonline.com: This is Susie Bramhall's fabulous site for gluten-free living and eating. You can also follow the link to her blog from the website.

ACKNOWLEDGMENTS

Jessie and Jilly would both like to acknowledge the following individuals, without whom this book would not have been possible:

First and foremost, a big thanks to everyone at Da Capo Press/Lifelong Books, especially Ms. Renee Sedliar for taking a chance on us and believing in this book.

Ms. Brandi Bowles and everyone at Foundry Media. Thanks for your constant support and hard work to help this little gluten-free engine chug on. We are so thankful.

Our amazing photographer, Chris Granger. We thank you for thinking outside the box—or in the birdbath as the case may be. Your humor, willingness to take a risk, and tolerance of our craziness has been a blessing. Thank you for being part of "part deux."

Our incredible food stylist, Ms. Sara Essex Bradley. Your patience, creativity, and incredible vision made this shoot such an enjoyable one. We are forever thankful for having you come on board this second time.

Our wonderful helpers, Miss Sarah Chatagnier and Miss Grace Treffinger. You gals were such a gift to us!! Truly, we couldn't have pulled it off without your help. Thank you so much!

Chef Dana Tuohy at the NOCCA Institute. Thank you for all of your help and for sending your fabulous assistants our way. Phew!

Ms. Charlotte Martory at Emeril's Homebase. Thank you for all your hard work and constant help. Truly, we appreciate it.

Ms. Maggie McCabe. Where do we begin to thank you for all you have done and continue to do to help us. You are beyond amazing!

Ms. Nicole Hunn. Without you, this whole thing probably wouldn't have happened. Beyond thanks to you for your vision and support. We are so appreciative!

Mrs. Sarah Sadler Worsley at Race and Religious. We are so grateful for all your help and for letting us make our cookbook dreams come true in that amazing lil' wonderland of yours!

Huge thanks to Lindsay Ross and Matt Owens for letting us "borrow" your truly rad house and its never-ending cool contents for this shoot! How lucky we were to have found y'all . . . thanks SEB!

Jilly would like to thank the following individuals:

I'd like to dedicate this book to Ms. Jackie and the Whittington family. For all you taught me in those years, I'll never quite be able to put into words just how grateful I am. You helped me to become the woman I am today. You showed me what being a constant friend, a wife, and a proper mum really IS, and you taught me how to always cook from the heart. The recipes you taught me still make me smile every time I prepare them and think of you. Being in the kitchen together with our cute aprons on, cooking away, are some of the fondest memories one could have. For all your love and support, for all you have given me and taught me, I am so thankful. I hope I've done ya proud, Mumsie.

I'd like to thank my parents:

Daddy and Aldie: This book wouldn't be possible without you and your constant love, guidance, and support. I am so blessed to have you. For everything, thank you.

Momma and Russ: For letting us take over your kitchen (and life!) once again to make this book and all these recipes happen, I am so thankful!! I hope we put it all back together? Thank you for your constant support, never-ending love, and taste tasting!

Jessie: For all your hard work, sacrifice, and endurance, I thank you. I hope you are happy with what we've accomplished. Thank you beyond.

E.J. and Meril: How I love you both so much!! You brighten up my days and world so much. Love you to bits, tater tots!!

All my family: The Lagasses, The Kiefs, The Burnsides, The Swansons. To my grandparents, cousins, brother-in-law, nephews . . . thank you all for your never-ending love and support.

A very special thank-you to our late Grandpa Kief, the most wonderful man. Every time I make gumbo, I will always think of you and smile. All my love to you, Gramps.

To all my friends:

To the Nemeth family: Tierney, Eric, and sweet Violet; thank you for all your love and taste testing!

To the Oakes family: Marybeth, Bobby, and Erin; thank you for all your fabulous taste testing, feedback, and constant support. You are all incredible.

To the Shinn family: Chris, Tarah, and Chad; thank you for years of friendship, encouragement, foodie taste testing, and support!

To the Fontaine family: Danny, Sareta, Dylan, Zac, and baby Ziggy; this is what Aunty has been up to back in the States, my loves. All my love and thanks to you all. I'd be lost without you!

To the Hulme family: Charlie, Charlotte, and my Emily May; for years of friendship, love, and support and for being my soul music brother, I am so grateful. Love you all so.

To my Mer Maggs; my soul sister!! My partner in crime! How I love you and am SO grateful for your friendship, kindness, and support. I'd be lost under the sea without ya!

To Kasia and Misa: my Claridges sisters!! Who would've thought. I thank you girls for being such true friends, constant supporters, and cheerleaders for my crazy gluten-free dreams.

To Jen O; you don't realize how much you put up with . . . I do! So thank you for all of that!! All my love and thanks.

To all my 822 girls; Drea, J, Nicole, Lizzie, and Melissa; thank you and love you so much . . . 822 for life!

And a very special thank you to D.S.; your love, patience, humor, gentle guidance, and support gets me through and makes all of this worth it. My eating partner in crime, I thank you for all you are to me. Pirates for life! All my love and thanks to you always.

Jessie would like to acknowledge:

My thoughtful, patient, loving, and visionary husband, Steven. Your never-ending encouragement and enthusiasm help me to be a better person every day. I love you.

My two greatest gifts: Jude and J.P. Thank you for bringing me purpose and joy. I smile whenever I think of you, and I am so glad to be your mother! I love you very, very much.

My super stand-in, Shelita Johnson. Without you, none of this would have been possible. Thank you for everything you do for us. I will be forever grateful!

My second super stand-in and all-time super supporter, my mom, Luz. Mom, you have given me so much help, time, and encouragement, and it means more than I can say. Thanks for always being there for all of us!

My father. Thank you for helping us with this second adventure. It is sincerely appreciated.

My mother-in-law, Patsy, for her tasty food, unwavering support, and sampling prowess. Thanks, Maw-Maw!

All of my extended family and friends who brainstormed recipes, shared food stories and memories, and gave me honest feedback after testing all my food! Thank you all so very much!

My sister, Jilly. Thanks for pulling this off! Your hard work and persistence will always be appreciated.